THE HISTORIES AND PROPHECIES
OF DANIEL

THE HISTORIES
AND PROPHECIES
OF DANIEL

By

G. H. LANG

KREGEL PUBLICATIONS
Grand Rapids, Michigan 49501

Library of Congress Catalog Card Number 73-81797
ISBN 0-8254-3104-2

First edition........................1940
Second edition 1941
Third edition.....................1942
Fourth edition 1950
First Kregel Publication edition 1973

Printed in the United States of America

CONTENTS

PREFACE

By the grace of God my interest in prophetic studies was kindled in my youth, and by that grace it has been maintained and deepened for sixty years. Some results of this reading and reflection are here offered to my fellow-pilgrims in this waste, howling wilderness for the end of which we long.

I say *results* rather than *conclusions*. Let no one conceive that he has *concluded* his study of prophetic scripture. For myself, I know that I know "not yet as I ought to know." The mass of details is so vast that it is more than a life-work to co-ordinate it, and the overlooking or the wrongly estimating of even one statement may lead to a false opinion, just as the omission or misreading of one figure will falsify a calculation.

If a book be only a repetition of positive and well-known truth it may still be of use, by introducing that truth to some not acquainted with it. But this book is offered as, it is hoped, a *contribution* to the study of *Daniel*.

More space than is usual is given to treating the historical chapters, on the grounds that actually these too are prophetical and also are full of urgent and practical lessons, lessons without which the prophetical chapters will never be rightly used.

Upon the more obviously prophetic parts some interpretations are offered not yet common, but which seem to me to follow closely the statements of the book, and to give them a more powerful practical bearing.

Of writers on prophecy known to me the most helpful are G. H Pember, B. W. Newton, R. Govett, and, on *Daniel*, S. P. Tregelles. The last-named book is happily still to be obtained, from Mr. G. H. Fromow, 9, Milnthorpe Road, Chiswick, London, W.4. The book by Pember here quoted (except on p. 180) is *The Great Prophecies of the Centuries concerning Israel, the Gentiles, and the Church of God* (Ed. 1941). Numbers in brackets after quotations are the pages of the work quoted. Other simple numbers in brackets are the verses of the chapter of *Daniel* under consideration. This can be easily remembered, because each chapter of this book deals with the corresponding chapter of *Daniel*.

The Revised Version is generally followed, *not* the Authorized. The inexact renderings of the latter put exact study quite out of the question ; and in prophecy pre-eminently exactness of rendering is indispensable to exact knowledge, and exact knowledge to learning distinctly the landmarks the pilgrim needs to see on his journey so as not to miss the way, and how he shall walk and act so as to please God. If this book shall help any in so walking its chief end will be served.

These pages were written in the summer of 1938. Matter in square brackets—[ ]—is mine.

G. H. L.

August, 1940.

Note to the Fourth Edition.

Sundry minor changes have been made necessary by lapse of time and the cessation of war. Some rearrangement and amplification will be found in Chapter VII. The exposition remains as before.

March, 1950.

THE HISTORIES AND PROPHECIES
OF DANIEL

CHAPTER I

THE PROPHET HIMSELF

THE TOOL MUST FIT THE HAND OF THE WORKMAN, THE SWORD the hand of the soldier. God's instrument must be adapted to His use, His co-worker must correspond to Himself. The character of the prophet must represent worthily the God before Whom he stands and for Whom he speaks.

This first chapter delineates Daniel himself. It shows his status in society, the discipline that developed him, the sphere of his service, the temptations that tested him, his associates, his strength of character. It reveals the secret overruling by God of his affairs, the direct divine enduement granted, the superiority over worldly men thus conferred, and the feature, altogether and miraculously exceptional in those lands and times, of his preservation to extreme old age, in spite of the changes and dangers of an eventful public career amid world upheavals.

We are not told who penned the description, but it is so masterly, so comprehensive though brief, as itself to manifest the heart-knowing God as its author, revealing the qualities He valued in the man who was to bear His name before kings and to describe to them, and to all succeeding generations, the course of world history. His messages were to be an exhibition of man and of God : of the one in his greatness and weakness, his skill and folly, his vice and cruelty, his pride and doom ; and of the Other in His divine wisdom, unfailing power, inflexible justice, His mercy and faithfulness, His present and final supremacy.

So special a service demanded a special servant. This prophet was to stand before kings in the highest offices of State, so he was chosen from royal, or at least noble, blood (ver. 3). For certain purposes there are advantages in aristocratic birth and inheritance. The training, culture, physical well-being (ver. 4), instinctive and acquired skill in ruling, the wide outlook, the ease in handling large affairs, make a man either more useful, or, of course, more hurtful to mankind. Every society, the kingdom of heaven in-cluded, must have leaders, if it is to prosper. Happy is the land that rears them, miserable the country denuded of them, as by

decay or revolution. The mismanagement of affairs public by men
unversed in great matters has produced vast miseries, of which
awful examples exist to-day, as heretofore. But when God needs
a servant He chooses one suitable to the work in view, and trains
him thoroughly. Such an one was Daniel.

He must learn to stand as a rock amidst the fury of vast and
violent public changes and grave personal perils. Therefore as a
youth he was permitted to endure the horrors of invasion ; to
witness the degradation of his king being bound with fetters. He
himself, with others of his rank, was dragged from home and
country to servitude in the land of the invader and oppressor, and,
as far as we know, he never again saw the land of his birth
(II Kings 24). He watched the rifling of the house of God itself,
a plain token that Jehovah was abandoning His people to the
consequences of their apostasy. This lad, who was already " skilful in all wisdom, and endued with knowledge " (ver. 4), could
not but have reflected much upon all these terrible happenings,
and have seen in them the dread fulfilment of Jeremiah's contemporary prophetic warnings, the solemn, yet to faith the strengthening, assurance that God keeps His word to the letter.

Arrived in Babylon he is quickly put into a new school, with
hard lessons and frightful perils. He is taken into the royal household to be trained for service at court. And what a court ! At
its head a terrible oriental despot, capable of most fiendish cruelties,
as was usual in those days, and as can be matched, alas, in these
days. He could slay a captive's sons before their father's eyes,
and then put out the latter, so leaving the wretched parent with
this as the last memory (Jer. 39 : 6, 7). He could throw his chief
officers into a furnace to watch them burn (Dan. 3) ; yea, could
roast his victims in a slow fire (Jer. 29 : 22). Yet modern poison
gas and liquid fire are not much behind this for barbarousness.
Such a man Daniel must study to please ! How shall the youth
maintain his godliness ? How shall a young officer of State preserve his probity in a court permeated with bribery, corruption, and
fraud ? How shall a young man keep clean his way amidst the
filthy immoralities habitual in heathendom, and pre-eminently in
its court life ? And how shall a captive courtier resist the terrible
pressure of the temptation to secure toleration and advancement
by worshipping the gods of the tyrant in whose hand is his future,
yea, his life ? (Comp. II Kings 5 : 17, 18).

Indeed, apart from formal prostration before the gods in the temples, there was the daily dedication to the palace deity of all the food to be eaten. One who ate of it did thus publicly acknowledge the false god and partake at his altar, for all the viands on the table were consecrated by the firstfruits portion being placed on the household shrine (I Cor. 8 ; 10 : 27, 28).

This vitiated atmosphere Daniel must breathe all day long : how shall his soul not be poisoned ? Through these snares he must pick his way : will his feet not be caught ? This pressure, powerful and constant, he must meet : will he succumb ? We may believe that the story of his ancestor Joseph, in the court of Egypt, guided and nerved him. The psalms of his royal father David must have directed and inspired him. God's word written has saving power, when believed and obeyed. Perhaps it was Daniel who afterwards wrote : " Wherewithal shall a young man cleanse his way ? By taking heed thereto according to Thy word," and " Thy word is a lamp unto my feet and a light unto my path " (Ps. 119 : 9, 105). At any rate, no other life down to his time yields so many situations that correspond to statements in this eulogy of the Word of God. Compare the following verses with the places in Daniel : ver. 10 with 6 : 13 ; 6 with chs. 2 ; 4 ; 5 ; 6 : 21, 22 ; 51, 61, 78, 85, 86, 87, 95, 109, 110, 121, 157, 161 with ch. 6 ; 63 with 1 : 7 ; 164 with 6 : 10 ; 165 with 6 : 22.

The first crisis came immediately with the first entrance upon palace life, and it at once revealed the stamina already developed in the soul of the youth. " Daniel purposed in his heart that he would not defile himself " (1 : 8). The actual occasion was secondary, the essential matter was the purpose to remain undefiled. Daniel will be holy because his God is holy. So the law commanded ; so shall it be with him, at whatever cost (Lev. 11 : 44, 45 ; 19 : 2 ; etc.).

This is the dominant lesson of the chapter. Oh, to learn it well ! For this is the primary, the vital, the indispensable qualification for high service to the Holy One. " Depart ye, depart ye, go ye out thence, touch no unclean thing . . . cleanse yourselves ye that bear the vessels of Jehovah," was the call Daniel had heard through the words of God by Isaiah (52 : 11). It is repeated to us (II Cor. 6 : 14 ; 7 : 1) : " Come ye out from among them, and be ye separate, saith the Lord, and touch no unclean thing ; and I will receive you, and will be to you a Father, and ye shall be to me sons and daughters, saith the Lord Almighty. Having therefore these promises, beloved, let us cleanse ourselves from all defilement of flesh and spirit, [persistently] perfecting holiness in the fear of God."

Daniel kept clean from defilement of the flesh by resolving not to eat of the king's dainties, seeing these were dedicated to his false god; for we assume that this was at least the principal reason, though doubtless there was the further ground that the food included articles prohibited by the law of Moses, as swine's flesh, etc.

And by keeping clean the flesh he at the same time, and thereby, kept clean the spirit also; for thus he preserved himself from a bad conscience toward God, from the corrupting principle of disobedience to His law, from a compromise which must have lowered moral stamina, enfeebled the will, dissipated courage, and blurred his spiritual vision for both the will of God and the depravity of the world. How pressing is the duty of bodily purity, and with what fabulous usury it recompenses! Hence Paul, that he might be approved of the Judge and win the incorruptible crown, enslaved his body (I Cor. 9 : 27). No wonder that our Lord included fasting in His early instruction on practical righteousness (Matt. 6 : 16-18). Cleanness of body will be the measure of cleanness of heart, and defilement of the body involves defilement of heart. John Wesley truly said that God commonly retrenches the superfluities of the soul in the same measure that we do those of the body.

It was not that Daniel became an ascetic or was morbidly scrupulous, for we learn later (10 : 2, 3) that ordinarily he ate pleasant food; but he would not touch *defiling* food. Wisely did he face this issue at once, and win the battle at the first brush with the foe. Thus he asserted immediately the supremacy of duty over apparent self-interest, of obedience over danger, of faith over fear, of the fear of God against general custom, of the spirit over the body, of the will over appetite, and above all, of the supremacy of God over man, whether himself or the king. To have shirked this fight would have lost the campaign, and after ages would never have heard of him; the winning it was the start of life-long victory, of final triumph; and Daniel stands in Scripture as one of the very few, whose lives are told at length, against whom no fault is recorded. He is an instance of what is meant by being " without blemish."

Nor was it that he had to depart from the world as to bodily presence. He could not, for he was a captive. Where a believer *can* leave a yoke with an unbeliever he is peremptorily commanded to do so, by words before quoted. "Come ye out from among them and be ye separate," is imperative. But it may not always be rightly possible. Slaves could not escape that yoke, and were directed how to adorn the Christian teaching while under it. A believing husband or wife may not break the already accepted yoke with an unbeliever (I Cor. 7). We are not called to go out of the world physically to secure our sanctification (I Cor. 5 : 9, 10), as monks and hermits would fain do. Indeed, it is precisely what the Lord did *not* ask for His followers, but rather that they, being sent by Him into the world as His representatives and to be the salt of the earth, should be kept from its evil and its evil prince (John 17 : 15). So Daniel shall live seventy long years at Babylon, the centre of the world, yet not be of it, nor be tarnished by it. And the grace that sufficed for him is more abundantly available for us, since Jesus went to the throne and the Spirit of holiness came down to dwell in us. Only we, like Daniel, must be, and must abide, in the place and calling clearly appointed of God for each ; and in this dispensation, unlike that, political office is not a sphere of God for us, as it was not for our Lord when here. Not till He rules should we.

Now the real, the God-intended separation from the world involves practical difficulties. For Daniel these were literally insurmountable, a mountain he could in no wise himself remove. The great king had prescribed a certain arrangement of life : who would dare to vary it ? To do so would " endanger the head " of the presumptuous officer that sanctioned it (1 : 10). But God is supreme, and will open a way for him who is determined to be holy. The very will of God is our sanctification (I Thess. 4 : 3), and He will make it possible. In Daniel's case He (1) disposed the heart of the heathen official concerned to be kind and compassionate towards the captive youth, a very rare circumstance that must have comforted and emboldened Daniel. Then (2) He gave Daniel tact and courage as to the test to be applied in the practical handling of the matter. (3) He made Daniel and his three friends to flourish physically on the spare diet. Thousands of Christians might well note this to their advantage. (4) He wrought in them humble submission to the official under whom they found themselves by His permission (1 : 13), coupled with secret and firm faith that God would endorse their course. With this sure confidence in God the believer can with quietness let his forbearance and yieldingness be known unto all men. Apparently he leaves the situation to them, while actually he commits it into the hand of God, knowing that He is at hand and is working. (Phil. 4 : 4–7). " Wherefore let them also that suffer according to the will of God commit their souls [better, their lives] in well-doing unto a faithful Creator " (I Pet. 4 : 19).

That Daniel's three friends were with him in this faithfulness which God endorsed, shows that this course of life was not for a specially great servant of God alone, but is for all. Indeed, as yet Daniel was not great, but lowly in station. What is before us was the first step to true greatness. Their adherence to the will of God brought accession of knowledge, skill, and understanding (17) ; so that these men of God proved vastly superior counsellors, even in practical and weighty human affairs, to the cleverest men of the world (20).

Thus purposing at all cost to please God, to be pure, thus endowed, and educated in the divine school of discipline, the young man set forward on the journey of life, thick beset with perils and trials ; and it was given to him to show to after-generations, to us, that God is El Shaddai, the All-sufficing ; for seventy years later, in extreme old age (9 : 1, 2) he was still, by his understanding and his prayers, a pivotal co-worker with his God and for the people of God. Such as will be holy must

> " . . . climb the steep ascent of heaven
> Through peril, toil, and pain.
> O God, to us may grace be given
> To follow in their train ! "

And the qualification for being a prophet is the qualification for understanding prophecy. The reader must be one with the prophet in this at least, the resolute purpose to be holy. For the immediate end of all prophecy is practical, moral : " every one that hath this hope set on Christ purifieth himself, even as He is pure " (1 John 3 : 3). Merely mental study of Scripture is idle, and being idle is mischievous ; but " if any man *intendeth to do* God's will, he shall know of the teaching whether it is of God " (John 7 : 17). Therefore, as we proceed to consider the visions and messages of Daniel let each ask himself, Am I a man of Daniel's moral purpose and resolve ? If so, the Spirit of truth will open the meaning of what He showed and said to Daniel ; if not, Daniel's book will remain a sealed book, even when the time of the end may have come (12 : 9).

CHAPTER II

THE EMPEROR'S DREAM

Section I. *The World Crisis that occasioned it*

SUPREMACY OVER THE HUMAN RACE WAS SECURED BY SATAN when Adam and Eve accepted his counsel in defiance of the will of God. He thus became the Prince of the world, and history exhibits two main purposes : that of Satan to maintain his rule, and that of God to regain His sovereignty. Satan rules in disregard of the true welfare of man : " The thief cometh not but that he may steal, and kill, and destroy " : God aims at the well-being of His creatures : " I came that they may have life, and may have it abundantly " (John 10 : 10). He who is a murderer from the beginning loves to destroy (John 8 : 44) ; but to God destruction is a strange work (Isa. 28 : 21) : " I have no pleasure in the death of him that dieth, saith the Lord Jehovah " (Ezek. 18 : 23, 32) ; and His judgements are executed as part, though an unavoidable part, of the process of restoring good government and peace among men (Matt. 13 : 41-43) ; for the true Ruler rules for the good of the ruled.

B.C. 1921. A chief step towards this divine end was the selecting of a portion of mankind to act as a nucleus of the recovery of the whole race and earth. For this purpose God chose Abraham, of Ur in Chaldea, and announced to him, " in thee shall all the families of the earth be blessed " (Gen. 12 : 3).

B.C. 1451. In pursuance of this purpose and promise Abraham's descendants were multiplied into a nation, and became the pivotal people on earth, in reference to whom as a people national and international relationships are regarded and regulated by God (Gen. 12 : 3 ; Deut. 32 : 8, 9). The divine installing of Israel in this position is the first key to the puzzle of international history, and the placing them at the geographical centre of the ancient world, Palestine (Ezek. 5 : 5), was an epoch-marking event. Their return there as the allotted period of Gentile domination ends, at which time international affairs will, as at the beginning, be found centred in those regions, will mark a corresponding epoch.

B.C. 1015. A further chief step in the divine plan was the

17

elevating of that people to national supremacy under David and Solomon, ancestors of, and a joint type of, Jesus Christ, the Son of God and son of David, in whom finally all the purpose of God for world blessing shall be completed.

But David's successors on the throne proved unequal to maintaining the supremacy he had won, nor were his people ever fired by the consciousness of the benevolent purpose of Abram's God towards all the families of the earth. Self-centred, they were found unadapted to the design of God, and it became needful to chasten them into humility and into fitness for the work required. This process would prove to be protracted, though it should at last reach its goal, as all divine purposes do and will.

B.C. 603. This dire necessity brought on a further chief epoch. The sovereignty of the earth was designedly transferred by God from Israel to Gentile hands, partly for the testing of the latter, and so as to show that these also are incompetent for producing world peace, by delivering the human race from the baneful rule of the Usurper and restoring the benign sovereignty of God. Nebuchadnezzar, king of Babylon, was permitted to attain world supremacy, and in the process to dethrone the kings of Israel and to remove the chosen people from their land.

This reveals a third great factor in world affairs. First, human rulers follow their own plans to further their own ambitions; second, and often unknown to them, the Prince of this world uses them for his fell purposes; and third, behind and above and through them both, God works towards His purpose of universal blessing. Blessed are the pure in heart, for amid all earth's darkness and confusion they see God at work, and are quietened and comforted amidst the raging storms.

Godly Israelites of Nebuchadnezzar's time needed this enlightenment and comfort, and it was freely granted to them. Nine centuries earlier Moses had disclosed the general development of Israel's future and chastisement, ending in their restoration of soul and of their outward position and service in the purposes of their God (Lev. 26; Deut. 32). Still nearer to their day (150 years before) Isaiah had shown that the power of Assyria* would be used to humble Israel, but that this accomplished, God would duly punish the Assyrian for the pride and cruelty shown as he did the

---

* A name which at that period sometimes included Babylonia; see Herodotus III, 155: "I could not endure that the Assyrians [meaning Babylonians] should laugh at the Persians." So also in Ezra 6: 22, and in the Apocr. (Jud. 1: 7; 2: 1, 4,; 5: 1) rulers of Babylon are called "kings of Assur."

work (Isa. 10 : 5–7, 12–14 ; etc.). This leading prophecy extends to the close of c. 12 and is there seen to stretch on to a point when Israel is restored to permanent favour, with the Holy One of Israel dwelling in Zion. This shows that its terms were not exhausted by the monarchs who commenced the judgments, such as Shalmaneser and Nebuchadnezzar, but that the final executor of the wrath of God against Israel, whose work will at last fit them as a people to fulfil the promise to their first father, will also be a king of Assyria.

And it may be that this last world-emperor will take the name of the first world-emperor, for, in connexion with the final destruction of Babylon and the final restoration of Israel, it is said : " Israel is a scattered sheep ; the lions have driven him away : first the king of Assyria hath devoured him (Shalmaneser, II Kings 17 : 3) ; and now at *last* this Nebuchadnezzar king of Babylon hath broken his bones " (Jer. 50 : 17). At the time this was written the Nebuchadnezzar of that day may have been in the mind of Jeremiah ; but God often had in *His* view more than the prophet saw (I Peter 1 : 10–12), and the next verse denounces against Babylon as complete an overthrow as had fallen upon Nineveh, and this in connexion with the restoration of Israel to their land, and the final removing of their iniquity. Here, then, the *last* oppressor of Israel is perhaps named Nebuchadnezzar. This is the more likely seeing that Jeremiah speaks here of the northern Kingdom, Carmel, Bashan, Gilead, Ephraim, and in distinction from Judah which is mentioned separately. Now the Nebuchadnezzar of that day did not " break the bones " of the ten tribes, for they had long before been carried away from their land. But the whole land will have descendants of Israel at the end times, and will be overrun by the Beast.

Such an overthrow of Babylon as is detailed in Jeremiah and Revelation 18 the city did not have in Nebuchadnezzar's day. It remained the centre of the world for over 200 years after his time, and continued to exist for another fifteen centuries. But Jeremiah foretells a destruction of the king of Babylon and his land like to that of Assyria. Nebuchadnezzar of old saw no fulfilment of this ; but the Beast will see it to the utmost degree and the last detail. That last king of Babylon, by grant from the dragon (Rev. 13 : 2, 3), will attain completely to the universal dominion granted to the first Nebuchadnezzar, but never actually attained by him, and God's word will be literally fulfilled. See my *Revelation of Jesus Christ*, ch. XII, which chapter may be had as a pamphlet.

Moreover, to direct and to strengthen the godly in that former awful time of transfer of sovereignty and of world chaos, Jeremiah had plainly and repeatedly explained the control of God in that fearful drama.   He had announced that world supremacy had been granted to Nebuchadnezzar ;   that all nations must submit or be destroyed ;   but that this Gentile supremacy would prove but temporary.   There would be a partial restoration of Israel after seventy years, and a complete and permanent restoration later, which Isaiah had already announced (Jer. 27 ;   28 ;   29 ;   etc. : Isa. 10 ;   11 ;   etc.).

These inspired messages would guide such as Daniel to the attitude they took of submission to their conquerors, and thus save them from futile attempts to rebel or to escape, and at the same time sustain them with the good hope of deliverance and of final prosperity for their people.

But yet clearer guidance and yet richer comfort were to be given, for both the godly in that crisis period and for their successors until the very end of that whole period of Gentile supremacy then commencing.   And it should be given first to the first head of world empire, so that he, and all subsequent world rulers, might know, if they will, the circumstances under which they hold power, by permission of the Lord of the whole earth, and might shape their course in His fear.

Nebuchadnezzar shall be made to see in a dream the character and course of world empires, of the first of which he was the creator and head.   And that it might never be justly questioned that this vision was God-given, and its meaning God-revealed, and therefore was true and also certain of fulfilment, the purely supernatural course was taken of a second man being caused to dream over again the altogether exceptional vision which the former man had dreamed, in both its general features and its detail, and then to explain its significance.   Nebuchadnezzar was shrewd enough to conclude that one who really had power from heaven to interpret a dream could also learn from heaven what had been dreamed.   The Chaldean diviners failed at this reasonable test ;   Daniel fulfilled it.

Section II.   *A Satanic Attack on Daniel*

It is a chief method of Satan to seek to turn to *his* ends God's measures for serving *His* ends.   Thus Adam, designed to rule this earth for God, is seduced into surrendering that rule to Satan.

God had now worked in an unusual way to instruct Nebuchadnezzar and exalt Daniel. Satan at once schemed to destroy Daniel. He would work through Nebuchadnezzar's craft and cruelty. Such a man is a ready tool for the craft and cruelty of Satan. A spirit like his is a good conducting medium for the energy of the " spirit that now worketh in the sons of disobedience " (Eph. 2 : 2). It offers no resistance to his moral force, but is susceptible to his impulses.

The blessed parallel to this is, that a pure, gentle, peaceable spirit is equally a suitable vehicle for the transmission of the impulses of the holy Spirit of God. Am I such ?

Thus the human spirit is the " transformer " through which the devices and forces of the invisible world are rendered active and effective in the world of mankind. Therefore, says God, " take heed unto your spirit, that none deal treacherously " and " be renewed in the spirit of your mind " (Mal. 2 : 15 ; Eph. 4 : 23).

It came into Nebuchadnezzar's mind to set a test for all his professional " wise men," a test quite impossible of fulfilment by them ; and that upon their failure they shall all be destroyed ; and as Daniel and his friends belonged to this order they would equally be destroyed. To Satan it were a trifling price that hundreds of his faithful subjects should perish, if he can thus compass the death of this dangerous young servant of God, Daniel, and of his three companions. He can easily provide a thousand more inspired sorcerers to deceive his dupe, the king ; but at all costs Daniel must be put out of the way. It is thus that Satan's human servants, ambitious monarchs and dictators, to serve some mad or selfish end, coolly hurl thousands of their fellow-men to premature death in war.

A man who purposes that he will not defile himself thereby provokes the utmost satanic hostility. But it is equally and blessedly true that one who thus purposes, thereby puts himself under the shadow of the Almighty, the righteous Lord who loveth righteousness. " The Lord knoweth how to deliver the godly," as Peter and Daniel proved ; and even when He does not deliver, yet finally not a hair of their head shall perish (II Peter 2 : 9 ; Acts 12 ; Luke 21 : 18).

Satan's scheme was not only frustrated, but was made to serve more brilliantly the purposes of God. There is a limit to the power of spirits : they can cause men to dream (Matt. 1 : 20 ; 2 : 13, 19) ;

but it seems that they cannot perceive what a man is otherwise dreaming, or else Satan could have glorified *his* servants by enabling *them* to tell the king what he had dreamed.   But only the all-wise Searcher of hearts can understand a man's thoughts when so far off from his own control as in a dream.   He revealed the king's secret to Daniel, and thus God was exalted before the king and his court, and Daniel, whose destruction had been plotted, was advanced to far higher position and influence for serving the purposes of God.

But the man who is to be thus honoured and used must be a man of prayer (2 : 18, 23), and also one who can be trusted to give all the praise to Him to Whom it is all due, and to give it in private as in public (2 : 19, 23, 27, 28, 30).   God cannot consent that His glory shall be stolen by a creature (Isa. 42 : 8) ; Israel must not vaunt themselves against Him (Judges 7 : 2).

Section III.   *The Dream*

All men trembled and feared before the ferocious Emperor (5 : 19 ; 1 : 10), but he before nothing, except *dreams* (2 : 1 ; 4 : 5). " Thus conscience doth make cowards of us all," including the mightiest.   Even the pious Job said, " Thou scarest me with dreams, and terrifiest me through visions " (Job 7 : 14).   And truly such dreams as Nebuchadnezzar saw were as calculated as they were designed to alarm a proud and ruthless conqueror and oppressor.

In the visions of the night there stood before him a mighty and magnificent human form, with head of gold, breast and arms of silver, belly and thighs of brass, legs of iron, and feet and toes part of iron and part of earthenware.   As he gazed, from a towering mountain a boulder was detached, which fell swiftly and heavily upon the image, smashed it to pieces, crushed all its parts to powder, and a mighty wind springing up swept all away, as the chaff of the summer threshing floor is carried before the breeze.   Then the stone that had fallen enlarged until it filled the horizon and covered the whole earth.

To gain something of the effect produced in Nebuchadnezzar it is needful to give time to think oneself into his position, and also to *visualize* the scene, not merely to read the record as simply description.   Imagination is a most valuable faculty, so long as, in spiritual subjects, it works only upon the material supplied by inspiration.

Its danger arises in introducing features not in the record, which mistake has too much blurred the study of scripture visions and their interpretation.

An imperious monarch, who had lived, fought, risked life itself to create a vast empire, might reasonably be fascinated and terrified by such a vision. For

1. It brought vividly to mind that sad and outstanding fact in all human affairs—degeneration. Silver, brass, iron, earthenware is each of lower quality than its predecessor, and the last spoke of frailty also, of that want of cohesion which assures weakness and collapse and is fatal to all institutions.

2. The vision reminded him also that there are powers superior to man that will bring destruction on all his boasted enterprises and glory. It was without human hands that the stone was cut out of the mountain, and winds are beyond man's control. It would seem that modern statesmen practically ignore this dominant factor in world affairs. But the heathen had observed and allowed for it. Hence the offerings to their gods on all occasions. Nor is it reasonable to suppose that so expensive, humbling, and mysterious a practice should have utterly deceived for thousands of years millions upon millions of men as shrewd as ourselves, and no more liable or wishful to be deceived. It is more reasonable to suppose that so universal and age-long a practice has *something* of reality behind it. It was not long after Nebuchadnezzar that Solon, the wisest of the Athenians, told (as is reported) another rich and powerful monarch, Crœsus of Lydia, that he had observed that the gods, after greatly prospering a man, and when he became proud thereby, had a way of suddenly plucking him up by the roots, and that therefore he could not adjudge Crœsus happy until he had seen his end. The tale is that the prosperous and haughty king scorned such a melancholy view of life, but when roasting in the fire, where Cyrus put him after conquest and capture, he remembered the Athenian, and Herodotus attributes his calamity to the anger of the gods at his pride.

Nebuchadnezzar was now to be instructed along that line: he was to be shown the end of human greatness, at its greatest development in universal empire. The vision gives but a brief sketch of the long and weary centuries of Gentile domination of the earth, but enlarges greatly upon its closing period. This is a characteristic of prophetic Scripture. It links the beginnings and endings, with often very little notice of the intervening time. The first prophecy reveals this distinctly (Gen. 3 : 15). The fall is linked directly with Calvary, and then with the final defeat of the serpent in the earth campaign then opened between it and God. Only two stages from start to finish of the, to us, so long drama of world history.

And that end of world affairs is destruction from the Almighty. How foolish, then, and ungodly it is for the godly to invest time, energy, money, and in time of war life itself, in buttressing and polishing an image that the powers of heaven have afore-doomed to destruction. This folly shall be manifest unto all when God arises to judgment.

3. To the acute mind that was watching the vision it would be evident that, whatever dire event the descent of the boulder might portend, it figured an action that would be sudden, violent, irresistible ; for the fall and crash would be a matter of but a few moments, indeed, all but instantaneous, and as unexpected as overwhelming. No more absurd, outrageous treatment of a figure can be found than the notion that all this smash-up of world empire, with the high winds of wrath sweeping away the very refuse, sets forth the quiet and unobserved birth of a Babe into the world, with the very, very gradual spread of a movement of peace that He would inaugurate, the very extension of which by force He should expressly forbid. Moreover, the stone does not commence to enlarge until after the image is wholly removed.

Here is notable proof of the profound importance of grasping accurately the figurative and symbolic method of instruction, so natural to the oriental mind, and therefore to the Bible, and so considerably foreign to the mechanized habit of mind of the modern Westerner. Rightly understood, a figure, so far from being a loose type of expression, teaches as precisely as a direct statement, and generally much more richly and pleasingly, thus making a deeper and more lasting impression upon the memory. The book of Proverbs is an excellent primer for the study of figurative speech.

Section IV. *The Interpretation.*

This vision being fundamental to understanding the divinely over-ruled course of world history we shall give in full the divine intepretation of it.

Daniel 2 : 36-45. This is the dream ; and we will tell the interpretation thereof before the king. Thou, O king, art king of kings, unto
whom the God of the heavens hath given the kingdom, the power,
and the strength, and the glory ; and wheresoever the children of
men dwell, the beasts of the field and the fowls of the heaven hath
he given into thine hand, and hath made thee to rule [better, with
Darby, *ruler*] over them all : thou art the head of gold. And after
thee shall arise another kingdom inferior to thee ; and another third
kingdom of brass, which shall bear rule over all the earth. And the
fourth kingdom shall be strong as iron : forasmuch as iron breaketh
in pieces and subdueth all things : and as iron that crusheth all these,
shall it break in pieces and crush. And whereas thou sawest the feet
and toes, part of potter's clay and part of iron, it shall be a divided
kingdom ; but there shall be in it of the strength of the iron, forasmuch
as thou sawest the iron mixed with miry clay [or, earthenware]. And as
the toes of the feet were part of iron, and part of clay, so the kingdom shall
be partly strong, and partly broken [or, brittle]. And whereas thou
sawest the iron mixed with miry clay, they shall mingle themselves with
the seed of men ; but they shall not cleave one to another, even as iron
doth not mingle with clay.

And in the days of those kings shall the God of the heavens set up
a kingdom, which shall never be destroyed, nor shall the sovereignty
thereof be left to another people ; but it shall break in pieces and consume all these kingdoms, and it shall stand for ever, forasmuch as thou
sawest that a stone was cut out of the mountain without hands, and
that it brake in pieces the iron, the brass, the clay, the silver, and the
gold. The great God hath made known to the king what shall come
to pass hereafter : and the dream is certain, and the interpretation
thereof sure.

The following matters require careful consideration.

i. Nebuchadnezzar personally was the head of gold. Writing
over sixty years ago (in 1886) Dr. Grattan Guinness, in his *Light for
the Last Days*, purported to draw out of Scripture a painfully
intricate set of periods connected with prophecy and history. The
calculations were based on the year-day theory, that in prophecy
a day *means* a year, so that 1,260 days means 1,260 years. This is
essential to the historical scheme of interpretation, which would
make out that almost all prophecies have been fulfilled except the
actual advent of our Lord. Dr. Guinness's scheme has been the
basis of later attempts to fix the end of the age.

All this elaborate reasoning started from an assumed and non-
Scriptural idea, and thus was wholly erroneous. The cycles varied
in their terminal points, being made to run out over a period of

some 135 years.   Hence it was indispensable to find a corresponding
period within which they could commence.   This was gained by
the assumption that the whole duration of the Babylonian kingdom
was included under the golden head of the image.   But this assumption, and the derived calculations now falsified, would have been
impossible had Daniel's emphatic terms been accepted : " *Thou*, O
king . . . *thou* art the head of gold."   When " thou " can be made
to mean a long succession of persons covering a century and a
half, grammar would seem to have lost all force.   Moreover, Nebuchadnezzar was the head of gold for a distinct reason that had no
application to any king of Babylon before him, even the grant of
universal dominion.

ii. An important feature of the image is the deterioration in the
quality of rule, indicated by the ever-lessening value of the metals
chosen, gold, silver, brass, iron, earthenware.   This process should
end in government by violence, as iron crushing all, but with a
brittle, easily broken earthenware moderating this extreme of force,
yet itself owing its preservation to the iron element persisting to
the last.

Nebuchadnezzar was an absolute monarch : as Daniel afterwards
said : " whom he would he slew, and whom he would he kept
alive ; and whom he would he raised up, and whom he would he
put down " (5 : 19).   Gold indicated *autocratic* rule.

The Persian sovereigns were limited by the power of the great
nobles.   See ch. 6, where Darius is seen restricted by the laws and
circumvented by the nobility.   The rule was *aristocratic*.   A similar
scene was King John forced by the nobles to seal Magna Charta in
A.D. 1215.

The Grecian authority was *military*.   Alexander succeeded because he was a great soldier.   After his early death his empire fell
to pieces by internal strife, there being no genius to prevent this,
but ambitious soldiers to hasten it.

The Roman power was ruthless : it crushed, it organized, it
legislated, but its authority was maintained always by severity and
lapsed when its strength to crush failed.   The Papacy dominated
the middle ages by the same ruthlessness, as witness the general
slaughters of Waldenses, Albigenses, and others, and the horrors
of the Inquisition.

For the past century and a half there has developed the power
of the masses.   It was seen in measure in the middle ages in the

power of trade guilds, free cities, and merchant princes, but it advanced notably in and since the French Revolution. As far as this *democratic* influence has modified the brutality of the " iron " it has been beneficial ; but earthenware is essentially weak under strain or against violence, and the stern dangers and emergencies of affairs public change democracies into autocracies, actually if not nominally. The excesses and weaknesses of the French Revolution demanded and produced Napoleon, and the Great War (1914–1918) put power into a few hands, even in the most democratic lands. The subsequent uncertainties brought the rise of dictators, and the Russian democratic movement has proved the most despotic and frightful tyranny that has ever cursed the world. The 1939–1945 War brought a distinct increase of despotic rule in Western lands (see my *World Chaos*).

Thus the elements of iron and earthenware commingle but cannot coalesce (ver. 43). The earthenware brings weakness, the iron lends strength, and thus will it be to the end of this age. And behind them both faith sees the God of heaven, watchful, merciful, strong, overruling and overturning, until He shall come whose right it is to reign.

Ideal government is by an autocrat, if he be a perfect being. But in the hands of fallen man it tends ever to tyranny. Yet it remains the ideal, for it is divine : God is the absolute monarch of the universe. He has determined that all things shall be subject to man (Gen. 1 : 26–28 ; Ps. 8 ; Heb. 2), but he must be a perfect man, in character, wisdom, and power, for only such an one can be trusted with such authority. The man Christ Jesus alone fulfils every requirement, and His kingdom shall stand for ever.

iii. It is to be especially noted that Daniel's interpretation ignores not only the kings of Babylon that preceded Nebuchadnezzar but also those who succeeded him. The second stage, the breast and arms of silver, was to come simply " after thee." It is the same as to the third stage. Some details of these will be given to Daniel later (ch. 8), but for the purpose of the instruction to be gained from the image the first three periods are comparatively unimportant. The stress lies upon the fourth part, and there again most especially upon the final stage, the feet and toes.

Daniel impressed this upon Nebuchadnezzar : " God hath made known to the king Nebuchadnezzar what shall be in the latter days " (or, at the *end* of days). The then current force of this term is easily learned. The great prophet Isaiah, in a leading utterance which lies at the base of prophecy, had applied it to the days of Messiah, when the house of Jehovah is to be established at the top of the mountains (Isa. 2 : 2). Daniel's contemporaries, Jeremiah and Ezekiel, employed it in prophecies concerning that same era. See Jeremiah 23 : 20 ; 30 : 24. The latter chapter is occupied with the final restoration of Jacob. It speaks of the "time of Jacob's trouble " ; of their consequent liberation from all thraldom ; that David is to be their king ; of a full end being made of their enemies (8–11) ; their Prince is to be one able to " draw near " unto God. that is, to be a priest as well as a ruler. Comp. Zech. 6 : 12, 13. See also Jer. 48 : 47 ; 49 : 39 for predictions concerning Moab and Edom still awaiting fulfilment in " the latter days." In Ezek. 38 : 16 the yet future invasion of Palestine by Gog and Magog is to be in the latter days. Read further Num. 24 : 14 ; Deut. 4 : 30 ; 31 : 29 ; Hos. 3 : 5, all to the same effect.

It is most important to observe this double feature of what the prophet does *not* explain and of the vision passing on to the end of the age, because much of the common explanations of this chapter ignores it and makes the image to teach concerning the long centuries of this era. Nor is the historical school alone at fault ; much futurist treatment is to the same effect.

For example, it is very generally taught

1. That the lower part of the trunk points to the earlier Roman days.

2. The two legs represent the Roman empire in division, the eastern and western sections.

3. That the empire passed away under the attacks of Vandals and Saracens.

4. That it is to be " revived " at the end of the age.

5. That its final limits are to be those of its greatest former extent, under Trajan or Hadrian, early in the second century A.D. This assumed area is spoken of as " the Roman earth " or " the prophetic earth."

6. That territory not within those limits will not form part of it at last.

7. That the ten kingdoms, the toes of the image, will be distributed five in the western section and five in the eastern of the old empire. (See Note at end of this chapter.)

Now all these details have been imported by interpreters. The divine explanation through Daniel does not suggest any one of them. They have been invented by attempting to explain what the wisdom of God saw fit not to explain, to fasten a special meaning upon things to which *He* did not assign a meaning. Let us examine each detail.

1. The fourth kingdom of prophecy bears no name in Scripture. Nebuchadnezzar is named, as also his city, Babylon. The name of the second empire, Persia, is given (Dan. 5 : 28 ; 8 : 20 ; etc.). Greece is mentioned by name, as overthrowing Persia (8 : 21). *The fourth power is unnamed.* It has been most confusing that writers have universally assigned to it the name of its place of origin, for thus thought has been concentrated intensely upon the city of Rome as its centre throughout its existence. But in prophecy Rome has no special place and is not even mentioned. Thus the " historical " interpretation is without foundation, and " futurism " also must be modified.

Babylon had existed since the days of Nimrod (Gen. 10 : 10), but the ups and downs of that state during those fifteen hundreds of years do not matter *prophetically.* It was when Nebuchadnezzar made Babylon the centre of a world empire that the first kingdom of *prophecy* arose.

The Medes and Persians had had an almost equally long history, but that is of no account *prophetically.* It was when Cyrus made Babylon the centre of his rule that the second kingdom of *prophecy* appeared.

The Grecian states had been fighting, developing, colonizing for long centuries before Alexander, but prophecy takes no account of this also. It simply does not matter. It was when Alexander made Babylon his world-centre that the third kingdom of *prophecy* became present.

It is thus with the fourth empire, as might surely be expected. The mutations of its long course are of small concern *prophetically.* The divine interpretation and the profound interest concentrate on the closing days, when Antichrist will make Babylon his capital. This may be inferred from the fact that a vertical image is employed to picture the whole period ; for the centre of gravity of each successive portion is exactly under that of the portions above, so that the feet stand directly beneath the head, breast, and body.

2. These facts rule out all attempts to fit the history of this age into the legs of the image. The attempt has involved some distortion of both history and the image, as when it is urged that all through the centuries there have always been ten or about ten

kingdoms in the Roman territory. This is as much as to say that the toes and the legs are contemporary, as if the toes had pushed out all down the legs. Obviously toes are the *final* stage of the image. But if the attempt to fit the legs to history could succeed it would be of no importance to the lessons of the vision.

If the two legs represented the divided Roman empire, why was not the image shown as standing on one leg for perhaps a third of its course ? for the western part succumbed in A.D. 476 while the eastern portion survived almost a thousand years, till A.D. 1453. That the image was *standing* is noted by the prophet (31).

A well-known and ardent historicist wrote to me that the image though presented as vertical, was to be interpreted as horizontal, lying with the head at Babylon and the feet at Rome. I pointed out that Persia, the second portion of the image, was further east than Babylon, and that Babylon lay between it and Greece, the third portion ; and that thus the image would present the curious feature, unperceived it would seem by Nebuchadnezzar, of the head being situate between the breast and the belly.

He further urged that the number of the toes was not to be taken literally : that since the division of the Roman empire its territory had been always occupied by that number of states more or less, sometimes thirteen, sometimes eight, but always about ten. And he added that had I lived in the east, as he had done, I would have known that the oriental does not treat numbers too literally. My answer was that *I had* lived in the east, in fact had just then returned from eighteen months in Egypt, and had never met an oriental who, when he spoke of his ten toes, meant that sometimes he had thirteen, sometimes eight, but always about ten ! To this question we shall return when dealing with the ten horns of the fourth beast of Daniel 7.

With all respect to good and learned brethren, one must feel that a system of interpretation which involves the grotesque is self-refuted.

3. Nor does the image show any breach of continuity from beginning to end. Nebuchadnezzar was not shown the legs as broken off and re-joined. The notion of the empire passing away and reappearing is a needless invention arising from the misleading attempt to fit into the interpretation a period that the Spirit of truth passes over untouched because it is unimportant to prophecy. The ups and downs of the fourth kingdom prior to its final stage are as immaterial to prophecy as are those of the first kingdom.

4. This idea of a reviving of the Roman empire is a result of misunderstanding a statement in Rev. 17. We read there of a " beast," " who was, and is not, and is about to come up out of the abyss, and to go into perdition " (ver. 8). But *this* beast is not an empire but a person. It is immediately shown that he is a king, not a kingdom (vers. 10, 11), and he will have ten associate kings (12). These will be the ten toes of the image. These kings are to make him their overlord (17). The Abyss is a locality quite well known to Scripture. It is the region within the earth whither all the dead have gone and still go. It is mentioned in Luke 8 : 31 ; Rom. 10 : 7 ; Rev. 9 : 1, 2, 11 ; 11 : 7 ; 17 : 8 ; 20 : 1, 3. No more blundering translation is to be found than the A.V. " bottomless pit," a term which, if it gives any sense, gives a wholly erroneous picture. The boy Spurgeon floored his ministerial grandfather with the query, If the pit has no bottom where do the people go when they fall out the other end ? A deep, vast, unexplored region is the idea.

Now *empires* do not descend into that place, though the individuals who once formed them go there ; and no *empire* will return thence, though God will suffer Satan to bring back a *man*, who has formerly reigned on earth, to reign again as his vicegerent (Rev. 13 : 2–10 ; Dan. 8 : 24 ; 11 : 37–39). This resuscitated king will " go into perdition," that is, he will not be sent again into the first death, into Hades or Tartarus (II Peter 2 : 4), which are parts of the Abyss, because he will have been there before, but he will be cast direct into the second death, the lake of fire (Rev. 19 : 20 ; 20 : 10). " It is laid up for men *once* to die, and after this judgment " (Heb. 9 : 27). This is wholly inapplicable to an empire corporately.

This fact of the future deceiver and emperor being a man now in Hades is, we think, the clue to a passage endlessly debated but never yet elucidated, II Thess. 2 : 1–12. It reads : " The day of the Lord will not be except the falling away come first and the man of lawlessness be revealed, the son of perdition. . . . And now ye know that which restraineth, to the end that he may be revealed in his own season. For the mystery of lawlessness doth already work, only there is one that restraineth now until he be taken out of the way, and then shall be revealed the lawless one," etc. This says that *lawlessness* is already working, *not* that it is being restrained ; but that the *lawless one* is being held back by some power until the season when he is to be permitted to work again on earth. The gates of Hades prevail against him. Who the restrainer of the dead is the Thessalonians knew very well, as Paul intimates ; for they had been mostly heathen, and all mythology, from the earliest Babylonian times, had taught concerning an angel ruler of the abyss, who received every one sent down to him but released no one, not even a goddess visiting Hades,* save by special order of the supreme god. This is one of some interesting points in which Scripture confirms mythology. The very name of this angel keeper of the Abyss is given in Rev. 9 : 11 in its Hebrew and Greek forms, the latter being actually akin to the name of one of the best known and most feared of the Greek gods, Apollo, the Destroyer. No wonder that the Greek Thessalonians knew about him. He is in view again, unnamed, in Rev. 6 : 8.

We therefore dismiss from prophetic study this whole conception of the fourth empire of prophecy being " Roman," of its passing away and reappearing, as well as the idea of its area being that of the old Roman world. We adhere to the picture employed, that the image, though in fact going through many changes in area and form and rule, is an unbroken continuity, and that the supremely momentous period is its end, and this will find its centre at Babylon under Antichrist. Dominance of the earth has continued to flow from peoples that have been connected with the fourth empire, and no others have attained it. This will continue until the fourth kingdom has absorbed all its predecessors, but by that time its centre will have shifted to Babylon and its area will be vaster than at any previous time.

Though it belongs rather to the exposition of the *Revelation* than of *Daniel* it may be well to add that the harlot of Rev. 17 is only temporarily associated with Rome. At the time John saw the visions she was connected with the Seven Hilled city (ver. 18), but, as her name indicates, she is properly Babylonian. The religious system that we know as the Roman Catholic Church commenced in Babylon after the Flood, and thence infected all nations (Jer. 51 : 7). As God's movements in providence and the gospel moved westward, from the Semitic to the Japhetic peoples, Satan also moved his centre westward, and at last to Rome. The bastard Christianity of the Roman Church is heathendom christened with Christian names and forms. Upon this see the first five chapters

* See the myth concerning Ishtar. S. H. Langton, *The Mythology of All Races*, Vol. V, *Semitic*, 326–335 ; Wallis Budge, *Babylonian Life and History*, 138 ; Spence, *Myths and Legends of Babylonia and Assyria*, 125.

of Alexander Hislop's *The Two Babylons* and G. H. Pember's *Mystery Babylon the Great and The Mysteries and Catholicism.* As God's movements return to the middle east so will those of Satan. Politically this is going on now, and the woman, in order that she may ride on the beast, that is, dominate politics, must follow suit. This is pictured in Zechariah's vision (5 : 5–11) of the woman in the ephah being taken back and re-established " in her own place," which is in the land of Shinar, that is, in Mesopotamia at Babylon (Dan. 1 : 2). As Zechariah saw her taken from his land to Shinar it may be presumed that her headquarters will for a time be in Palestine. She is already the owner of many historic sites and fine properties. It is to be remembered that this Church is not tied to Rome. She does not call herself Roman Catholic but simply Catholic ; and during the War of 1914–18 it was stated in the Press more than once that the then Pope had expressed a willingness to remove from Rome. This was repeated during the late war (1940). By the time the system reaches her own place in Babylon she will have absorbed many of her daughter systems and will have become a much more powerful organization than at present (see p. 105).

That the city Babylon is to be rebuilt is required by the fact that the divine predictions concerning it have not yet found fulfilment. The whole proof is too long to be given here, but

(1) Babylon is to have an overthrow as sudden and complete as that of Sodom, like as when a stone is flung into deep water (Isa. 47 : 11 ; Jer. 50 : 40 ; 51 : 61–64). The city has never been thus overwhelmed, but only very gradually decayed. That this destruction was still waiting at the close of the first century after Christ is seen from the repetition of this detail, the stone flung into water, in Rev. 18 : 21. As late as the fifth century A.D. Babylon was still a town of size, and Jews were living there— see *The Jewish Encyclo.*, vol. II, 400, s.v. " Babylon." It is highly doubtful if the site has ever been wholly uninhabited, as is required by Jer. 50 : 39, 40, and Isa. 13 : 20. The last passage says that the Arabian shall never pitch his tent there after the destruction. Now in a diary of Dr. W. E. Blackstone, the author of *Jesus is Coming*, which I read in Egypt many years ago, just after he had toured Babylonia, he stated distinctly that he had tested the point with his Arab guides and they made no objection at all to pitching in the midst of the ruins.

(2) This sudden destruction is to reduce the city to heaps of ruins, and it is to be effected by the Medes (Jer. 51 : 27, 28 ; Isa. 13 : 17). Now Herodotus testifies explicitly that when Cyrus captured the city of old he did not destroy it at all and that its gates and walls were left intact. Indeed, Cyrus made it his capital under Darius the Mede (Dan. 5 : 31). Cyrus' own account confirms Herodotus on this point—see Sayce, *Ezra, Nehemiah, and Esther*, 12, 16. It was some two centuries later that Herodotus visited and described the city (Her. Bk. III, 159).

(3) Various other such details waiting fulfilment can be adduced, but it is clear that Rev. 18 has not been fulfilled and that it refers to the city Babylon. Its every detail belongs to a literal city. The " Mystery Babylon," the woman, of Rev. 17, is a system that is to be destroyed by the kings of the earth to make way for the supremacy of Antichrist (ver. 16, 17). But when the *city* is destroyed it is by no such process as a cannibal orgy as in the case of the harlot, nor do the kings in question bring it about, but on the contrary they mourn over its destruction (Rev. 18 : 9).

(4) Again, the harlot is destroyed before Antichrist reigns supreme in order and that he may do so ; but in Rev. 16, after the pouring out of the bowl judgments upon his kingdom, and the gathering of his armies for the last battle, at Har-Magedon, the city Babylon the great comes into remembrance for judgment (Rev. 16 : 19). Thus the woman and the city though connected are not the same. The former is judged before Antichrist rules, the latter at the close of his career. The kings hate the harlot but bewail the city. The former is Babylon only in mystery, by a secret spiritual association ; the latter is the actual city.

From shortly after the Flood Satan made Babylon his world centre. It was there that idolatry was instituted and that the great false systems of philosophy were commenced. About the same time God chose Jerusalem as His world centre. At the end of the days God will return unto Zion and Satan to Babylon. World movements have now set steadily in this direction. Napoleon said that whoever held Babylon held the key to India and the world, and no doubt he had this in mind in his expedition to Egypt and Syria. But the British thwarted his scheme at the battles of the Nile and Acre, and adopted for themselves his far-seeing suggestion. It has ever since been a dominant, if undeclared, factor in world politics. By geographical necessity Mesopotamia is the great land route between east and west, for the vast mountains on the north and the deserts and ocean on the south compel this. On this subject the reader may consult B. W. Newton's *Babylon and Egypt*, Pember's *Antichrist, Babylon, and the Coming of the Kingdom*, and *Mystery Babylon the Great*, as well as my own treatise before mentioned (p. 19).

(5, 6) As the empire is not *Roman*, from the prophetic viewpoint, there is no ground for limiting its area to what it has been in the past. That an ambitious statesman planned to make Italy the centre of a rule as co-extensive as that of the past was very natural, and it portended international trouble, but it was no guide to the interpreting of the oracles of God for the end days. God's plans are not framed by His enemies, nor are revealed to them, unless they learn them from His Word. The plan did not succeed. Italy may become one of the four beasts of ch. 7, but that will not make it the centre of Antichrist, nor Rome his capital city. To suggest that Ireland cannot be in the " revived " kingdom, nor north Scotland, nor Germany, and so on, because they were not in the Roman empire, is being wise above what is written.

The suggested limits can be plainly refuted from Scripture. The final stage of the image includes the gold, silver, and brass, as well as the iron and the earthenware, for all are present and are crushed when the stone falls (Dan. 2 : 45). Thus the final area must include all the territories of the four empires. In ch. 7 this principle is shown again, but with application to a more restricted area, by the fourth beast stamping its predecessors with its feet, and yet they are still present at the last stage, and the three outlast the fourth a short time (ver. 7, 19, 23 and 12). See also Appendix A.

Now the second and the third empires extended as far as India. As to Persia see Esther 1 : 1, and it is well known that Alexander penetrated over the frontier of India, reducing all the lands as he went. But Rome of old did not rule effectively beyond the Euphrates : she never really absorbed Mesopotamia, and the vast eastern lands she never touched. But the authority of Antichrist, at its height, will be *universal*. See Appendix A.

(7) With this falls the attempt to locate the ten kings as five in the east and five in the west of the old empire. It is unwise to assume which of the now existing powers will be of the ten. No one can tell what present kingdoms will be removed by the " nation rising against nation and kingdom against kingdom " as foretold by Christ. (See p. 85 f.)

The great lesson taught by the vision is that " in the days of those kings the God of the heavens shall set up a kingdom which shall never be destroyed, nor shall the sovereignty thereof be left to another people ; but it shall break in pieces and consume all these kingdoms, and it shall stand for ever " (44). Faith anticipates with joy the great voices in heaven which proclaim " The kingdom of the world is become the kingdom of our Lord and of His Messiah ; and He shall reign for ever and ever " (Rev. 11 : 15). What God requires of His own people in the meantime is not that we participate in the rule, ambitions, strife of world empires, but that, as foreigners in a world where His authority is not owned, we submit to present rulers as far as they demand nothing that a child of God may not do consistently with the highest duty to render unto God the things that are God's ; that we endure patiently what may be inflicted by rulers when we are bound in conscience to refuse aught that they demand, and thus stand forth as witnesses to God and His rejected Messiah ; that at all times we pray for rulers, and especially that we pray " Thy kingdom come, Thy will be done, as in heaven, so on earth."

Into this 44th verse of Daniel 2 is condensed the soul of all prophecy from Enoch to Malachi. In the light of this glorious expectation the psalmist sang this ecstatic apostrophe (96 : 9–13) :

> O worship Jehovah in the beauty of holiness :
> Tremble before Him all the earth.
> Say among the nations, Jehovah reigneth :
> The world also is stablished that it cannot be moved :
> He shall judge the peoples with equity.
> Let the heavens be glad, and let the earth rejoice ;
> Let the sea roar, and the fulness thereof ;
> Let the field exult, and all that is therein ;
> Then shall all the trees of the wood sing for joy ;
> Before Jehovah, for He cometh ;
> For He cometh to judge the earth :
> He shall judge the world with righteousness,
> And the peoples with His truth.

And thus at last shall mankind know that most blessed of all conditions, absolutely righteous rule.

In this vision granted to Nebuchadnezzar the glorious prospect was set forth in simple essential outline unaccompanied by any excess of detail, and thus the mighty consummation stood forth in clearest light. It has been at a loss of distinctness, perspective, and impressiveness that expositors have beclouded it with so much inserted matter. Let the lesson be taken afresh to heart that, when God has made Himself His own interpreter, we do well to confine ourselves to His explanations. To labour every detail of a picture or parable is to risk obscuring the vital lesson. To impose some fixed counterpart upon each separate item is unwarranted. Some background and surrounding is needful to make a picture, but the skilful portrait painter does not hide the beauty of the face by overloading or overcolouring the details of dress or furniture.

NOTE.—The following remarks upon Melchizedek by Adolph Saphir suggest an important principle of interpretation. They are from his *Lectures on the Hebrews*, ch. VII.

But the Scripture *purposely* does not mention who he was. Genesis abounds in genealogies, and in full and minute genealogies ; but the genealogy of this man is not given. If we knew who he was, should we not counteract thereby the meaning of the Holy Ghost in this instructive omission ? If he was Shem, then we know who his father was, and when he lived, and how old he was ; and this is just the very point which the Holy Ghost does not wish us to know . . . all we are told is, Melchizedek was one of those still left on earth, who retained the primeval knowledge of God, who worshipped Him, and who ruled in righteousness. With regard to all other circumstances, our *ignorance* is *knowledge*. The negative element is a positive element. Let no man attempt to supply that which the Holy Ghost has purposely left out ; for, in the first place, he must be unsuccessful ; in the second place, if he were successful, it would only militate against the purpose and the word of God, and only hinder us from learning those lessons which the Scripture intends us to derive. . . .

Instead of indulging in morbid and fanciful speculations about the historical individual, let us look at the important spiritual realities which in the inspired commentary are given us in this parable or type. Let us learn also from this instance and the other New Testament comments on Old Testament types that the typical meaning is always deduced from what *the Scripture itself says concerning them.*

CHAPTER III

NEBUCHADNEZZAR'S IMAGE

THE HISTORIES OF *Daniel* ARE PROPHECIES. THEY ARE A revelation of principles that will operate throughout the times of the Gentiles, typical events the like of which will be ever recurring.

Ch. 1 shows the type of man God will always need, make, and use. The present chapter reveals the attitude of Gentile rulers to religion and the duty of the godly in relation thereto. For the people of God this has been ever a truly serious subject, and it has suddenly become so again in modern Europe. The right to freedom of conscience and worship is being challenged, and in several countries the battle has become open and stern.

1. In ch. 2 world empire was represented to Nebuchadnezzar by a great image. It may be presumed that this idea was still in his mind when he made his own great image. He had created an empire such as never had been, and he would have all men own and honour it.

2. In the *vision* the head of gold had spoken of absolute sovereignty. But Nebuchadnezzar's conception was that the whole State shall be thus characterized; his whole image was of gold. The ancient proverb ran : " The life of the State is the law of the State," which during the Great War of 1914–1918 the then Leader of the House of Commons quoted to justify a certain un-Christian course. When a pious man pointed out that this was a pagan saying, the Leader admitted this, but said that it is a true saying. God be thanked that this is not yet the working principle in every land, but it is the doctrine of the modern totalitarian State. The State is all : its needs are paramount, its demands imperative, its commands absolute law. No private conscience or right can be admitted as against it : the individual is merely part of the State and exists for its advancement. And this is held forth as the ideal, the *golden* condition of society. See *World Chaos*, chap. XI.

3. This golden image, the State, is to be *worshipped*. Nothing less than divine honour is to be rendered to it, and it is to be

rendered to none other. Great statesmen have always been too astute, too conversant with human nature, to ignore its ineradicable religious element. Man *must* tender homage to *something* outside of himself, so religion must be acknowledged, but in such manner that it shall be subordinate to the State.

4. But an impersonal somewhat like the " State " will not long stir the deep enthusiasm of the human heart. It will lose its fascination unless it becomes embodied in a person, who can be known and revered, or at least feared.

The Babylonian empire, the golden image, was the expansion of its Founder, the head of gold, and he was the embodiment of it. To honour it was to honour him, and by requiring all men to worship the image, the State, he secured that they should worship himself, its creator, genius and inspiration. Thus the personal element was supplied, and the fascination of hero worship employed.

This constant feature of history is being repeated to-day. Not to speak of vast statues being erected to certain modern dictators let this instance from the Continent suffice to show the principle and practice : " Modern paganism, as the paganism of all ages, heads for idolatry ; in this case emperor worship—the Head of the State worshipped as the incarnation of the divine nation. Herr Baldur von Schirach, who has charge of the entire youth of the nation, thus addresses them (*Times*, July 29th, 1936) : ' One cannot be a good German and at the same time deny God, but an avowal of faith in the eternal Germany is at the same time an avowal of faith in the eternal God. If we act as true Germans we act according to the laws of God. Whoever serves Adolf Hitler, the Führer, serves Germany, and whoever serves Germany serves God ' " (*Dawn*, March, 1938).

5. In consequence, religion is an affair of the State and its outward forms are to be regulated by law.

(*a*) There is to be only one religion for the " peoples, nations, and languages " (ver. 14), and so when " *all* the peoples, the nations, and the languages heard . . . *all* the peoples, the nations, the languages fell down and worshipped." As it was at first in century 6 B.C. so it was again in century 2 B.C., when Antiochus Epiphanes issued a decree to his whole kingdom that they should be one people with one code of laws and one religion (I Maccab. c. 1). The godly of the Jews stoutly resisted and were fiercely persecuted. And so it shall be at last : " The whole earth wondered after the beast, and they worshipped the dragon, and they worshipped the beast " and the image of the beast (Rev. 13 : 3, 4, 15).

(*b*) In particular, all *officials* must conform to State worship : " the satraps, the deputies, and the governors, the judges, the treasurers, the counsellors, the sheriffs, and all the rulers of the provinces were gathered together unto the dedication of the image " (3).

Government service, and especially official position, is more dangerous for children of God than private employ.   Public servants are the first who are required to bind their conscience and actions by the oath of allegiance and obedience, which in itself is a promising to a man a *degree* of obedience which is due to God alone. Every such oath is a rendering unto Cæsar something that is God's, and His alone.

In its full development the totalitarian State conception requires that every one of its subjects shall regard himself or herself as bound absolutely to that State, to further its interests, to fulfil its utmost demands, as against every other State or race, and irrespective of the commands of even God.   Dr. Niemöller's last sermon before arrest was on the words " We must obey God rather than men " (Ac. 5 : 29), and that led direct to prison and concentration camp.

The Christian is required by God to love his " neighbour " as himself, that is, each and every individual of the human race.   The love of God is to the world (John 3 : 16) ;   Christ died as pro-pitiation for the whole world (I John 2 : 2) ;   His disciples are to take the message of love to the whole human race (Matt. 28 : 19 ; Acts 1 : 8) ;   they are to do good to all men (Gal. 6 : 10), including those who hate and injure them (Luke 6 : 27–36).   Only so will they resemble and reveal their heavenly Father and serve His desire to bless all men, and only so will they gather out from the nations that people for His name which is to include members from " every tribe and tongue and people and nation " (Rev. 5 : 9 ; 7 : 9).

Thus is already realized in the true Christian that love and good-will toward the whole of mankind, which alone can produce uni-versal peace.   To this longed-for goal nationalism is an inevitable enemy, because these conceptions, this spirit, and these consequent duties are utterly incompatible with the theory and practice of the totalitarian State ;   for the latter is based on affinity of blood, race, or land, which refuses therefore to be universal in its outlook and schemes, and requires its members to concentrate on itself, however hurtfully this may work out to other races or peoples.

Thus is precipitated an inescapable and irreconcilable conflict. He who worships Nebuchadnezzar's golden image accepts a false religion and denies the only true God; whereas he who, like Jesus our Lord, will worship Jehovah his God, and serve Him only, cannot and will not worship the image, no matter how terrible the present and personal consequence. (For further remarks on this subject see Appendix B.)

It is to be much observed that the New Testament lays upon the child of God no duty to the *State*, none whatever. Where therein is there a sentence that told the Roman Christian that he owed a duty to the Roman *empire*? On the contrary, such an one as Paul showed no sense of duty to even the Jewish State, though Israel was the chosen people of God. The very precepts given for Christian obedience forbid the idea. Paul, for example, by natural civil status was both Jew and Roman. When these two States were at war to which of them was one so circumstanced to render allegiance? which master was he to serve? which army should he join? against which State should he fight? which land should he ravage, and serve Christ in doing it?

The precepts of the New Testament are that we should obey whatever *king* or *governors* we may happen at any time to be under, the reason being that they are appointed by God for the double and associated ends of repressing crime and supporting virtue (Rom. 13 : 1–7 ; I Peter 2 : 13–17). For this beneficial work rulers of all ranks have divine authority; but for their *State* schemes and measures they can plead no warrant from God, and the precepts commanding obedience to them cease to apply. It has been the perpetual habit of rulers to extend their actions into matters for which God has *not* given them authority. Love of personal glory, of power, of wealth, with fear of neighbours like themselves, have swayed the corrupt hearts of sovereigns and subordinates and have fostered those racial and national prejudices, hatreds, ambitions which provoke international complications and wars.

It is in this way that " States " are formed and State aims and policies arise; for powerful personalities exploit the idea of the " State " to further grand ends for which rulers are *not* appointed by God and for which they hold no divine warrant. It is very true that God, by His secret and angelic authorities, *over*rules these doings for purposes of general justice on earth, using a bad ruler to chasten a corrupt people, and then punishing the king that has

thus abused his power (Zech. 11 : 6, 15, 16, 17) ; or causing one
nation to punish another for its wickedness, and afterwards bringing vengeance on the former for its cruelty to the vanquished
(Isa. 10 : 5–19).   But this *super*vising and *over*ruling of the wicked
is an affair that heaven alone can effect ; it leaves unchanged the
proper duty of rulers and its limits according to God.

There is therefore a vital distinction between " Cæsar " and the
" State." . The one is a person owned by God for a needful and
definite work : the other is a conception and creation of man for
purposes of his own ; and the Lord did not say, " Render unto the
State the things of the State," but " Render unto *Cæsar* the things
that are Cæsar's."   Nor does the New Testament contain the
slightest allusion to the affairs of State of the Roman empire or the
least intimation that Christians should share in them.   Neither will
this be thought strange by one who considers the nature of the
imperial schemes and the crafty and cruel measures by which they
were served.   The same nature and methods have marked in
measure every world kingdom and will do so until they are superseded by the kingdom of the Son of God.

Careful reflection will show that this must needs be the line for
the child of God.   The Son of man obeyed all the laws in force in
His land and taught others to do so (Matt. 8 : 4 ; 23 : 2, 3).   The
difference between Him and other teachers lay in showing the true
force of those laws (Matt. 15 : 1–20 ; Luke 6 : 1–11 ; 11 : 37–52 ;
etc.).   But in the affairs of the Jewish *State* He took no part, and
indeed refused to do so.   His people was then ground under the
heel of the ruthless Roman State.   They nursed the deepest hatred
for their oppressors, and only waited opportunity to free themselves from the cruel yoke.   Now all men will justify this, and
such as will not join in so natural and national an aim will be
accounted traitors.   Yet the Lord Jesus refused to serve this end
and to allow himself to be made the leader of the national hopes
(John 6 : 14, 15).

How could He have done so without trespassing upon the
*over*ruling of affairs by God His Father, Who had permitted the
Romans to gain dominion over Israel, Who had indeed foretold
it a thousand years and more in advance (Deut. 28 : 49) ? Cæsar,
and Pilate his representative, had been given their power " from
above," as Christ Himself said (John 19 : 11), for " there is *no*
power but of God " (Rom. 13 : 1), and therefore the Son of God
could not, would not resist them, not even when in this case the

power was misused. This last point is of deep meaning for those who would follow His steps, for the common argument used to persuade Christians to join in war is that the other country is in the wrong, is acting unrighteously, and it is a sacred duty to resist the wrong.

Mordecai served the Persian monarch in the civil administration, for this was for the support of virtue and the punishment of vice ; but he would not have obeyed had he been called upon to support the scheme of the Prime Minister, Haman, to massacre the Jews, not even though it was ratified by the royal seal. Daniel and his friends served Nebuchadnezzar in the like sphere, but no one will believe that they would have served him in the ravaging of Palestine, had they been so commanded. The former was Nebuchadnezzar's duty from God : the latter was an affair of State, of empire, which God indeed overruled for an end of His own, but for which in due time He overthrew Nebuchadnezzar's empire (Jer. 50 : 18). And thus it will be at the end of the age with the last emperor (Isa. 10 : 12). No Christian can rightly support a ruler in anti-Semitic persecution, or any such *State* affair.

It is also to be observed that it was not God's wish or plan that Israelites should be in such relations to world empires as those in which Daniel, Mordecai, and others found themselves. It was purely a result of Israel's sin that they were so found. It was as *captive slaves* that they so served. Neither is it the mind of God that His heavenly people should fill such positions in world affairs in this age. Daniel, Esther and others being where they were through no fault of their own, God used them for gracious purposes ; but they would have been out of His will had they sought or accepted such relations of their own will.

In the same way now pious men, uninstructed as to the thoughts of God in this matter, remain slaves to the world system, serving it in ruling positions or otherwise, and they do so with no challenge of conscience. God similarly uses such to good ends, as the freeing of slaves, and the softening of conditions of labour or of prisoners. But they are not in the line of God's primary thoughts for His children, the disciples of Christ. God's day for Israel and the church of God to share in the government of the nations is yet future, when His King shall return and take over the government.

Meanwhile it is ours to submit cheerfully to present authorities, going willingly two miles when the law demands only one (Matt. 5 :

40, 41). The limit of obedience lies where rulers require what God does not permit or trespass into spheres not sanctioned by God. Of these spheres religion is a chief example, and the making a religion of serving the State is one of the worst forms of such idolatry. It begets in its devotees ambition, duplicity, lying, hardness of heart, ruthless cruelty, all in an intense degree scarcely ever otherwise produced; so that the great empire builders have been the most terrible destroyers of mankind, as witness Napoleon replying to the appeal of Metternich to spare human life with a curse on human life, as that for which he cared nothing.

It is deplorable that Christians often do not discern the distinction between rulers as sent of God for necessary and beneficial moral ends and rulers as builders, organizers, defenders, and destroyers of States. They then suffer themselves to be entangled in the affairs of the latter, and are beguiled into the worship of the golden image of race, State, country, sharing in politics and wars, and failing to answer to the thoughts of their Lord for them as spoken to His Father concerning them: " I have given them Thy word; and the world hated them, because they are not of the world, *even as I* am not of the world " (John 17 : 14).

(*c*) To rulers external religion is thus an affair of the State, to serve ends of State, and to be regulated by State decree: " Thou, O king, hast *made a decree* that every man . . . shall fall down and worship the golden image " (Dan. 3 : 10).

This religion shall be attractive, by being :

(i) External and visible : an image that can be seen.

(ii) Magnificent : an image of great size and splendour, all of gold.

(iii) Seductive to the senses : associated with it there shall be " all kinds of music."

(iv) Impressive : the throng shall be vast, representative, comprehensive.

(v) United : all shall worship in a set place, at a set time.

(vi) Orderly : regulated by royal decree, under the direction of a State-appointed minister, a herald.

(vii) Dignified : the monarch himself shall be present, the head and observer of the proceedings.

It is noticeable how all of these features are found in all State religions and State churches. Let the student examine three stages of English history and he will find these marks in each.

(*a*) Before the Reformation they characterized religion as maintained by the Roman Church, the Pope being the general head over all lands, but the sovereign carrying out his behests locally. (i) The Church was a visible institution, with external buildings. (ii) It was rich and magnificent, with stained glass, images, sculptures, vestments. (iii) It was seductive with music, incense, and sensuous attractions. (iv) It claimed universality, comprehensiveness, representatives from all classes, particularly the upper classes. Officials especially were required to support it. (v) Attendance at the appointed church and services was compulsory by law, under criminal penalties. (vi) Spontaneous worship from the heart, impelled and controlled by the Holy Spirit, was prohibited as disorderly. All was regulated by the Breviary or Prayer Book, and conducted by the State-licensed minister. (vii) The king himself must attend public worship, by his presence lending dignity, sanction, and command to religion.

(*b*) When Henry VIII renounced Papal supremacy all these things continued as they had been, the king displacing the Pope as head of the English Church.

(*c*) When Elizabeth established the Protestant religion the doctrines were modified and the ceremonies altered in measure, but the features in question remained as part of the State-church system, as was the case in the other Reformed State churches. It continues so to this date, with the later modification in this country that subjects of the crown are not now compelled by law to attend the State church; but all members of that Church are expected still to attend at its set places and ceremonies.

(*d*) Even in those lands where the *State* is the image the same features prevail in principle. (i) The State as a corporate entity is set before the mind as its visible object. (ii) The State is to be rich, great, splendid. (iii) State provides theatres, concerts, and other sensuous attractions. (iv) The State insists on universality within its territory: every person without exception must be devoted to its schemes and glory. (v) Each individual must attend its appointed functions, central or local, as may be dictated by authority. Non-compliance is punishable. (vi) Individual life, spontaneous religion, or other personal or sectional aim is suppressed. (vii) The head of the State shall be ever to the front, the pattern, controller, inspirer, and the adored of all. In 1938 in one room in a Continental house, and that a Christian house, I saw five different portraits of the then head of that State!

Worship from the heart Nebuchadnezzar cannot compel : outward form he can order.   Spiritual adoration of God is a realm into which no man may trespass as regards his neighbour.   *Of the church of God the Son of God is the sole head, and therefore no earthly ruler has any rights in the house of God (the church), or in regulating its affairs.*   A Minister for Religion is a direct challenge and affront to the Son of God.   No Christian or assembly of Christians should negotiate or compromise with such an official, beyond perhaps informing him, as authorized by government to inquire, what his or their beliefs and practices may be.   What had Shadrach and his companions to do with the king's herald or his commission to secure obedience to the royal decree as to worship ?   They simply ignored him and his proclamation, acting as if he had not published the king's order.

In one of his later sermons Dr. Niemöller said that the celebrated preacher, Dr. F. W. Krummacher (*d.* 1868), when warned of the displeasure of the Emperor if he did not conform to a certain decree concerning the Lutheran Church, replied : Tell His Imperial Majesty that I am ready at any time to lay my head on the block at His Majesty's command ; but when His Imperial Majesty presumes to be lord of the gospel, I despise His Imperial Majesty !

How strikingly complete was Nebuchadnezzar's scheme ; how strikingly it has persisted all through this period of world empires ; how striking and instructive is the Bible account of it.   May God give His people eyes to see, and Caleb hearts to follow the Lord Jesus wholly.   For history is repeating itself still, and increasingly, and will unto the end, when the Beast will lay waste the church.

6. The penalty of not conforming to the State religion was extreme—death, and death by the awful form of burning.   The emperor will simply exterminate non-conformity, nor will hesitate at the most savage barbarity to secure this.   The records show that he failed : piety defeated ferocity.   In the long run it has always been so.   The lamb overcomes the dragon.   Yet rulers blindly refuse to learn this lesson of the long centuries, and have continually justified our assertion that the histories of *Daniel* are prophecies.   The cruelties of Antiochus Epiphanes in his frenzied endeavours to compel the Jews of the Maccabean period to apostatize ; the fierce zeal of Saul of Tarsus striving to compel Christians to blaspheme ; the fiendish barbarities of the Roman and Papal

persecutions, were all to the same ends and inspired by the same spirit as those of Nebuchadnezzar.

But perhaps in the sight of high heaven the atrocities committed upon simple godly non-conformists by the Protestant States and State churches are the worst of all exhibitions of this worship of the golden image, for they were perpetrated by those who professed gospel truth. At first the great Reformers claimed full freedom of conscience, and won it from the Roman Catholic Church and Princes by vast toil and suffering. But no sooner had they gained it for themselves than they resolutely refused it to others, and Luther, Melanchthon, and their helpers in Germany, with their co-Reformers in other Continental lands, as well as the bishops and rulers in England, persecuted unto fines, bonds, tortures, and barbarous executions Baptists and others who would not enter State churches or accept infant baptism.

It is a lamentable story, yet by no means to be forgotten. It were well if Foxe's *Book of Martyrs*, the story of the Covenanters in Scotland under Charles II, of Bunyan in prison, and of thousands and thousands of other such saints and martyrs were read again by their ease-loving non-conformist successors. For these were not maltreated and martyred by pagans or papists, but by Protestant ecclesiastics using the civil power as their agent. And still this ruthless spirit animates the fanatical ecclesiastic. "The Church" is his idol, his golden image, and woe unto death be to him who will not worship it : still will he stir up officials to suppress at any cost by any means those who stand erect when he has constrained the law to cry, Bow down !

7. When this issue is forced there is but one course open to the godly—a refusal, absolute and unwavering ; resistance, passive, but uncompromising. "We do not need, O king, to ponder carefully our answer. The issue is simple ; our duty plain. Be it known unto thee, O king, WE WILL NOT serve thy gods, nor worship the golden image which thou hast set up. This is final."

In several European countries to-day this is the real, the vital issue. Is the State supreme or is God ? God be praised for all who are resolute upon this point, though prison, concentration camp, or exile be their place of witness.

Jewish rulers pressed the apostles with the same sharp issue and drew forth the same determined refusal. "We strictly charged you not to teach in this name : and behold, ye have filled Jerusalem with your teaching, and intend to bring this man's blood upon us.

. . . We must obey God rather than man " was the simple direct answer (Acts 5 : 28, 29). " We are not able *not* to speak the things which we saw and heard " (Acts 4 : 19, 20).

8. The promoters of the worship of the image, whether secular or clerical, recognize quite clearly that their claims and those of the Lord Jesus Christ are simply irreconcilable. They feel that it is of the essence of the gospel of Christ that they are the persons responsible for His rejection, whether they unjustifiably profess His name, or whether, as the Jews, they repudiate Him. The Sanhedrin were trying to shelve the plain but unwelcome truth that they were the parties already and actually responsible for the death of Jesus. It was no question of the apostles bringing His blood upon them : they had taken it upon themselves by saying : " His blood be on us and on our children."

The late rulers of Germany tacitly owned this conflict. The court acquitted Dr. Niemöller of endeavours to subvert the State, but the Secret Police knew quite accurately that, whatever political bias the prisoner may have shown, his assertion of the supremacy of God was the crux of the dispute by denying the claim of the State to absolute supremacy, and so they incarcerated the preacher in a camp without form of law or justice.

Behind all this bitter antagonism is the Prince of this world. For a time his agents may moderate the expression of their master's hatred to Christ ; *but the fire is there*, and will blaze yet again, as at the first. " Then was Nebuchadnezzar *full of fury*." Formerly from his high throne he had smiled graciously upon these he had honoured, but now " the form of his visage was changed against them " by the rage of his heart at being resisted and his image contemned.

Thus it was with the Sanhedrin against Stephen : " They were cut to the heart, and they gnashed on him with their teeth " (Acts 7 : 54). Let these scenes rise distinctly before our vision— raging wild beasts ; livid, furious faces ; gnashing teeth, yelling voices, fiery flames ! But the Lamb that was led to the slaughter had said to his followers, " Behold, I send you forth as sheep in the midst of wolves," and had foretold that these conditions would persist to the end of the age, for, at that final period, for His name's sake they shall be " hated of all men."

In the overruling of God, and that His gospel might spread to the ends of the earth, He granted to His church the late century of tranquillity. But this is wholly exceptional, nor may we count upon it being renewed. We do well to arm ourselves with the mind of Christ (1 Peter 4 : 1), Who came into the world knowing from the first that He must be lifted up (John 3 : 14 ; 12 : 24, 32), that the path to glory lay through suffering, and in faithfulness told us that " in the world ye have tribulation," it being the normal condition for His followers (John 16 : 33).

Yet the disciple need not be daunted. He must face the Devil as a roaring lion ; but, if he withstand him through a steadfast faith, he shall share the victory of the Lamb and trample Satan under his feet shortly.

But on no account let Shadrach dream that Nebuchadnezzar will be anything less than *furious* when his golden image is despised. On the contrary he will urge on the persecution to such extent that his own servants may be destroyed in the endeavour to cast Christ's servants into the furnace, even as armies of persecutors have suffered severely in wars to exterminate heretics. But for this Nebuchadnezzar will care nought so long as his malicious, ferocious hatred is glutted upon despisers of his religion.

And at last the " harlot " shall " be drunken with the blood of the witnesses of Jesus " (Rev. 17 : 6 ; Luke 21 : 12) ; and at the very last, under the Beast, those who will still " keep the commandments of God and the faith of Jesus "—therefore Christian believers—(Rev. 14 : 12), and who will not worship his image, will need endurance beyond all that have run the race of faith before them. " Behold your calling, brethren . . . unto you it hath been granted in the behalf of Christ, not only to believe on Him [and so to save your souls], but also to suffer in His behalf," and so to share His throne (Phil. 1 : 29).

It is most noteworthy that the very apostles who so plainly laid down the general rule that followers of Christ must obey rulers in all things for which rulers were appointed by God, themselves so flatly, and so persistently, refused obedience when religion came into question. *The justification is that in this sphere rulers have no appointment or authority from God. When they enter it they become themselves transgressors, trespassers against the rights of God, and then they who respect those rights must refuse the demands of Cæsar.* " Let none of you suffer as an evil doer [a criminal] . . . but if any suffer as a Christian let him not be ashamed ; but let him glorify God in this name " (1 Peter 4 : 15, 16).

9. But there is deliverance for the faithful.

In the case of the three Hebrews it was immediate, physical, sensational : in countless other cases it has not been thus. These three " quenched the power of fire," but " others were tortured, not accepting their deliverance," that is, by abjuring or compromising their testimony to Christ (Heb. 11 : 34-40). It must surely have been with these three in mind that a later sufferer for Christ assured his fellow-sufferers that " the Lord knoweth how to rescue the godly out of trial " (II Peter 2 : 9). If therefore in most cases He does not deliver so promptly or sensationally it is not that He is not able, but because other and worthy ends are to be served.

It must surely have been with those three in mind that the Lord assured His followers that, though persecuted, prosecuted, hated, killed, yet " not a hair of your head shall perish. In your patience ye shall win your lives " (Luke 21 : 12-19). And again : " He that endureth unto the end, *this one* shall be saved " (Matt. 24 : 13), that is, saved from the Day of the Lord by the Rapture.

If Abraham immolating his son on the altar, and seeing him set free, was, in the heart experience of Abraham, the equivalent of the death and resurrection of his son (Heb. 11 : 17-19), then these three also went through death and resurrection ; and, without actually dying as to the body, their experience is a prophecy of the deliverance by a literal resurrection of all who have died, or shall yet die, for Christ's sake. They have felt the bodily pangs which the three were spared, but they shall be more than recompensed in the resurrection of the just. For " Faithful is the saying : For if we died with Him we shall also live with Him : if we endure we shall also reign with Him " (II Tim. 2 : 11, 12) ; even as it is also written that if we are children of God then are we His heirs ; " heirs indeed (μέν) of God, but (δέ) *joint-heirs with Messiah, if so be* that we suffer with Him that we may be also glorified with Him " (Rom. 8 : 17).

Faith must give substance to this hope, so that it may be a confident expectation, a working reality, nerving the soul to high endeavour and final endurance. Nor be it overlooked that if the three had shirked the fire they would have missed the wondrous company of the Son of God in it, just as they to-day who will not bear their cross after Him forfeit the sweetness of His presence in trial. Also they would never have been partakers of the great deliverance wrought for them by God, even as they who refuse to share the sufferings and death of their Lord now will not share in that first resurrection that ushers into His glory. For it also stands written in His inviolable word, in the place just above quoted, that " if we shall deny Him, He also will deny us : if we are faithless, He abideth faithful ; for He cannot deny Himself," which He would do if He were not to deny those who had denied Him (II Tim. 2 : 12, 13).

10. To the individual, to a people, and to the race God may allow a period in which they seem to triumph at their will and He is silent. He is long-suffering while His chosen are afflicted by the godless (Luke 18 : 7). This in part is to afford to the impious time to reflect and repent, if they will (II Peter 3 : 9, 15). But when it has become plain that their will is *not* to repent (Rev. 2 : 20–23), when they have gone to the extreme and justice can no more rightly forbear, then God executes a swift judgment, or effects a striking deliverance of His people. The effect is sometimes a sudden re-action in the beholders and they give glory to the God who so works for those who have been faithful to Him and His word.

The bringing of these three Hebrews out of the fire unscathed is an instance, and the resuscitation of the two witnesses in Jerusalem in the days of the Beast (Rev. 11 : 11–13) will be another. The glorifying of the church with Christ, after the weary centuries of His rejection and her oppression, and the sudden deliverance of the godly of Israel from the very maw of the Beast (Joel 2 : 15–18, etc.), will be yet greater examples, of which personal deliverances all through the ages have been types.

When the world beholds the saints of God radiant in bodies of glory, and also perfected in character by the very fiery trials kindled by the godless, then will some, like Nebuchadnezzar that day of old, give glory to the God of heaven and will honour those who trusted their God, defied the king and his impious order, yielded their bodies to suffer rather than prostitute them to a false religion, and thus remained utterly faithful to their own God, the only true God (ver. 28).

In principle this is the path for faith at all times. " Present not your members unto sin, but present them unto God as weapons of righteousness . . . present your bodies a living sacrifice, holy, acceptable unto God, which is your reasonable service " (Rom. 6 : 13 ; 12 : 1). May we not think that Shadrach and his friends rendered to God that dreadful but glorious day worship more acceptable than did Solomon at the grand pageant when he dedicated his splendid temple ? This at least is clear, that Solomon shortly tarnished the brightness of his homage, but theirs is imperishable.

11. And even as they were promoted to higher dignity and office in the service of the king (30), so " if we suffer with Christ we shall be also glorified with Him . . . if we died with Him, we shall also live with Him : if we endure we shall also reign with Him " (Rom. 8 : 17 ; II Tim. 2 : 11, 12).

History ever repeats itself because the principles of conduct in both man and God ever operate : and of these one of the deepest was declared to Eli by a man of God, unknown but spiritually instructed, in the words : " Jehovah saith . . . them that honour Me I will honour, and they that despise Me shall be lightly esteemed " (I Sam. 2 : 30). Our Lord emphasized this by His words : " He that owneth Me before men, I will own before My Father who is in heaven ; but whoso shall deny Me I will deny " : statements repeated once and again (Matt. 10 : 32, 33 ; Luke 12 : 8, 9 ; II Tim. 2 : 12, 13) and at last reasserted from heaven by Christ in glory (Rev. 3 : 5). To these words He will be faithful ; He will deny or own each of us then according as we deny or own Him in this perverse generation. The present determines the future as the unavoidable consequence of moral law ; and while these statements of the Word of God are not to be connected with final salvation, but with status and reward in Christ's kingdom and in the estimation of His Father, yet is their import so solemn as to demand searching of heart and courageous fidelity in the evil day.

CHAPTER IV

BY THE KING—A PROCLAMATION

CHAPTER II GAVE A VISION OF WORLD EMPIRES. CHAPTER III showed the attitude of such empires to religion. The present chapter gives a picture of the kind of ruler such empire demands, by which it is created and which it in part creates. The picture is typical. All empire builders more or less conform to it, but especially the great conquerors. The soul shudders at the spectacle of these mighty monsters striding over the earth in pride and cruelty, their track a pestilential swamp of blood and tears. " The land before them is as the garden of Eden, and behind them a desolate wilderness " (Joel 2 : 3). " Their feet are swift to shed blood; destruction and misery are in their ways; and the way of peace have they not known : There is no fear of God before their eyes " (Rom. 3 : 15–18). Can there be clearer proof that the heart of man is perverted and blinded than that he honours the most highly these very men who must ruin his race and world ?

Here we are shown how such men are estimated and dealt with by high heaven. Would that sovereigns and subjects would all learn the lessons here taught. Let the Christian at least do so, and thoroughly.

1. The chapter opens by a universal proclamation by the emperor : " Nebuchadnezzar the king, unto all the peoples, nations, and languages, that dwell in all the earth."

We have before remarked that, though Nebuchadnezzar did not actually rule the whole earth, it had been granted to him by God, and that the grant will be realized literally by the last emperor that shall succeed to Nebuchadnezzar's sovereignty. Thus this proclamation stands in Scripture as applicable universally ; its lesson is for all nations to the end of Gentile dominion.

That such a proclamation was issued was in the line of that universal testimony by which God from time to time reminds mankind of Himself and leaves them without excuse in their rebellion against His government. The argument of Romans, chs. 1 and 2 to this effect is well based on history.

(a) The world down to the Flood had full knowledge available of the creation of man and of the Creator. For example, Adam lived more than half of that period, Methuselah was his contemporary for over 300 years and he survived to the year of the Flood. This covered 1,656 years to 2348 B.C.

(b) Noah had been contemporary with Methuselah 600 years before the Flood, and he brought over that accurate knowledge of God for 350 years after the Flood. His son Shem continued (at least as to the possession of knowledge) that testimony for 250 years more, that is to 1846 B.C. He had been alive at the same time as Methuselah for 100 years. The Flood itself left the race deeply impressed with the fact of God and His power, as the universal traditions of it show. But the race, loving sin, did not like to retain the knowledge of the Holy One (Rom. 1 : 21, 25, 28, 32). The rejection was deliberate and against light possessed.

(c) Immediately after the time of Shem Melchizedek is found continuing the testimony as priest of the Most High God. At the same time Abraham is raised up to maintain and enlarge the witness. This was at the centre of the then peopled lands, and in the same period came the terrific judgment upon Sodom and Gomorrah, in the same central region.

(d) Some four hundred years later the world was forcibly reminded of Jehovah by His drastic dealings with its then greatest monarch and empire, Pharaoh of Egypt, and by the consequent settlement of Israel in Canaan. By these events the name of Jehovah was to be " declared throughout all the earth " (Exod. 9 : 16). Both Scripture and profane history show the widest possible and frequent intercommunication between the peoples at that period (about 1450 B.C.), and Canaan was the great highway from north to south and east to west.

(e) Four centuries or more later the glory of Solomon and the grand temple for the worship of the true God were talked of to the ends of the earth (Matt. 12 : 42). About 1000 B.C.

(f) And now, after some four centuries more, in which Israel should have been, and in declining measure was, a witness at the world's centre, their national testimony had become so corrupt and false that it was caused to cease, and their lampstand was removed out of its place. The name of God was blasphemed among the heathen because of those who professed to be His people, and now they were scattered among the heathen. As individuals and as a race they were indeed some testimony to the God of their fathers, to His existence, rights, claims, justice, power; they kept the fact of God before men, yet rather repelled men from Him than drew to Him.

But God would not leave Himself without distinct world-wide witness. He pressed Himself upon public attention by His dealings with the great emperor who rose to power. He gave him a public explanation of how he had come to his dominion, and what course world empire would take to reach its destination and destruction. By delivering the three from the furnace He showed how easily He could thwart him, and now He deprives him of position and of reason till he shall learn and own that the government of earth is really in the heavens, and that the greatest of men is a nobody before the Most High God, to whom alone of right belong worship, authority, power.

(g) This lesson to all races will be repeated before long by the royal proclamations of Cyrus and Darius. In truth it is being ever repeated, and is seen by those who have eyes to see, ears to hear, and hearts to bow before the God of heaven. It is the lesson that some rulers of to-day sorely need to take to heart for the welfare of themselves and their peoples. But blindness falls still upon self-willed Gentiles, as it did upon rebellious Israel, until at length there is no healing. At last the sentence goes forth, " Cut it down : why doth it cumber the ground ? " Kings, dictators, nations, crumble to dust, and well is it if mercy suffers the stump to remain to sprout again.

It is not always so. Princes fall never to rise : nations wither never to revive. It shall be thus with the last empire and its last emperor (Dan. 11 : 45 ; Rev. 19 : 20). Yet for the Gentile peoples as a whole there is a future. At the close of this age the axe of divine wrath shall cut down Gentile dominion, yet the nations shall come to the rising Sun of righteousness, and in His healing rays shall flourish with a beauty far surpassing their utmost former growth. Thus it was with Nebuchadnezzar when he had humbled himself before God : " excellent greatness was added unto me " (36) ; which is a picture for all men, all nations, all times : for " he that humbleth himself shall be exalted."

2. The second feature of the proclamation is also noteworthy. This savage, ruthless soldier, this devastator of whole countries, now wishes that " peace be multiplied " unto all men. We may hope and believe that this was no mere formal and customary introduction, but that the heart of the emperor had learned that peace, not war, is the need of mankind.

The philosophy of men like Neitzsche, that war is a necessity, in truth a blessing for a people, steels men's hearts till they become inhuman. It prepared them for the cruel doings of 1914-18 and bore more deadly fruit in Nazi atrocities and the late war. Yet it is but one application of the theory of evolution, which, by inculcating the doctrine of "natural selection," suppresses the kindly instincts of human nature, teaches that the weak *ought* to go to the wall, that it is indeed good for the race that the strong should trample them to death. Nietzsche was but a son of Darwin.

The cruel philosophy of such men recognizes acutely, and from their point of view justly, that Christ is their deadliest foe, that the doctrine of grace based upon One suffering for His enemies is the utter condemnation of their doctrine, its irreconcilable, implacable contradiction. It was no wonder that Nietzsche hated Paul.

Let every lover of the Lord Jesus, especially such as live in totalitarian and military states, face this issue. However carefully at present such rulers may phrase their statements as to Christianity, however cautiously they may as yet act in respect to evangelical religion, at heart they *know* that the Bible proclaims love, peace, mercy, gentleness, illustrated in the character, ways, and sacrifice of the Son of God, and also proclaims forgiveness of wrongs as the glory of God and the true excellence of man, and they *know* that not thus can *their* schemes be carried through. "Ambition should be made of sterner stuff" than meekness, forbearance, pity for the poor, and that poverty of spirit set forth by Christ as the first and indispensable quality for sharing in the kingdom of the heavens (Matt. 5 : 3).

In this thorough change of outlook and of desire for the earth Nebuchadnezzar was a prototype of the peoples at the end of Gentile history. When the dealings of God with the nations have had due effect they will at last honour Him and be at peace under the rule of His King, Jesus Christ. But only the most drastic treatment will effect so unsought yet blessed a change. As with Nebuchadnezzar so the only cure of *national* pride is national *insanity* (Jer. 25 : 15, 16). "Whom the gods would destroy they first make mad" holds an element of truth (II Thess. 2 : 8-12). The saying might well have arisen in Babylonia after the dread experience of its first great emperor and before his recovery. But the desired end of the true God was recovery, not destruction. He aims at restoration, wherever possible ; and the nations at last, like Nebuchadnezzar, become bestial in nature and habits, will realize the folly and sin that brought such humiliation and will lift up their hearts unto God.

3. What Nebuchadnezzar needed to learn is what present-day rulers also need to learn.

(i) *The Supremacy of God.* He is "the MOST HIGH God." Before Him "all the nations are as nothing; they are counted to Him as *less* than *nothing*," a startling superlative, since strictly there cannot be less than *nothing*. To Him they are but "a drop in the bucket" (Isa. 40 : 17, 15). The father of a friend of mine was so exceptionally strong that he could hold a stable bucket of water on his little finger and swing it round and round at arm's length. To such an one an extra drop in the bucket were of no account. Such are the nations of the earth to God. What stupidity to ignore and resist the Most High God!

(ii) *His greatness and might.* "How great are His signs! and how mighty are His wonders!" And He is always doing such, in nature, in providence, and in government. The sun, moon, and stars are for signs (Gen. 1 : 14). The perpetual provision of food for billions of living creatures on earth—what a sign of benevolence is this! "He gave you from heaven rains and fruitful seasons, filling your hearts with food and gladness" (Acts 14 : 17).

And what wonders are wrought in the overruling of world movements. In our own days how have thrones that have stood for centuries, even millenniums (as Persia and China), been overthrown as in a day, and proud monarchs have been suddenly swept from the garish day in which they strutted across life's stage, into obscurity or eternity.

All this Nebuchadnezzar had seen, yet not seen; all this present rulers have seen, yet have not seen. The responsibility of neglecting this witness to the great and mighty God, or of rejecting it, he incurred, and they, for the more part of their number, are incurring it.

(iii) But when his eyes were at last opened, Nebuchadnezzar discerned that the vicissitudes of international affairs were not mere matters of chance, but that behind all the shifting scenes of world kingdoms there works an everlasting kingdom, a dominion that endures through all the changes of all generations.

Into that kingdom none enter but children; of such it is composed (Matt. 18 : 3, 4; 19 : 14; etc.). Nebuchadnezzar had now humbled himself as a little child, and forthwith that kingdom and its King became to him the dominant reality. Thus he could be trusted by its Sovereign with a nobler sphere in one of its small earth divisions, for now he would rule in the fear of his Overlord, the God of heaven : " Excellent greatness was added unto me " (36).

The British Empire reached its zenith under the godly Victoria. Of her chief statesmen several were God-fearing men. Only under such rulers can it retain its place if it is to retain it. (See p. 20.)

(iv) Having learnt all this for himself, now the king is impelled to the duty of instructing others. How evangelical he has become! " We cannot but speak the things that we have seen and heard " ; " woe is unto me if I preach not the gospel " ; " out of the abundance of the heart the mouth speaketh." Is each of us as faithful in this as Nebuchadnezzar ?

4. The proclamation goes on to point out the danger of success and prosperity. They easily gender carelessness and pride, which develop a callous disregard of God and His warnings. Nebuchadnezzar deemed that the wide dominion that was his, the vast capital he had built, the magnificent palace he inhabited, were his creation, and his alone : " Is not this great Babylon which I have built for the royal dwelling place, by the might of *my* power and for the glory of *my* majesty ? " (30).

Few, surely, have been the successful princes that have not fallen into this snare of the devil. The Pharaohs, the Nebuchadnezzars, the Cæsars, where are their mighty cities and grand palaces ? Gone entirely, or only ruins left to show how God overthrows the proud. Though the potsherds of the earth strive against their Maker, yet shall neither London, Berlin, nor Rome be earth's final centre, nor that last and greater Babylon that, as the capital of Antichrist, shall outshine Nebuchadnezzar's proud city. No ! Jerusalem is the city of the great King, as He himself has styled it, and " it shall be exalted above the hills, and all nations shall flow unto it " (Isa. 2 : 2). This most impossible figure of speech, streams flowing uphill to the summit of the highest mountain, is used to arrest attention, to point out the impossible work that God Himself will do.

" Behold, this was the iniquity of thy sister Sodom : pride, fulness of bread, and prosperous ease was in her and in her daughters ; neither did she strengthen the hand of the poor and needy. And they were haughty, and committed abomination before Me ; therefore I took them away as I saw good " (Ezek. 16 : 49, 50).

Deep in the valley of the Jordan, 1,300 feet below sea-level, 4,000 feet lower than the flanking mountains of Moab and Judah, the Sodomites lived in the most tropical climate that men inhabit. The deep cleft conserved the rays and heat, the waters of the river and the springs made growth luxuriant and supplies abundant ;

cultivation was at the minimum ; leisure at the maximum ; the devil found mischief enough for these idle hands, and " the men of Sodom were wicked and sinners against Jehovah exceedingly " (Gen. 13 : 10–13).

They mocked the pious Lot who so foolishly went to live amongst them. Their path led to a sudden and fiery destruction. Thebes, Athens, Rome followed their ways and suffered similar judgments, yet still men follow the enchanted road. Still they protest against toil, still invent every conceivable device to avoid labour ; still they fight for shorter working hours and longer leisure, higher wages, restless pleasures, godless indulgences. Still shameful vices increase, still cities and races fester in their sins and reek with corruption. Again and again God speaks and warns, but Nebuchadnezzar's instruction is disregarded, though reinforced from time to time by the sudden destruction of a Pompeii, a Messina, a San Francisco.

Wealth, leisure, idleness, luxury, amusement, for these man still toils and fights as the *summum bonum*, the all-inclusive good ; yet when he has scaled laboriously the dazzling pinnacle of prosperity all too often he turns dizzy from success and pitches headlong to perdition.

Oh, to heed the royal warning of the superbly successful Nebuchadnezzar ! Oh, to heed from the heart the simple but profound remark of Henry Martyn, when he had taken the premier mathematical degree of the world and was senior wrangler when only twenty, " I obtained my highest wishes, but was surprised to find that I had grasped a shadow." Oh, to believe the words of the poor, despised, yet deeply satisfied Son of man, " Take heed and keep yourselves from all covetousness : for a man's life consisteth not in the abundance of the things which he possesseth " (Luke 12 : 15).

5. Because of its deep importance we must emphasize again the failure of the magicians to interpret the king's dream. To-day fortune-tellers, fraudulent or spirit-inspired, lure thousands back to heathenism of thought, spirit, and ways. Yet, as ever, are they lying spirits, deceivers. Demoniacally shrewd they couch their oracles in equivocal language, and thus apparent fulfilments occur ; but at any keen and real test they become most uncertain or utterly untrustworthy. Themselves deceived by demons they are their agents to deceive others.

Crœsus of Lydia inquired of the most renowned oracle of the ancient world whether he should fight against Cyrus of Persia. The subtle answer was that if he crossed a certain river he would destroy a great kingdom. Blindly supposing this to refer to the kingdom of his enemy he went forward, only to find his own kingdom fulfilled the answer of the priestess.

Their chief deceit and bait is to assert that it is the departed dead that return to guide and succour their inquiring loved ones. Powerfully does the prophet of God protest against this in the words : " And when they shall say unto you, Seek unto them that have familiar spirits and unto the wizards, that chirp and that mutter : should not a people seek unto their God ? on behalf of the living should they seek unto the dead ? To the law and to the testimony ! if they speak not according to this word, surely there is no morning for them " (Isa. 8 : 19, 20).

But again the true God, Jehovah, reveals Himself, and accredits His servant Daniel by giving the true meaning of the vision.

6. *The Dream.* The Creator of the mind of man knows the surest way to impress upon it His thoughts. Such a dream as Nebuchadnezzar saw was peculiarly calculated to arrest his attention and provoke enquiry.

It should be remembered in what danger of assassination tyrants generally pass their days. In Constantinople I was told that the late Sultan of Turkey never slept in the same room two nights in succession, nor said in advance in which room he would pass the coming night, nor ate of a dish till someone had eaten of it in his presence ; a fearsome state of mind in which to live. It is difficult not to think that Nebuchadnezzar had a secret surmise as to what the felling of the tree might portend, though other details, and the inward desire for certainty, led him to call for a supernatural interpretation.

That the lesson should be taught to him pictorially, not by direct statement, made it more impressive and thought-provoking. It also harmonized with that natural mental habit of the oriental mind to clothe thought in imagery, to use symbolical and figurative language.

The concordance will show the use in Scripture of the figure of a tree to represent men. The picture suggests :

(i) That which is established, as against the transitory and shifting.

(ii) That which is living, not mechanical.

(iii) Something that is spreading ; as Nebuchadnezzar had continually extended his dominion.

(iv) Then the tree has beauty, which is the first thought attached in Scripture to a tree : " Out of the ground made the Lord God to grow every tree that is pleasant to the sight, and good for food " (Gen. 2 : 9). The divine thought for man is first beauty of character then fruitfulness of service. But man's perverted heart reverses the order to-day, and asks for utility. Let the factory or home be only cheap and serviceable, then may its exterior be the distressingly ugly structure in fashion just now.

Then next the tree suggests :
(v) shade ; (vi) rest ; (vii) food ; all of which desirable features were seen in the great king. He afforded to his subjects protection from their foes, with security and quiet while they bowed their necks before him ; and thus were needful supplies assured through agriculture and commerce.

This short analysis of the figure of the tree may emphasize a previous remark that a figure of speech may be most exact, and more rich in meaning than a plain statement can be in brief compass. It has also the benefit of stimulating enquiry and exercise of mind.

7. The vision impressed upon this autocratic monarch that he was but a subordinate of " the only Potentate, the King of kings and Lord of lords " (I Tim. 6 : 15). But it revealed also the *agents through whom* the Most High governs the kingdoms of men. This is a theme of great importance and fascination. " I saw, and behold, a *watcher*, and a *holy* one, came down from heaven " (13). This title and description Daniel repeated (23).

1. Thus there are beings greater in might and power than man (II Peter 2 : 11), whose office is to watch what men do ; nor are kings exempt from their scrutiny, but rather are particular subjects thereof.

2. These watchers discern the moral state of our hearts. They noted the pride of the king.

3. They are holy in their nature and actions. This does not mean that unholy spirits do not watch us and discern our state. They do. Satan had watched Job (Job 1 : 9, etc.). But it meant for Nebuchadnezzar that he could indeed count on just and not unjust treatment. Demons and their Prince are malevolent in their desires and therefore malicious in their doings. But they cannot act against a Job until, and only as far as, God expressly permits (Job 1 and 2).

But the character of this watcher meant also that, unlike demon gods, he could not be bribed by sacrifices and gifts to tolerate in the king what was contrary to God. A truly solemn reflection. The godly can rejoice that this is so ; but let the wicked tremble.

This passage is by no means the only window through which Scripture enables the eye of faith to look into that wondrous and dominant world.

(i) In Zechariah 3 : 9 we read of " seven eyes which are [fixed] upon [=which are watching over ; Variorum Bible] one Stone."

(ii) Rev. 4 : 6–8 describes in symbols four heavenly beings who are at once intimately related to the orders of creatures on earth, but also stand nearer to the throne of God than do any other of the heavenly beings, and these are " full of eyes, round about and within " ; they see all that is " around," the things open, and " within," things inward and secret.

(iii) The prophet Micaiah (I Kings 22) had a vision of a heavenly assize, at which Jehovah presided in person, as He had twice done on the occasions when Job was discussed.   At this sitting of the court of angels Ahab was condemned to death, and the sentence took effect in spite of the king's craft in going into battle dressed as an ordinary soldier.   Whereas Jehoshaphat, though marked down by the enemy because of his royal attire, nevertheless escaped.

These prominent instances may suffice without considering in detail (iv) the general and so frequent reference to the activities of angels in judgment and mercy.   The *Revelation* is one long panorama of God effecting His will by these heavenly servants.

(v) Psalm 82 begins : " Elohim (plural) standeth in the assembly of El (singular).   He judgeth among the elohim " (plural).   Will the reader please read the Psalm ?

There is no instance of God in person taking His place among a company of earthly judges and remonstrating with them.   There are the three instances cited where He does this exact thing among angel rulers.   Nor would His threat, " Ye shall die like Adam " (lit.) be of special weight with men, for in any case they will die like Adam.   But when we remember that certain angels who re- belled of old were cast down from heaven to the deepest part of Hades, and are there reserved unto the final assize of the universe (II Peter 2 : 4), the warning to these elohim, " Ye shall fall like one of the princes," has solemn import, and shows why Jehovah says to these : " I said, Ye are elohim, and all of you sons of the Most High."   The use Christ made of these words (John 10 : 34) does not at all challenge this : the only description of these beings which He gave was that " the word of God came to them," which does not refer to the Bible but to the words which God spoke to them as quoted in this psalm.

Thus there is a court of superior angels who judge men on earth, and are themselves supervised and judged by Jehovah.   It would be natural, and Job 1 and 2 and I Kings 22 suggest it, that at any rate their more important decisions require the personal endorsement of God. For Nebuchadnezzar heard the holy watcher announce the sentence against the tree (14), and it was added (17), "The sentence is by the *decree of the watchers*, and the demand (decision, *Darby*) by the word of the holy ones"; but upon this Daniel comments, "It is the decree of *the Most High* that is come upon my lord the king" (24).

(vi) To give one other instance, it was thus that Jehovah came down to inquire personally as to the reports that had reached Him as to the state of Sodom, before He would confirm the death sentence upon whole cities (Gen. 18 : 20, 21).

All this has its lessons of warning to the godless but of comfort to the godly. The triumphing of the wicked is short; the final deliverance of a Job is certain. Nor is any class of men exempt from this heavenly jurisdiction. A heathen king and a king of Israel are alike punished. The righteous Job is purified and perfected; the sinning brother in Christ of the church at Corinth is likewise delivered to Satan for chastisement leading to ultimate salvation (I Cor. 5 : 3-5); for when we [believers] are chastened we are *judged* by the Lord in order that we may not be condemned when the world will be condemned (I Cor. 11 : 32). The unforgiving servant (Matt. 18 : 21-35) is delivered to the exactors *till he shall have paid all that is due*, which cannot scripturally be forced to mean that the *sinner* can at long last escape from *hell* by enduring his sentence there. Satan is not the agent but the object of wrath *there* : now he inflicts it, then he endures it. It can only mean that a child of the Father, whose sins have been forgiven, if he deal with hardness of heart with his brother (ver. 35), may be subjected to the chastisement of this heavenly court; for it is to believers it is said later, by one who heard the Lord give this instruction, that "judgment is without mercy to him that hath showed no mercy" (James 2 : 13); and with what judgment and measure one deals with another shall he be dealt with by these judges (Matt. 7 : 1, 2).

4. James adds that "mercy rejoiceth against judgment." Is not this well illustrated in the case of Nebuchadnezzar? For (i) the court gave him notice of their impending action. (ii) They then gave him a respite of a whole year, that he might seek mercy and escape judgment. (iii) Daniel was directed to show him a path walking on which he would meet Mercy. And (iv) even when at last the sentence had to be executed it was not a final irremediable

punishment, but for seven years Mercy waited in the vicinity until chastisement had done its blessed work ; and then, when the proud at length humbled himself, Mercy rejoiced against judgment.

It all shows with what exactness these holy watchers weigh each person and with what strictness of equity they administer justice. But they can and do take extreme measures.   Ahab likewise received repeated and timely warning through Micaiah (I Kings 22 : 8, 16), but proving obdurate the tree was at last cut down and no stump was left.   Similarly, some of the church at Corinth had been cut down, as trees, in their sins, as Ananias and Sapphira before them (I Cor. 11 : 30 ; Acts 5 ; James 5 : 19 ; I John 5 : 16).

5. Thus these dealings of God with the great monarch are lessons for all persons in all periods.   This Nebuchadnezzar recognized and sent the account to all peoples.   And Daniel's words of counsel point that way of escape from these righteous dealings of the holy watchers : " Wherefore, O king, let my counsel be acceptable unto thee, and break off thy sins by righteousness, and thine iniquities by showing mercy to the poor ; if there may be a lengthening of thy tranquillity " (27). To cease from sin and show mercy, to live in holiness and love—these are ways acceptable before God from those who know Him not, such as a Nebuchadnezzar or a Roman officer (Acts 10 : 1–4, 34, 35), as from His own people.

Such a walk is in no degree the *ground in law* upon which mercy is extended to the guilty :   that ground, that which makes it right in law that mercy be shown, is the atoning death of the Son of God, which satisfies justice by meeting the full claim of the law against him.   To this sacrifice God was ever looking, upon this basis He showed grace, as well before it had been actually offered as now thereafter.

There would not have been, there is not, any merit in a man breaking off his sins and doing good :   he does but do what he ought always to have done.   But, on the other hand, such repentance and change becomes the just and fit occasion for the extension of mercy, and without that change it were not right in law or morals that mercy be allowed to rejoice against judgment. Ahab himself had earlier afforded an instance of this (I Kings 21 : 29). When he had humbled himself before the word of God the dread sentence that had been announced was postponed, so that it should not fall in his lifetime.   But when later he returned to iniquity, the personal part of the sentence fell upon him, though the full judgment that should sweep away his whole house had been deferred.

6. Lastly, the action of this court of angels has no bearing upon the *eternal* destiny of men. This court sits only as far as to the day when Christ and His glorified saints will take over the rule of heaven and earth. Then its senior judges will give up their sovereignty to God the Father : they will place their crowns at the foot of the Ancient of days (Rev. 4 : 10) ; for " not unto *angels* hath God [in His plans] subjected the inhabited earth to come " (Heb. 2 : 5). " Know ye not that the *saints* shall judge the world and angels ? " (I Cor. 6 : 2, 3). This is millennial.

But further ; when the solemn *final* session of God's court shall be held, the decision of which will declare destiny, from which there will lie no appeal, beyond which there seems no hope of moral change and therefore no hope of mercy, *then* not to angels or to men will judgment be entrusted, but God himself will act alone through the Son (Rev. 20 : 11-15), to Whom He has committed all judgment (John 5 : 22). It is to be noted that the context of this last passage is occupied with such judgment as assures *eternal* life or *eternal* death (ver. 24). That Judge will be omniscient, His decisions infallible, and beyond appeal. Praise God that destiny is in His hands alone. Acting on His perfect principles of justice and mercy He may banish to perdition some who lightly deemed themselves secure, and may show mercy to others that shallow thinking dogmatists had already consigned to damnation. His answer at last to the question He has not yet answered, " Lord, are they few that be saved ? " may have vast surprises in both directions.

Seeing then that we know such things, what manner of persons ought we indeed to be, walking in all holy living and godliness, giving diligence that we may be found of Him in peace, without spot and blameless in His sight (II Peter 3 : 11, 14), knowing that " our God is a consuming fire " ? (Heb. 12 : 29).

How beautiful are the last words of David ! He had learned to find all his salvation and all his desire in God (II Sam. 23 : 5). How striking are the last words of Nebuchadnezzar, as far as Scripture records them : " Now I Nebuchadnezzar praise and extol and honour the King of heaven : for all His works are truth, and His ways judgment : and those that walk in pride He is able to abase " (37).

Here we take leave of the first great emperor, in hope that he had learned this lesson so well as to walk thus to the end of his days, only two years later, and that we shall hear him praising the King of heaven in resurrection life. Be it thus with us also.

CHAPTER V

"THOUGH THOU KNEWEST"

PIETY DOES NOT RUN IN THE BLOOD. NEBUCHADNEZZAR HAD learned publicly to extol and honour the God of heaven; his grandson Belshazzar as publicly defies Him. His hatred of the holy God who humbles the proud could not be satisfied merely by maintaining the worship and praise of demon gods, and the idols that represented these. Nay; in the midst of the drunken orgy Belshazzar—possibly (as was Ahab, I Kings 22 : 20–22) suddenly inspired by a deceiving spirit, sent to assure the doom of the impious sinner—openly desecrates the vessels that had been consecrated to the worship of the God he hates.

God has no pleasure in the death of the sinner (II Peter 3 : 9–15 ; Ezek. 18 : 23, 32). He desires repentance ; He delights in mercy ; He is long-suffering. But there is a limit ; at last justice must replace mercy ; Belshazzar had reached that limit and sealed his fate.

How easily God can terrify the godless. The infidel boasted loudly as he and two Christians debated while they drifted down the river and neared Niagara. But when awakened to the danger he cried to God for help, and afterwards owned that, while infidelity may not be a bad thing with which to drift down the river, it is a very bad thing with which to go over the falls. That man was in time to cry to God, but Belshazzar's pale face, troubled mind, and shaking knees availed nothing now. Oh, it is an awful hour when a hardened sinner as life closes awakes to his fearful state, but too late to find mercy.

Again are the servants of lying demons called in, and explanation of the mystic writing on the wall is demanded. But their cunning fails, nor would they have dared to tell the truth, even had they guessed it.

Daniel had been superseded, and was in retirement. The queen-mother simply remarks : " there is a man in thy kingdom " (11). A counsellor of such integrity, an officer of such probity, suited not a young and licentious king or his court. Belshazzar is, or feigns to be, ignorant of him, saying, "*I have heard* of thee that the spirit of the gods is in thee " (11, 14). How easily men give the glory of the only God unto others. Even the queen-mother did not, or did not care to, acknowledge the true God to Whom Daniel had ever borne uncompromising witness.

Yet never had Babylon more needed Daniel's God and Daniel. For long the Persian hosts had been around the city, and now its hour of doom had struck. At the time that God had announced the sovereignty of Nebuchadnezzar He had also declared that in the days of his grandson the punishment of Babylon should come (Jer. 27 : 7). That grandson had now filled up the cup of wickedness that should compel that punishment ; the man whose counsels, if followed, would have deferred or avoided the doom had been thrust aside, and the judgment was both merited and executed. Let any servant of God who is rejected and superseded take comfort : the plans of God are fulfilled by the rejection of His own Son, as they will be in due time by His acceptance. It is enough that the servant be as his Master.

It is observable how different is Daniel's manner towards Belshazzar from that towards Nebuchadnezzar. The latter he addressed with full respect : " My lord, O king . . . Wherefore O king " ; and from him had accepted position and honour. But Belshazzar's offer of gifts he scorns : " Keep thy gifts for thyself and give thy rewards to someone else," and to him he says with pointed emphasis, " O thou king ! " (17, 18). A man who with determination was defying light and truth, was deliberately outraging God, and whose doom was sealed and announced, Daniel could not countenance or from such an one accept gifts. With what loathing must the aged saint have looked around upon the disgusting debauchery of that drunken royal revel.

All sin is sin, but guilt is proportionate to knowledge. The sting of Daniel's charge was " Though thou knewest " thou hast so acted (22). Men are responsible to take to heart the lessons of the dealings of God with others. Belshazzar knew right well how God had humbled his grandfather, and yet dared to defy the Most High. Knowing of those events he could scarcely *not* have known of Daniel. It is upon this just principle that God judges.

(i) All men have the testimony of nature that there exists a Creator of eternal power and divine nature (Rom. 1 : 21), and that He does good, sending rain and sunshine, supplying all needs of all creatures (Acts 14 : 15–17 ; 17 : 24–26), and not discriminating against the evil or His very enemies (Matt. 5 : 45). And this testimony is universal (Ps. 19 : 1–4).

(ii) All men have the witness of conscience, with the law of right and wrong written in the heart. They *know* that the abominations they commit are wicked. The ordinance of God that sin brings death cannot be avoided or its testimony be denied.

(iii) The general providential dealings of God with men emphasize this inward knowledge, and particular dealings with individuals accentuate its voice to those who know of these. This was the special aggravation in Belshazzar's case, and he was without excuse.

(iv) Some men have God's law in written form, as Israel since Sinai, and all who through them, or through the Book itself, have been given knowledge of that law. What a ponderous weight of guilt the printing press has added to millions, even as it has multiplied the privileges and opportunities offered in the Book.

(v) Some have the fuller light of the good news of salvation by faith in the Son of God and His sacrifice for sinners.

Each will be dealt with in judgment according to the light available (Rom. 2 : 12–16) ; and the Judge has afore-announced that it will go easier in the day of judgment for Sodom and Gomorrah than for Bethsaida and Capernaum (Matt. 11 : 20–24).

These principles hold in the present dealings of God with nations, as well as cities, or persons. The writing on that palace wall reveals this for all times, all nations, all rulers. Not again has a visible hand scared a godless king ; but that hand was only making visible for once what had been already done in that dominant realm which is unseen by men. The words are a revelation of divine government.

" MENE. God hath numbered thy kingdom and brought it to an end." His actions are not haphazard, but *calculated*. The duration of an empire is not left to chance, to human enterprise, to Satanic capacity ; it is reckoned out by God. Antichrist will endeavour thus to act : he will think to change the times and seasons (Dan. 7 : 25) ; but he will stand only till that which is " determined " has been done (Dan. 9 : 27) ; and the exact duration of those most dreadful days has been both fixed and announced by God (Dan. 8 : 14 ; 9 : 25 ; 12 : 7, 11, 12) ; for out of compassion for His own chosen people He has set a strict and short limit (Matt. 24 : 22).

This is made known to strengthen faith, and to give quietness of heart when days of trouble come, whether personal, local, national, or universal (John 14 : 29 ; 16 : 33). God knows exactly how long it shall be to the end. The little child fears as the train plunges into the dark tunnel, but the father knows it has a deter-mined limit, and he sits in peace ; the end and the daylight are not, cannot be, one foot further off than the length of the tunnel.

" TEKEL : Thou art weighed in the balances and art found wanting."

But God acts not only by calculation : He *weighs* the value of actions, and measures out justice with exactness. There is no rough-and-ready action in His court. The Judge ponders, weighs up the various considerations that affect each case—mental, moral, physical inheritance ; environment, opportunity ; inducement, en-ticement ; motive, pressure ; present consequences, painful or pleasant : and none but God is competent thus accurately to weigh even one life, or even one act of a life. Who then but One who is himself God can be capable of judging the innumerable myriads of moral beings, heavenly and human ? Jesus *must* be God or He *could* not perform such a task as that of universal judge (John 5 : 22, 23).

The ancient Egyptians had a true idea of this divine judgment, though misapplied to their god, Osiris. They said that after death the man was taken to the hall of judgment, where his heart was removed and weighed in the scales of justice against a feather. If it were the lighter, he had been pure ; if the heavier, it was weighted with sin, and he must suffer due punishment.

Thus speaks Scripture also : " As a man thinketh in his heart (or reckoneth within himself, R.V.), so *is* he " (Prov. 23 : 7) ; therefore " keep thine heart above all that thou guardest ; for out of it are the issues of life " (Prov. 4 : 23). A lustful desire in the heart is the equivalent of adultery (Matt. 5 : 28), hate is murder (I John 3 : 15). This is the view of Him of whom it is written that " Jehovah is a God of knowledge. By Him actions are *weighed* " (I Sam. 2 : 3).

Man pictures Justice with scales and sword, but blindfold. But God is a God of knowledge, and acts with full light upon each case and each act, with conscious, infallible, incorruptible accuracy.

In those perfect scales Belshazzar was found light ; let us each ask : Shall *I* be found wanting ? Royal estate, glory, riches, which sway so heavily the judgment of men, do not influence the balance of divine justice by which all shall be tested, save as such possessions brought fuller and larger opportunity and responsibility. There it is character that turns the scale.

" Peres : Thy kingdom is divided, and given to the Medes and Persians." Empires do not stand by horses and munitions, not even when these cost annually thousands of millions of pounds sterling. Babylon was deemed impregnable, but it fell. The *Titanic* was deemed unsinkable, but she sank. Herodotus points out how easily the Babylonians might have defeated the Persians. For the river bed by which the latter entered was not only protected by the great gates which the Persians had not been able to force, but under which they crept at night as the water of the Euphrates sank when drained off by Cyrus, but the openings in the banks, by which access to the waters was gained by the inhabitants, were also defended by gates. If the defenders had been normally alert they could have closed these gates, mounted the banks, and have caught their attackers in a veritable death-trap. Herodotus visited the city not such a great while after, and when the memory of the deeds of Cyrus was still fresh, and he says it so happened that a great feast was in progress that very night, and the city proved an easy prey to the Medes and Persians.

We say " it happened " ; but no ! in truth the divine sentence was fulfilled, and " in that night Belshazzar the Chaldean king was slain " (30). The first empire of prophecy had run its aforedeclared course. So will the last. History is prophecy.

CHAPTER VI

THE DEN OF LIONS

WHERE WAS DANIEL WHEN HIS FRIENDS WERE TESTED BY THE fiery furnace ? It is not known : but now, as life is well advanced, an equally severe test reveals that he, like them, has strength to be faithful unto death.

Men are ruled mainly by self-interest ; yet God overrules them. The time was near when Israel must be restored to Palestine, and " an Israelite indeed, in whom is no guile," was re-exalted to the highest office in the new empire that shall grant this restoration and fulfil God's purpose and prophecy (Jer. 25 : 11, 12 ; 29 : 10). Whether the proverbial wisdom of Daniel (Ezek. 28 : 3) had reached the ears of the kings of Persia, or whether the events in the palace on the night of the capture of Babylon were told to him, or what other reason led Darius to exalt him, we do not know. Perhaps the fact that the Persians were not idolaters, in the common meaning of the term, may have made them more likely to appreciate and protect the Jews, the only other non-idolatrous nation. It is enough that we see the hand of God in the triumph of the Persians and in the exaltation of Daniel, for both events were for the good of Israel.

The coffers of Darius would be better replenished by having a Grand Vizier of unassailable integrity, and his burdens of State be greatly lightened by the aid of one intimately acquainted with the conquered realms and their government. But for these very reasons Daniel would be thoroughly obnoxious to the subordinate officials for *they* could not so easily replenish *their* coffers, at the expense of the king and the public, seeing that this trained eye was ever upon them and this experienced hand held directing power. Thus often is the godly man in the difficult position of being the centre of antagonistic interests and influences.

The chapter gives a vivid and painfully accurate picture of the corruption in high places that has ever cursed every land where the fear of the Holy One has not had power through His word and Spirit, and which corruption is again increasing in lands that have been blessed with these purifying influences but are rejecting

71

them.   The western nations are being steadily saturated with pagan philosophy, and the issue is, and must be, pagan morals, or rather immorality, in every walk of life.   See *World Chaos*.   In this experience of Daniel let the Christian see the situation that, in principle, must become general in the world.   Let him learn of Asaph (Ps. 73), as surely Daniel had done, lest the ease and triumph of the wicked cause his feet to slip.

In such circumstances what course shall the godly take ?   Peter was well acquainted with these conditions, and he answers : " Let them also that suffer according to the will of God commit their lives (ψυχή) unto a faithful Creator *by doing good* " (I Peter 4 : 19). By doing what is right, according to the standard of God, a man places his life in the ordering and safe keeping of God ; and he takes it out of the keeping of God when he does wrong.

Daniel's enemies saw that his conduct afforded them no occasion whatever to accuse him to the king.   Here is the standard and possibility for every servant of God.   Unimpeachable integrity and unwavering fidelity in all duties and relationships.   But here also is seen the *limit* of a Christian's duty to the sovereign, the State, to all men.   " We shall not find any occasion against this Daniel *except* we find it against him concerning the *law of his God* " (5). Note well this exception to the general rule that rulers are to be obeyed.   In any matter upon which God has declared His holy will obedience must be to Him and none other.   He is the Most High, the King of kings, and we must obey Him rather than men, if He has spoken upon a matter.   *The rulers of the earth are His subordinates, appointed by Him and removed at His pleasure, and the orders of subordinates may not prevail against the commands of the Superior.* How deeply important therefore it is to be well versed in His Word, and to be imbued with His Spirit to understand and apply that Word in all its precepts and at all costs.

How dangerous a disease is vanity : it blinds the eyes of the mind, dulls the perceptions, and leaves its victim helpless before impending perils.   Darius knew well enough the cunning and duplicity of oriental courtiers, and had he not felt flattered by their proposal virtually to deify him he might have reflected upon the likelihood of some false reason for their so extravagant desire to honour him.   If he was to replace the gods at all, why should it be for only a month ?   Surely he might have suspected a trap in this singular proposal.   And then again : why was not his aged and valued Prime Minister at the head of the official body in presenting this petition? A moment's reflection might have reminded him of the sheer impossibility that this chief Jew should abjure his God before his people and all men, the God he had served so long and honourably. But pride went before and lured him into the snare.

What shall the godly do when his duty to God is attacked? If he can flee he has the Lord's counsel to do so (Matt. 10 : 23). But it is not always possible to escape from the situation. Gethsemane and Calvary were the path of God for His Son. Sometimes a Nehemiah must say, " Should such a man as I flee ? " (Neh. 6 : 11). In such a case the attitude of uncompromising obedience to God, and of consequent disobedience to the law of man, is right, noble, and wise, the Christian's only course. " When Daniel knew that the decree was signed, he went into his house (now his windows were open in his chamber towards Jerusalem) ; and he kneeled upon his knees three times a day, and prayed, and gave thanks before his God, as he did aforetime " (10). This was to court disaster ; but consequences must be left with God. It was thus that Christ, by asserting Himself to be the Son of God, gave advantage to His enemies, yielding to them the ground of condemnation they had sought in vain. Against false charges He said nothing : to the vital truth He confessed, though it assured His condemnation. How vividly Bunyan has detailed in his *Relation of his Imprisonment* the exercises of his soul when faced with arrest if he should preach against the orders of officials ; yet he felt he dared not shirk the test, and so went to the meeting and thence to the prison.

> " Dare to be a Daniel,
> Dare to stand alone ! "

How easily it is sung !

> " They climbed the steep ascent of heaven
> Through peril, toil, and pain :
> O God, to us may grace be given
> To follow in their train ! "

How many sing it sincerely? Who really seeks *such* grace? Who does actually believe that the way to heaven is like that?

" The tender mercies of the wicked are cruel." The princes sprang their trap and the king and Daniel were their victims, both helpless in the toils. They pressed their advantage to the full. How great respect Daniel had won from Darius is shown by the painful, persevering efforts the king made to rescue him. But he was in the iron grip of his national laws. He was no absolute sovereign as Nebuchadnezzar, no head of gold; authority had degenerated to a limited monarchy; the next best, as silver is to gold, but a lower and weaker condition. So he yields, pays the bitter penalty of his foolish vanity, and Daniel is lowered into the den of lions.

Let us visualize the situation. At the Basel Zoo I was watching the lions just before feeding time. Hungry, restless, fierce, they paced swiftly to and fro, and, oh, with what voracity they tore the great joints of raw meat and gnawed and crushed the bones. I was outside the den; but *Daniel was inside* !

The hungry, roaring lion is a picture of the Devil, roaming restlessly around seeking for a Job that he may devour him (I Peter 5 : 8). *Why* are the godly so often left in his power ? *Why* should the most upright man of the whole Persian world be found in the den ? *Why* shall Paul be slain by Nero ? Yea, most enigmatical of all, *why* shall Jesus be crucified by Pilate ? *Why*, indeed ? The noble, eternal results of Calvary, for God and man, give answer, for Christ and for all who suffered for and with Him, as well before He came here as since.

" Many are the afflictions of the righteous : but Jehovah delivereth him out of them *all* " (Ps, 34 : 19). Indeed, David ! Is this so ? It is so : but there are two kinds of deliverance. The three Hebrews, Daniel, and Peter (Acts 12 : 11) were delivered physically : Jesus, James, and Peter (John 21 : 18, 19 ; II Peter 1 : 13,14) were *not* delivered physically. But when the *man*, Christ Jesus, crucified, dying, forsaken, nevertheless justified God in so treating Him, saying, " But Thou are holy ! " ; and when Paul, aged, facing death, and likewise forsaken by his brethren when most needing encouragement, yet prayed that they might be forgiven their fear and faithlessness, both the Master and the servant had been " delivered out of the mouth of the lion," as Paul puts it (II Tim. 4 : 17 ; Ps. 22 : 20, 21). For in heart they had been preserved from doubt towards God and bitterness towards men, which deliverance is, in truth, more wonderful and divine than that the body be saved from a lion. Moreover, the latter is exceptional, whereas the former God will work for every man of faith, of righteous life, of definite testimony.

The control of angels over creation is here strikingly illustrated : they can " shut the mouths of lions." The manner of this influence we are not told. It is easy to conceive that they who can give to a man the nature of a beast, as to Nebuchadnezzar, can suspend, as here, the fierce destructive nature of the wild beast, which, after all, is a foreign nature. It was not found before man fell from God, and it will be removed upon his general restoration (Isa. 11 : 1-9, etc.).

And how puny is man against these wondrous agents of the will of God. How easily they thwart his designs. How foolish to provoke their hostility. What terrific force lies in the words, " The Son of man shall send forth His angels, and they shall gather out of His kingdom all things that cause stumbling . . . shall sever the wicked from among the righteous, and shall cast them into the furnace of fire : there shall be the weeping and the gnashing of teeth " (Matt. 13 : 41, 42, 49, 50). That will be more awful than its type, when Daniel's accusers were cast where they had cast him, to their destruction. How exact is divine retribution. A barbarous king cuts off the thumbs and toes of conquered foes, and duly loses his own when captured (Judges 1 : 6, 7), which is the only instance known of Israel mutilating a captive in those wars. So to the exact fate to which the princes sent Daniel they are sent. What they meted out to him was meted out to them.

But equally blessed it is to know that these powerful beings are sent forth to do service for them that shall be heirs of salvation (Heb. 1 : 14). Daniel they saved from the lions, Peter from Herod (Acts 12 : 11), and a thousand more from other and otherwise inescapable perils.

Once again is Daniel because of his faithfulness privileged to be the occasion of a royal and universal testimony to the living, steadfast, and eternal God, and again he is exalted to a prosperity that gave vast opportunities to serve God and men.

All this is prophetic, a revelation of principles perpetually operating. Antichrist will claim for himself divine honours ; he alone shall be worshipped. The alternative will be death (Rev. 13 : 14, 15). Again the saints will need endurance to keep the commandments of God and the faith of Jesus (Rev. 14 : 12). As they will keep the faith of Jesus must they not be Christians ? They who are not delivered physically will, by suffering and death, secure an especial blessing (Rev. 14 : 13 ; 6 : 9–11 ; 20 : 4). They who endure to the end of those dread days shall be saved physically by rapture at the descent of the Son of man (Matt. 24 : 13, 14 ; Mark 13 : 13) ; and at the same time by resurrection shall all who are accounted by the Lord worthy to rule in His kingdom be brought up out of a deeper region than the den of lions ; for Hades itself shall surrender them at the voice of Christ, and it shall be found that " not a hair of their head had perished." " Then shall the righteous shine forth as the sun in the kingdom of their Father " (Matt. 13 : 43), and enter upon a vastly nobler service and glory than Daniel reached in his sphere. Yet in that great era Daniel is promised his share (Dan. 12 : 13), with all the faithful of the ages before Christ (Luke 13 : 28).

 " So run that ye may attain " (I Cor. 9 : 24). " Let us run with steadfastness the race that is set before us," looking away from earth to heaven, from the present to the future, from circumstances unto Jesus, and finding in Him the author and the perfector of faith. Full of point is Spurgeon's reason why the lions did not eat Daniel, even that one half of him was grit and the other half backbone. Equally to the purpose, when he saw an advertisement, " Tons of bones wanted," he said, Yes, backbones ! " Thou, therefore, my child, be strengthened in the grace that is in Christ Jesus " (II Tim. 2 : 1): " I can do all things in [the power of] Him that strengtheneth me " (Phil. 4 : 13).

CHAPTER VII

THE WILD BEASTS

I. THE COMMON EXPLANATION OF THESE FOUR BEASTS FROM THE sea is that each corresponds to one part of the image of ch. 2. The main difference, it is suggested, is that the image shows world empire as seen by a worldly-minded empire-builder, even a grand, imposing, strong creation, whereas the wild beasts reveal the inner, essential character of human rule as shown by God to His favoured prophet.

That these two aspects are presented will not be questioned; but (1) this is not adequate ground for interpreting the present vision as a virtual repetition of ch. 2. The earlier vision was as distinctly God-given and God-explained as that of ch. 7. Nebuchadnezzar did not form the picture for himself, and it does not represent a merely human idea of things. Moreover (2) the fourth part of the image, the iron subduing, breaking, crushing all opposition, as plainly reveals the cruel ruthless nature as do the beasts. And (3) it is a general feature of Daniel's visions that each repeats only as much of what has been before given as to reveal how it connects with the former, and then *each adds* something material as its main burden. " Repetition is very rare in Scripture " (Anderson, *The Coming Prince*, p. 274).

II. Many years ago I read a brief remark by Sir Robert Anderson that he saw no ground for the identifying of these two visions. I have come to believe he was right in this, though, as I venture to think, not in some of his other lines of exposition, such, for example, as the " postponed kingdom " and " interim dispensation " theories, and the much that follows thereon.*

Some reasons are :

1. The first detail of the vision is that " the four winds of the heaven break forth." The action was familiar to the minds of men. Readers of the *Aeneid* will remember how that four winds of heaven were set in motion by the gods to sink a fleet. In

---

* After the first draft of this book was written, I read for the first time Sir R. Anderson's *The Coming Prince*, and was gratified to see how many of the distinctive views on *Daniel* I had advanced he had suggested, if but tentatively.

Revelation 7 four angels are shown standing upon the four corners of the earth restraining the four winds of the earth until the time for a certain judgment to be executed.

How is it that trade winds blow with so considerable a degree of regularity and direction that sailors could more or less order a voyage by them? On the other hand, how is it that at times most destructive and violent tempests arise out of season? May not both facts be evidences of *control*, control that usually assures well-being to man, but when needful effects deserved judgment. Psalm 48 is millennial, and verse 7 shows that a fleet from the west is yet to be destroyed by a wind from the east.

The four winds breaking forth together from all quarters signifies a general commotion arising in all directions simultaneously. Now no such conditions attended the rise of either of the four empires of ch. 2. The disturbances were local, gradual, the more part of the areas being at rest while this or that district was being subdued.

2. This storm arises in the Mediterranean Sea. In Hebrew usage " the great sea " is a proper noun and means invariably the Mediterranean. The Hebrews were acquainted with several seas. One was the Euphrates (Jer. 51 : 36, 42). Another was the Nile (Isa. 11 : 15 ; 19 : 5), perhaps so termed because of its sea-like appearance when in flood and covering the wide valley. This usage continues. In Upper Egypt an Egyptian told me to cross the " sea " to reach a certain ruin. Then there were the Red Sea, the Dead Sea, the Sea of Galilee. In contrast to these the Mediterranean was naturally the Great Sea. The occurrences of the name are as follows :

(1) Num. 34 : 6, 7. " And for the western border [of the promised land] ye shall have the great sea for a border : this shall be your west border. And this shall be your north border : from the great sea ye shall mark out for you Mount Hor," etc. Mount Hor lies right against the Mediterranean. This first occurrence shows indisputably the sense stated.

(2) Josh. 1 : 4 : " the great sea toward the going down of the sun shall be your border." " The going down of the sun " fixes that the west of Palestine is meant, that is the Mediterranean.

(3) Josh. 9 : 1 : " all the shore of the great sea in front of Lebanon." There is only one sea " in front of Lebanon." Every visitor to those fine mountains will have gazed out over it.

(4) Josh. 15 : 11, 12 : " the goings out of the border were at

the sea. And the west border [of Judah] was to the great sea, and the border thereof."

(5) Josh. 15 : 47 : " Ashdod, her towns and her villages ; Gaza, her towns and her villages ; unto the brook of Egypt [the Wady el Arish, just where the land turns west towards Egypt], and the great sea and the border thereof."

(6) Josh. 23 : 4 : " Behold, I have allotted unto you these nations that remain, to be an inheritance for your tribes, from Jordan, with all the nations that I have cut off, even unto the great sea toward the going down of the sun." Jordan is specified on the east in contrast to the Mediterranean on the west.

This group of passages shows unmistakably the usage at the beginning of the national history of Israel, 1400 B.C.

(7) Ezek. 47 : 10 : " their fish shall be after their kinds, as the fish of the great sea, very many." The term here is in contrast to the sea of the eastern region, mentioned in verse 8 as that which the waters of the river shall heal, that is the Dead Sea, notorious for its saltness, and called " the salt sea " (Gen. 14 : 3 ; Josh. 3 : 16, etc.). That Ezekiel means the Mediterranean is seen in the next instance, only five verses later.

(8) Ver. 15 : " This shall be the border of the land : on the north side, from the great sea, by the way of Hethlon, unto the entering in of Zedad ; Hamath, Berotha, Sibraim, which is between the border of Damascus and the border of Hamath ; which is by the border of Hauran." The great sea, Hamath, Damascus, Hauran, describes a course from west to east, showing what is meant. The passage shows that Ezekiel is dealing distinctly with real things, not speaking symbolically. He gives what will be the borders of the same land in the time of Messiah as the former passages did of that literal land in ancient times. The next place reverses the direction and runs from east to west.

(9) Ezek. 47 : 19 : " And the south side southward shall be from Tamar as far as the waters of Meribath-Kadesh to the brook of Egypt, unto the great sea."

(10) Ver. 20 : " And the west side shall be the great sea, from the south border as far as over against the entering in of Hamath."

(11) Ezek. 48 : 28 : " at the south side southward, the border shall be even from Tamar, unto the waters of Meribath-Kadesh, to the brook of Egypt, unto the great sea."

This is repeated from No. 9 above.

(12) Dan. 7 : 2 : "the four winds of heaven brake forth upon the great sea."

It is clear that from the time of Moses the term had one regular meaning, and that this was still current in Daniel's day, as witnessed by its use by his contemporary, Ezekiel. There is no ground for giving it in Daniel 7 the symbolic sense of a time of international disturbance; especially seeing that, in the explanation, the angel says that the kings who will war " shall arise out of the *earth*." If " sea " means unrest of peoples, then " earth " must mean quietness of peoples. But both cannot be their state at one time.

The vision does declare such a period of international disturbance, but it is of great importance to retain the normal, literal sense of " the great sea " because it fixes the exact area of the disturbance whenever it shall come. The four beasts are to arise in the Mediterranean area ; they " came up from the sea," the Great Sea just mentioned.

Now this was not the case with the two first empires of the image. Babylon was 500 miles from that sea in a straight line, or perhaps 600 by the only route available. It had existed as a kingdom long before it touched the Mediterranean under Nebuchadnezzar. Before that its route to the sea had been blocked by the power of Assyria centred at Nineveh. It reached the coast only by gradual conquest.

The same was true of Persia. It was still further from the Mediterranean, being east of Mesopotamia. It also had existed as a kingdom for centuries before it reached the sea.

By no forcing of language can either be said to rise out of the Great Sea. It were as incorrect as to say that Great Britain rose out of the Mediterranean because she gained possessions there in the last century.

3. The interpretation informed Daniel that the four beasts were still in the future : " they shall arise." But Babylon had already risen to world supremacy, and was actually quite near its fall, for the vision was in the first year of the brief reign of its last king.

4. Sir Robert Anderson (*The Coming Prince*, p. 274) points out that the second beast does not truly correspond to Persia and Media with the accuracy to be noted in prophetic scripture. The rendering " it was raised up on one side " has been supposed to mean that one partner in the kingdom—the Persians—was dominant over the other—the Medes. But the true rendering, as given by

Tregelles and followed in the margin of the R.V., appears to be, " It made for itself one dominion," that is, it consolidated conquered lands into a unified kingdom.

5. He further remarks that the third beast does not answer to Alexander's empire. That arose as a single-headed kingdom under his undivided sovereignty, and became four-headed only after his death ; but this leopard has four heads and four wings at the time that it arises from the sea.

6. The four beasts all came up during one tempest, each struggling for supremacy, only to be vanquished by the last. No such terrific tornado has ever swept the Mediterranean region. The conflicts between Rome and Carthage or Cæsar and Antony were mere passing whiffs, with long intervals between, as compared with the tempest described by Daniel. Nor have four such powers in rapid succession ever struggled for supremacy. History shows nothing that at all answers to these features.

The common view can be studied fully in G. H. Pember's *The Great Prophecies of the Centuries concerning Israel and the Gentiles*. We consider this author the most illuminating writer upon prophetic scripture of modern times, but differ from him on this matter. The vision, as we believe, shows what has yet to take place in the Mediterranean area. Whether recent events are preparing for this convulsion, or are even its commencement, it is not for us to say, though this is quite possible ; but it *is* ours to watch the Great Sea, for there this terrible tempest will burst.

It has been said truly that " Control of the Near East is the key to world influence."

III. As to the symbols employed, it is not possible to identify the separate beasts with existing kingdoms. It is true that we speak of the British lion and the Russian bear, but here the apparent clue fails as regards warranting the present identifying of the beasts. For (1) Russia has never been, and still is not, a Mediterranean power ; (2) no Mediterranean country has the leopard as its emblem ; (3) the fourth beast is nondescript, like to no animal, no kingdom before known.

But the symbols will help the wise to a right understanding when the time of fulfilment shall have come.

1. The first of these powers will, at the time for fulfilment of the vision, be majestic, strong, lion-like, swift in its movements as the eagle, and as voracious as both the beast and the bird named. But presently its " wings will be plucked," it will lose its swiftness,

its power of rapid extension, and become like a man standing rather than a beast roaming or a bird swooping upon the prey. Also it will become humane instead of bestial, " a man's heart was given unto it," with which is to be compared Nebuchadnezzar and a beast's heart being given unto a man. Probably this humanizing of the government will prove its weakness in those rough times and will enable the bear to overcome it, for what chance has an ordinary humane man against a bear ?

2. The second power will be ponderous, slower, but terrible as a bear in destruction of life. Its activity will be in the direction of consolidation, rather than mere expansion : " it raised up one dominion." Its blows will be fearfully destructive : " three ribs are between its teeth, and they [the angelic superintendents of God's judgments] said thus unto it, Arise, devour much flesh " (5). That the ribs are between its teeth as it rises from the sea may suggest that it has just seized three lands, but not yet incorporated them into its empire.

3. The third beast will be as attractive and as cruel as a leopard, and as swift as a four-winged bird. It will also have a fourfold government, probably being a confederacy of four powers, pictured as four heads, and it will have real and great authority : " dominion was given unto it." That when it rises it already has four heads and four wings may similarly show that the fourfold confederacy had been formed immediately before. Men's minds are working in this direction. In 1947 the Secretary-General of the Arab League envisaged such a confederation of Arab countries adjacent to the Mediterranean and possibly to include Greece and Turkey. It is to be a " buffer State." Between what parties ? (*Daily Telegraph*, October 3rd, 1947). Four wings will mean uncommon swiftness in action.

4. It will be followed by the fourth beast, which will be recognizable by it being unlike any creature, any kingdom hitherto known among men. It is upon this power that the vision concentrates and enlarges. Its three predecessors are described briefly, no more being said than will suffice to identify each when it arises. But the details of the fourth beast are many and arresting and are the subject of the angelic interpretation.

From his youth and through a long career Daniel had witnessed frightful doings by kings and kingdoms. But though thus accustomed to terrible things yet the appearance of this monster fascinated, perplexed, and troubled him. As we observe what he observed let us remember that it reveals events really to happen on this very earth, and in its western area to which we belong, and so may our hearts be solemnized, our minds be enlightened, and our souls be made to feel the real nature and coming final expression of world-empire in the hands of man under the influence of Satan.

Though evolution in the realm of nature, as taught by modern theorists, is a fiction and deception, yet is there an evolutionary process in the affairs of *man's* world and history. This beast pictures the full development and outcome of the evil that lies in the human heart, which has worked there since Adam fell from God, is working there still, and in this monster will attain its full stature, horror, impiety, and will reach its doom. Hence the large place and much detail given to it in the prophecy and its interpretation.

(i) It is " terrible." It acts to the full upon the cruel maxim that a war is soonest won by ruthless terrorizing of the enemy people, that they may the sooner submit.

(ii) It is " exceedingly strong," implying that the resources of mind, men, and material are ample and are organized.

(iii) Its power to tear to pieces is irresistible : it has " great iron teeth."

(iv) It leaves no opposition existing : it " devours," absorbs all it attacks, annihilates all that opposes. No toleration is shown. It is the spirit lately revived in the west and seen equally in Nazi, fascist, and communistic rule.

(v) What it does not positively annihilate it crushes and stamps into helpless subjection with its brass-nailed feet, " breaking to pieces " all organized resistance as a threshing machine reduces the corn-stalks to chaff (23, marg.).

(vi) In size, appearance, strength, cruelty, and rapacity it will bear no resemblance to any kingdom that has preceded it : " it shall be diverse from all the kingdoms."

(vii) This will be seen very distinctly in its extent : " it shall devour the whole earth." No empire ever yet has fulfilled this prediction. All the old empires knew of vast territories that they did not and could not subdue. But Antichrist will fulfil this prediction (see Appendix A). Yet the *beast* is not the whole earth ; it devours it but is not it. Antichrist will be given his throne by the ten kings : their territory will be his own proper empire, but this will be so strong that all outside regions must submit, willingly at first, though later some will rebel (Dan. 11 : 40, 44). See further at pp. 89, 100.

This strongly emphasized dissimilarity (7, 19, 23) from all predecessors is important. It shows that the old Roman empire is not in view.

(viii) It had " ten horns on its head." This detail gives the true clue to the whole vision. The horns correspond to the toes of the image. The horns grow out of the beast : " out of this kingdom shall ten kings arise." Now the toes grew out of the feet, not out of the legs of the image. The feet and toes are the *final* stage of the image, and it is upon these that the " stone " falls (2 : 34). Therefore the beast and its horns are also the *final* period of world empire, not a picture of its course but of its conclusion. Similarly it is this beast that is destroyed at the coming of the Son of man and to make way for His kingdom.

Thus the vision of the beasts shows the political movements by which the feet and toes of the image will develop. It is not a repetition of the whole image, but an expansion in detail of that final stage of world-empire which is to be the culmination of " man's day " and is a chief subject of prophecy.

As the number ten connects this vision with the feet of the image so also does it (with other details) show that the beast of Rev. 13 is the beast of this vision, that chapter being an expansion of this as this is of Daniel 2.

IV. At the time this fourth beast is destroyed utterly (" given to be burned with fire ") is is said : " And as for the rest of the beasts, their dominion was taken away : yet their lives were prolonged for a season and a time."

This has greatly perplexed expositors, and must continue to do so as long as these three are supposed to represent the ancient empires of Babylon, Persia, and Greece, and the fourth Rome. For

(i) Babylon and Persia, as the empires of Daniel's visions, had ceased to exist when Rome came to supremacy, having been incorporated, first Babylon into Persia and then both into the Grecian empire ; and after the destruction of the Roman empire neither rose again to dominion or separate existence. The phrase " their dominion was taken away, yet their lives were prolonged " had no application.

(ii) Rome never trampled upon or dominated Babylonia or Persia, and certainly never consolidated its power there.

(iii) Greece it annexed and ruled, but that land also did not recover dominion when Rome fell. When the western empire collapsed Greece remained under the rule of Constantinople, and when that city fell it passed with it under the dominion of Saracens and Turks.

(iv) In any case the time limit for the prolonging of their lives, " for a season and a time," has no meaning in their history.

But the difficulties fade when all four kingdoms are seen as coming into existence quickly upon one another, during one period of political disturbance, and the three being crushed by the fourth, yet not wholly destroyed. They will remain as subordinate to the fourth; and when the Word of God utterly destroys this last (Rev. 19 : 10–21) they will be suffered to continue for a short period, presumably until the government of earth can be rearranged at the commencement of the millennium.

V. It is therefore to be expected that further great political disturbance will convulse the Mediterranean regions, for four successive kingdoms were pictured striving for mastery, and the fourth attaining it. This fourth will develop a ten kingdom form : " out of this kingdom shall ten kings arise " (7 : 24). The symbol of a horn is frequent. For horned beasts it is the weapon of defence and offence, and aptly signifies power to protect and attack, that is, political strength.

After this tenfold arrangement has been established an eleventh king shall arise within their territory : " There came up *among them* another horn " (8). The permutations of politics make all things insecure, and the ten will tolerate this new-comer, or find themselves unable to hinder the change. The full interest of the vision, and of much other Scripture, now concentrates upon this latest power. It is shown :

1. That at his rise he will be insignificant, " a little horn." Antichrist will not burst on the world in full Satanic splendour and power. Rather will he prove his fitness for supremacy in Satan's sphere by winning it through fraud and force.

2. Having secured a position among the nations of the league he will attack and subdue three of his neighbours : " before him three of the first horns were plucked up by the roots " (8, 24). Their overthrow is thorough; they are uprooted. It appears, however, that, as is frequent with conquerors, he reinstates these as his subordinates, for Rev. 17 : 16 shows that, when the later development is reached that he shall be elected overlord of the fourth beast, there are still ten kings who give him their kingdom.

The commotion among the confederates which will be caused

by him conquering three of their number must be considerable.
Naturally it will provoke hostilities against the aggressor. We
suppose that this period is opened up in seals 1 to 4 of Rev. 6 as
follows :

Seal 1.   The rise of Antichrist going forth on a career of conquest
(" conquering ") which leads to supremacy (" and to conquer ").
Seal 2.   The western powers seeking to reduce him to order, but
failing.   Seal 3.   The scarcity that will result in the regions affected
by the desolating wars raged.   Seal 4.   The eastern nations joining
in the welter.   Thus will he hack his bloody path to supremacy ;
and the summit reached, seal 5 refers to the final persecution of
the saints by Antichrist, and seal 6 to the intervention of Christ
immediately after that tribulation, according to Matt. 24 : 29-31.
Seal 7, interpreted by the Old Testament, covers the destruction
of Antichrist by Christ.

The detail proof of this may be seen in our exposition of the
Revelation, but it will be of interest to remark that in seal 2 the
word for " sword " ($\mu\acute{\alpha}\chi\alpha\iota\rho\alpha$) depicts the weapon used in John's
day by the Roman armies, whereas the word in seal 4 ($\acute{\rho}o\mu\phi\alpha\acute{\iota}\alpha$)
is that for the long eastern blade.   Some forty years ago Mr. Pember
pointed this out to me, and said he could only understand it to mean
that seal 2 speaks of western military activity and seal 4 of eastern
nations joining in the wars of the end days.   Pursuing this line I
examined the word " bow," the weapon of the rider of seal 1,
and found that the Greek world spoke of themselves as relying on
the " might of the spear," for that had been their great weapon
since the days of Alexander's phalanx, but they referred to their
eastern enemies as " drawers of the bow " (see Lid. and S. Lex.,
s.v., $\tau\acute{o}\xi o\nu$).

From this it is to be seen that the first readers of the *Revelation*,
being Greek by language and culture, would think of an oriental
monarch as being represented by seal 1.   *It cannot mean Christ*, for
at that very time He is shown to be in heaven opening the seals,
that is, ordering the events on earth these forecast ; nor does he
come forth to fight on earth until long after seal 1, when He is shown
in ch. 19 as the Word of God, and then His weapon is the oriental
sword ($\acute{\rho}o\mu\phi\alpha\acute{\iota}\alpha$), for He will be acting as King of Israel.   Now
this rider goes out on a career of conquest (" conquering ") that
ends in his supremacy (" and to conquer "), and the Scripture shows
only one such personage in the end times, Antichrist.   He wears
a crown, because he is not a commander fighting for a king, but is

himself a king, and he rides the white horse that symbolizes victory, as it will afterwards do for the final and eternal Victor, Christ.

3. He will have the personal powers necessary for succeeding and dominating.

(i) " Eyes like the eyes of a man." All commanding person- alities have notable eyes, revealing discernment and penetrating insight into men and affairs. But the eye is also expressive. It displays the nature and it diffuses influence. Man dominates wild animals by his eye, and also allures or alarms his fellows. This masterly power Antichrist will possess in high degree.

(ii) He will be also an orator : he has " a mouth speaking great things " (8). He will have great schemes and will know how to state them plausibly and persuasively, with that hypnotic energy which carries the crowd with it and moves masses of men to obey and co-operate. If mechanical production can survive the wide destruction that will have taken place, what a commanding influence over millions the radio will afford to fiery and seductive oratory, as it already does.

(iii) His appearance will correspond and will aid his progress : " his look was more stout [or imposing] than his fellows " (20). He will be the complete contrast to Jesus, the Lamb. In nature the Lord was meek and of lowly heart : He did " not strive nor cry, nor cause his voice to be heard in the streets "—He was no demagogue, stirring the passions of men to violent deeds ; and in His appearance there was none of that superficial beauty that fascinates and deceives (Isa. 53 : 2, 3). Of recent years Europe was familiar with portraits of just such men as Antichrist will be— proud, stern, resolute, despotic, yet fascinating. Such men are types, precursors of the mightiest of such rulers, and thank God, the last.

(iv) His attitude towards God is defined : " He shall speak words against the Most High." His power of oratory will be *super*human, demonic : " there was *given* to him a mouth speaking great things and blasphemies." It is well known in the spiritist seance that mediums suddenly display powers of elevated speech not possessed by them ordinarily. Antichrist will be Satan-inspired, and like all such will " open his mouth for blasphemies against God, to blaspheme (*a*) His name, (*b*) His tabernacle, even those taber- nacling in the heaven " (Rev. 13 : 6).

That is, the person, character, claims, and deeds of God, all that the name of a person represents and suggests, will not be simply ignored as by the many now, but will be positively blasphemed. God will be treated as deserving of the greatest disrespect and abhorrence. Some renowned modern philosophers, and some recent dictators (as in Russia), have shown something of what Antichrist will express to the full.

(v) But what must this of necessity portend for such as fear and love God? If "whosoever loveth him that begat [the father] loveth also him that is begotten of him" [the child], it is equally certain that he that hates the parent will hate the child (I John 5 : 1). Then will be fulfilled completely, what has been in process of fulfilment all through this age, even that which our Master said to us on the night when He was betrayed, " if they persecuted Me they will also persecute you" (John 15 : 17-25).

For this little horn, now become great, will " wear out the saints of the Most High" (25), or, as some render, " the saints of the high places," who will be of the same company as those " tabernacling in heaven" of Rev. 13 : 6. There will have been already removed to the heavenly world some saints who " had prevailed to escape all these things that shall come to pass" through Antichrist (Luke 21 : 34-36; Rev. 3 : 10; 12 : 5, the man-child; 14 : 15, the firstfruits). These will be beyond his power, but he will pour against them the blasphemous oratory that he will use against their God who has preserved them from his grasp.

But there will be other godly men within his reach : " the rest of the woman's seed" (Rev. 12 : 17), and thus the brethren of the man-child, but who had not escaped to the heavens and with whom the dragon will make war after he is cast down from heaven. To conduct this war he will bring up the wild beast from the sea (Rev. 12 : 17 and ch. 13). This beast is easily identified with the fourth of Daniel's vision, by the ten horns it carries, and in that it also combines in itself the characteristics of the three former beasts it had conquered and reinstated : it is like a *leopard*, with the feet of a *bear*, and the mouth of a *lion* (Rev. 13 : 2).

This beast will shortly be ruled by a head that had been wounded to death yet healed (Rev. 13 : 3), which is further explained in Rev. 17 : 8-11. This coming head has lived before, has died, and gone into the abyss, the world of the dead, and will be brought back thence to rule the earth for the dragon, and especially to " make war with the saints." He will " wear them out" (Dan. 7 : 25) and " overcome them" (Rev. 13 : 7), that is, as to their bodily life. But in the real fact the men of faith will defeat him by maintaining their witness to God and His Son : for it is not his particular desire to destroy their bodily life but rather their testimony to the true God and His Son, and in this he will fail. This is the essential battle of this age.

In this war there will be a religious test imposed by the beast, as before by Nebuchadnezzar and Darius. " He will exalt himself above all that is called God or is an object of worship ; so that he that sitteth in the temple of God, setting himself forth as God " (II Thess. 2: 4). Then will be seen " the abomination of desolation standing in the holy place " at Jerusalem (Matt. 24 : 15). And as many as will not worship the image of the beast shall fall automatically under sentence of death, as it was in the foreshadowing of all this in the days of Antiochus Epiphanes and the Roman emperors.

To make detection easier and punishment more certain there will be a complete economic boycott against the saints : they shall neither buy nor sell unless they bear the mark or the number of the beast (Rev. 13 : 14, 17). In principle and practice this has been seen in our day in measure, especially in Russia. But elsewhere also identity cards and ration cards intimate methods by which such a boycot could be enforced. To strengthen men of faith and warn men in general there will be at this very juncture a divine proclamation, made by angelic agency, that eternal torment awaits those who succumb to this pressure and worship the beast (Rev. 14 : 9–12).

This will develop that never equalled, or to be equalled, period of distress and tribulation of which Christ spoke (Matt. 24 : 21, 22) ; that hour of trial which shall try all them that dwell on the whole earth (Rev. 3 : 10 ; Luke 21 : 34–36) ; the " time of Jacob's trouble " (Jer. 30 : 7) ; but when also saints who " keep the faith of Jesus," and who therefore are Christians, not Jews, will require patience (endurance, steadfastness), and will by suffering and death secure a high and heavenly inheritance (Rev. 6 : 9–11 ; 7 : 9–17 ; 14 : 12, 13 ; 20 : 4 ; Rom. 8 : 17 ; II Tim. 2 : 11–13).

It has been remarked above that the territory of the ten kings will be the region of the fourth beast and Antichrist's own proper kingdom, though its military and economic strength, ruled by a sovereign of such superb powers and consummate ability, will constrain " the whole earth to wonder after the beast " and to worship him and the dragon.

But it was also observed that in time the fascination will wear off, and regions south, north and east will rebel. This will provoke him to great fury (Dan. 11 : 44). It can be understood that thus his edicts will be less well enforced in remoter parts than in his own home territories ; and when Christ, after having destroyed him, shall send such of his host as escape at that time back to their own lands to declare His glory (Isa. 66 : 18–21), and, sitting upon the throne of His glory, shall gather all the living nations for judgment (Matt. 25 : 31–46), it will be found that, even in that fearful era, there were those who never indeed had openly espoused His cause or avowed faith in Him, but who had sheltered and aided those who were known definitely as His followers and were being persecuted. The Lord will count such service as rendered to Himself. The notion that the Lord will remove from the earth all believers before the end days set in and that the day of grace and salvation then closes, is contrary to Scripture.

The great wrath of the dragon (Rev. 12 : 12) and the great fury of the beast, working through the wild passions of unbridled, demon-driven masses, will produce such a fearful tempest that the race would exterminate itself in an orgy of blood had not God set a limit to the duration of the storm ; " but for the elect's sake those days shall be shortened " (Matt. 24 : 22 ; Isa. 26 : 20, " a little moment ").

The period during which he can work as he will is " a time and times and half a time " (25), three years and a half. During this period " he will think to change the [appointed] times and the law " (25). He will study to organize mankind in every affair upon a new basis under new arrangements, which will be designed to banish the remembrance of the past and to usher in an entirely new order and era, and for the time allotted he will succeed ; " they shall be given into his hand." It can be easily conceived that mankind, utterly wearied by the complete failure of all previous civilizations and arrangements, will be ready for the new experiment and will accept the changes gladly.

An effect of the scheme will be to make illegal the whole divine programme of the Jewish year, its time of commencement, sabbaths, months, seasonal feasts, and all else that, from its institution and ever since, has severed Israel's national life and routine from that of every people. This was its design, and this Antichrist will seek to reverse in the interests of his programme of the unity of the

world under himself. That "very small remnant" of Israel (Isa.
1 : 9 ; Joel 2 : 15–17 ; etc.) that will be turned by Elijah unto Jehovah
and will be remembering and doing the law of Moses (Mal. 4 : 4–6 ;
Rev. 11 : 1–13), will be indeed hard pressed by this measure. The
endeavour to follow the old religious seasons and law will throw
them out of gear with the whole world machinery, and will expose
them to the full penalty of the criminal laws of the empire.

In *The Great Prophecies* (pp. 112, 113) G. H. Pember
wrote :

> But it is probable that the changes will extend far beyond the
> circle of the Hebrew festivals. For since this prophecy is given to
> us, not in Hebrew, but in the world language of its day, we must
> not confine its application to the Jewish people, but understand it
> to refer to the whole prophetic earth. Times and law may thus be
> regarded as the fundamental conditions of human life and action in
> the world, which are ordained by God Himself. These would in-
> clude the divisions of time as derived from the relations between the
> earth and the sun and moon, or as appointed by direct command ;
> also the primal laws given, neither to Hebrews nor Christians, but
> to every inhabitant of earth without exception. Such are the laws
> of the Sabbath with its resulting week (Gen. 2 : 3), of the subjection
> of women (Gen. 2 : 18–23 ; 3 : 16 ; I Tim. 2 : 11–14), of marriage
> (Gen 2 : 24 ; Matt. 19 : 4–9 ; Rom. 7 : 2, 3), of propitiation by
> blood (Gen. 4 : 3–5), of the use of flesh for food (Gen. 9 : 3), of
> capital punishment for murder (Gen. 9 : 6), and of unrestrained
> procreation in the case of the married (Gen. 9 : 1).
>
> The crime which is a special violation of this [last] law seems now
> to be common in England, as it has long been in France and the
> United States of America. It is to be feared, too, that the infamous
> "Fruits of Philosophy" has spread the corruption even among the
> poor. The impatience of mankind would evade the curse of Gen.
> 3 : 16, as well as the toil and care which are involved in bringing up
> a family. But it will presently appear that far more pain and trouble
> result from breaking God's laws than could possibly be incurred by
> keeping them. Moreover, apart from all consideration of the
> Great Judgment, those sorrows which are evolved from the duties
> of life are disciplinary, and, if submissively borne, may obviate the
> necessity of more severe afflictions, even in the present life.
>
> These are the laws which God has ordained as the basis of all
> human society on earth and, wherever they are rejected, there is
> rebellion against the Creator. Hence the assaults to which they are
> now continually subjected warn us that the shadow of the coming
> Antichrist is already projected over the world.

Perhaps we may see a miniature rehearsal of the near future in the proceedings of the French revolutionaries, who in 1793 abolished Christianity, and adopted in its stead the prostitute-mirrored goddess of reason. For, with the institution of the new religion, they deemed it congruous to change weights and measures, together with divisions of time, and to apply the decimal system to everything. As regards time, they made the year to begin with September 22nd, and wished to divide it into ten months. Here, however, they were unable, even for their little day, to set aside the arrangements of the Creator, for, since it was absolutely necessary to make the months correspond to the revolutions of the moon, they were compelled to accept twelve months. But each of these was made to consist of thirty days, and divided into three decades which were to take the place of the four weeks ; while the tenth day of each decade was set apart for rest.

Possibly, the fact that the Fourth Empire is finally to be divided into Ten Kingdoms may be an indication of the universal adoption of a decimal system at that time.

It will be well also to remember, in connection with this subject, that a prohibition of marriage and a command to abstain from certain foods—probably the flesh of animals—are mentioned, in another prophecy (I Tim. 4 : 1-5), as prominent features amid the general lawlessness of the last days.

From these hints, compared with opinions and theories which are already spreading throughout the civilized world, we may, perhaps, get some idea of the changes in times and law which the Antichrist will attempt, and for a short while carry out. He will aim at an entire reconstruction of human society, upon principles which have long been working beneath the surface in a mystery of lawlessness, but which he will openly develop and establish on the face of the earth, in spite of their direct antagonism to the times and law of the Creator. Therefore it is that Paul terms him the Lawless One.

The foregoing was written in 1895. Since then the principles and the attendant evil practices have been witnessed on a far larger and more terrible scale in Soviet Russia, and are far more rampant in the world at large. Pember continues :

For a while there will be no interference on the part of God. Satan's prince will have full power to do according to his will for a period designated as " a time, times, and half a time."

In this curious formula it is probable that the plural stands for the dual, the latter being rarely found in Chaldee ; so that we might read, " a time, two times, and half a time." And enigmatical as the expression may at first sight appear, its meaning is to us an open secret ; for, as we shall presently see, Scripture itself reveals it.

The Chaldean word for " time " may be used indefinitely, as it is in Nebuchadnezzar's reply to the pleading wise men of Babylon : " I know of a certainty that ye would gain time." But, that it is also applied to a definite period, we may see by the passage before us, as well as by the " seven times " of Nebuchadnezzar's humiliation. Hence we have to discover what period is signified by the word in its definite use.

Now we have already seen that the " seven times " in the vision of the Tree are rendered simply as " seven years " in the Septuagint Version, and also by Josephus. The presumption, therefore, is that a " time," when used definitely, stands for a year. And, so far, at least, as the present passage is concerned, this presumption is strengthened to absolute certainty by a reference to the thirteenth chapter of the Apocalypse (ver. 5). There we shall find another description of the monarch represented by Daniel's Little Horn, whom John sees as the Beast. And it is plainly declared, that he will be permitted to continue his blasphemies against God for forty-two months—that is, for three years and a half. Hence a " time, two times, and half time," or three times and a half, are equivalent to three years and a half ; and consequently a " time " is equal to one year.

But why, it may be asked, is so strange an expression as " a time, two times, and half a time," used, instead of the more simple and natural phrase three times and a half ? Apparently, not without sufficient reason : for, according to the Jewish mode of calculation, three years coming together would involve the addition of an inter-calary month ; so that the period would be twelve hundred and ninety instead of twelve hundred and sixty days. But by naming one of the years separately this result is avoided. See Houghton's *Lateinos*, p. 29.

Rev. 11 : 2 and 3 confirms this. The holy city (Jerusalem) is to be trodden underfoot by the nations for the same period of forty-two months. It settles that these are literal months, that the term is at once varied to the equivalent in days—God's two witnesses will prophesy in that city for 1,260 days. This is in the period of the Beast, for he will at last kill these witnesses (ver. 7).

Already in our day the age of toleration is dying (see Appendix B) ; then it will have died. The State will be all, its head divine, its law absolute, individual rights and freedom will be annulled ; mankind having elected a tyrant will be his slaves, *or* his enemies at fearful peril. Under such conditions the three years and a half will seem an age, a prolonged nightmare, a darkness too deep to expect a dawn. But they will end—and THEN . . . ?

VI. It is a priceless feature of the visions of the Bible that they show the intimate interacting of earth and heaven. Thus in Rev. 12 both the " woman " and the " dragon " are shown as at once in heaven and on earth, a particular little noticed or weighed by expositors, yet crucial to the meaning of the vision. So also in our chapter the doings of earth are shown as watched and dominated by heaven. This is a chief secret of faith and patience in dark days.

When earth's evils and misery culminate in the Lawless One, WHAT THEN ? Then " THE JUDGMENT SHALL SIT " (26). That heavenly court which the ages through has supervised the doings of men, and especially of monarchs, shall hold its last session before it is dissolved to give place to the new government of Messiah and His saints (Heb. 2 : 5 ; Rev. 11 : 15-16 ; I Cor. 6 : 2, 3).

" I beheld till thrones were placed " (9). The A.V. " till thrones were *cast down* " is an instance of how completely that remarkable version sometimes hides the meaning, especially perhaps in prophetic scripture. To cast down thrones suggests the overthrow of monarchies, which thought has nothing whatever to do with this verse. As a young man of about twenty I set out to read through the R.V. It was a simply invaluable experience. My mind was fresh, the memory retentive, and the effects of that perusal have never subsided. Ever since, through over fifty years, I have studied the R.V. with ever greater care, and, while admitting imperfection, as in all man does, I am more than ever convinced of its superiority.

The statement " till thrones were placed," that is, placed in position for some to sit upon them, illuminated the whole vision, and instantly gave the clue to its nature and the time for its fulfilment. I saw at a glance that it is the same scene as Rev. 4 and 5, and a comparison of detail establishes this. Here one point will suffice : The issue of the transactions in heaven is that the Son of man receives universal and everlasting dominion. In Rev. 4 and 5 also the Lamb receives the same authority. Now it is impossible that this should occur *twice*, for the very reason that the dominion once received by Him is to last for ever.

Other details concur.

(i) The great throne, and One ancient of days sitting upon it.

(ii) The accompaniment of fire, a symbol of judgment.

(iii) Other thrones around the central throne.

(iv) The surrounding angel hosts. The numbers of these are identical—thousands of thousands, ten thousand times ten thousand.

(v) And, as stated above, the issue is the same in both visions and is one that cannot be repeated.

There are details in each not in the other. The later vision is considerably richer as a picture, which suits the introduction to the lengthy and elaborate drama that follows ; while that in Daniel is no longer than is needful for the purpose of the more concise vision. But the identity is clear. And this helps greatly to the understanding of the Revelation.

For *this* judgment session is not concerned with the whole course of world-empire, but with its conclusion : it is the *taking away* of the kingdom of the beast, its consumption and *destruction* (26) that is effected by this session of the heavenly court, in order that the government may be transferred to the Son of man and the saints. And therefore the book of the Revelation also is *not* an account of world-empire through the centuries, but only of the steps by which, at the end, that empire will be wrested from Antichrist and conferred upon its rightful sovereign, the Lamb, and His followers.

VII. And the end of man's protracted, toilsome efforts at world rule, what shall it be ? This, and only this—" the beast was slain, and his body destroyed, and he was given up to be burned with fire " (11). And its superb, God-defying head, the emperor, what of him ? Shall he, like Napoleon or the last German Kaiser, slip away into ignoble security while his palace burns and his servants perish ? Nay, verily ; " the beast was taken, and with him the false prophet . . . that deceived men . . . these two were cast alive into the lake of fire that burneth with brimstone " (Rev. 19 : 20) Truly

> the peoples labour for the fire.
> And the nations weary themselves for vanity.

Yet is this " not of Jehovah of hosts " (Hab. 2 : 13) : and least of all is it of Him that His own chosen saints should thus labour in vain, spending money, strength, time, yea, life itself in this vanity. Nay, nay ! It is the purpose of the Lord that " the knowledge of His glory shall cover the earth, as the waters cover the sea " (Hab. 2 : 14), and it is His will that to *this* glorious and certain purpose His people should devote themselves body and soul, in life and, if need be, in death. Such labour shall *not* be in vain, for it is wrought in the Lord (I Cor. 15 : 58 ; II Peter 3 : 11–13).

VIII. Concerning that kingdom which is to supersede all others not much detail is given in Daniel. His theme is *world*-empire, not the kingdom of the heavens, save as this will succeed the others. Nor was there need for more for his own sake, because the law, the Psalms, and the prophets had exhausted language and eloquence in describing and praising that coming era and kingdom.

Yet in this book what is essential thereto is emphasized by repetition.

1. It is the kingdom of the God and King of the heavens (2 : 44 ; 4 : 37), Who is the God of gods and the Lord of kings ; to Whom moreover secrets and things future are known (2 : 47). What a material advantage is this to a Sovereign dealing with a rebellion with the view of re-establishing his rightful authority. All advantages that rulers seek by a Secret Service are secured in perfection.

Also He is a Sovereign able to give His servants wisdom in every perplexity and to extricate them from every peril (chs. 2 and 3). And He can show signs and work wonders that give faith and courage to those who serve Him and bring awe upon the hearts of all (4 : 3). If His people of late have not needed this cheer very much let them remember that times are bringing again that oppression by the world which will supply the need for it. The Bible was written for all times, especially the end time.

He is also the living God, steadfast for ever (6 : 26), and the Most High (5 : 21 ; 7 : 22, 25, 27).

2. His kingdom is everlasting, invincible, indestructible, universal, and ruled by truth and justice ; the very qualities that human rule lacks, and lacking must perish (4 : 3, 34–37 ; 6 : 26 ; 7 : 14, 27).

3. But what seems to have astonished Daniel was the position in that kingdom of " One like unto a Son of man." How could *a man* be found in that upper world before the Ancient of days ? Why was one of this human race to be so supremely exalted to universal dominion ? Enoch and Elijah had indeed gone alive to that world above, but Daniel does not suggest that he thought this One was either of them. One day we may be able to ask him what came into his heart as he watched the vision ; but already *we* know Who is that Son of man ; it is " Jesus crowned with glory and

honour because of the sufferings of death," to Whom every knee shall yet bow.

And the " saints of the high places " shall reign with Him with Whom and for Whom they suffered ; their dominion, like His, being over heaven as well as earth, over angels as over men ; for the Lord shall preserve Paul, and all others who have *loved* His appearing, unto His *heavenly* kingdom (II Tim. 4 : 6–8, 17, 18).

" The greatness of the kingdoms *under* the whole heaven shall be given to the *people* of the saints of the high places," that is, Israel (27), even as it is said to that people, " that nation and kingdom which will not serve thee shall perish " (Isa. 60 : 10–12). For of their and our Lord it stands written for ever in heaven that " His kingdom is an everlasting kingdom, and all dominions shall serve and obey Him " (27). Let us serve and obey Him now, for He has promised that " the one overcoming, and keeping My works unto the end " [that period so dreadful, so fiery, so scorching], " to *him* will I give authority over the nations . . . as I also have received of My Father : and I will give him the morning star " (Rev. 2 : 25–29).

" Here is the end of the matter," the goal to which the Most High is leading and overruling, and which He will reach. And if there remain with us, as with Daniel, things which trouble our thoughts ; if the lightness and brightness of our face be changed into soberness by the lowering of such dark storms on the horizon ; if questions not yet answered press upon our mind ; then let us, like him, " keep the matter in our heart." Let us not be repelled, nor be rebellious against the divine programme, nor lapse into indifference, nor set aside these themes on the ground that they are not of practical consequence or are too complicated to be grasped ; let us " keep the matter in our heart " and see and ponder what was later shown to Daniel. Then, though shadows deepen, we with him can gain the light we need to keep our garments unspotted as we pick our way through this squalid world till the Day Star arise (II Peter 1 : 19) and the shadows flee away.

In the first and second editions of this book I assumed, as others had done, that the first beast will be conquered by the second and the second by the third. But this is not stated as to be the case. All that is shown is that the fourth beast will trample upon the three that preceded it. Thus the three former beasts, though (1) rising successively, will (2) exist simultaneously, and are (3) all to be reduced by the fourth, but are (4) finally to outlast it.

It would be premature to assert positively that the recent conflicts in the Mediterranean are the beginning of this vision, or a fulfilment of specific prophecies, though this may be so. But what seems probable is that the late wars in the Far East and Europe and the Near East are being overruled to work those changes which seem required for the development of affairs that *are* subjects of definite predictions.

I. Some further details connected with the four beasts from the sea are here noted.

1. In Appendix C, IV, it is suggested that Antichrist, the eleventh horn which is to rise among the ten horns of the fourth beast, will probably appear in Armenia. Further, that Ezekiel 38 shows that he will be ruling Persia (Iran), and Cush and Put (Elam), a region to the north of Persia and south of Media. It thus appears that these two lands will be part of the territory of the ten kings, of which Antichrist will become overlord.

2. But since he makes a covenant with Israel in Palestine (Dan. 9 : 27), and a little later overruns that land in war, it seems likely that before that invasion it is not part of his dominions, nor, therefore, of the territory of the ten-horned beast.

3. Further; since the king of the south (Egypt) long resists him (Dan. 11), and finally Egypt is invaded and ravaged by him, that monarch likewise can hardly be one of the ten kings that exalt him to supremacy, nor his land be part of their empire.

4. It is added that, at the time of that late conquest of Egypt, " the Libyans (Cyrenaica) and the Ethiopians (Abyssinia) shall be at his steps " (11 : 43). He will thus secure his south-west frontiers. But this implies that up till that late stage these areas also had not been part of his own territory proper.

5. Antichrist, being ruler as far as Persia and Elam, will, we learn, " wax exceeding great toward the east " (Dan. 8 : 9), as well as toward the south and Palestine, as just noted. " East " here will therefore mean further east than Persia and Elam, because these are already part of his dominions, their eastern frontier. That is to say, as Alexander pushed his conquests beyond Persia into Parthia and onward, so will Antichrist. For this the recent war and changes proceeding in the Far East may well be preparing. But

this again implies that those regions farther east were not before part of his ten-kingdom empire.

6. Once more. It is the kings of the Medes who will at last destroy Antichrist's capital, Babylon (Isa. 13 : 17 ; Jer. 51 : 11, 28). Their ancient enmity to his country and capital will flame afresh. It is therefore unlikely that Media will be one of the ten lands to exalt him to supremacy.

7. But again. While he is engaged in his conflicts with Egypt " ships of Kittim shall come against him " (Dan. 11 : 30). To the Easterns of that time Kittim meant principally Greece. See p. 165.

From these particulars it would seen probable that the territory of the ten-horned beast, in its earliest stages, will (1) centre in Asia Minor ; (2) on the west will not include Greece ; (3) on the south will not include Palestine, Egypt, Libya, or Ethiopia (Abyssinia) ; (4) on the south-east will include Persia and Elam ; but (5) on its eastern end will have its frontier west of Media, that is the land which lies to the south of the Caucasus, at the present east end of Armenia, and between the north end of Irak and the southern part of the Caspian Sea.

If this is correct, the ten kingdoms will be in the north-east end of the Mediterranean area, which leaves the central and western parts of the sea as the regions of the three earlier wild beasts. These the fourth beast will attack, trample upon, but not annihilate, because they will outlast its destruction by Christ. See section IV above, p. 84.

This original area for the ten kingdoms differs radically from a map of the fourth empire that has considerably influenced prophetic study for a century. But that exposition proceeds upon the assumption that, in our time, the three earlier beasts have long since come and gone, and that the fourth beast has been on the scene for some two thousand years or more, and only awaits its final phase. These present suggestions presume that this whole vision is still future.

Having thus conquered the three former beasts, and being thus master of the whole Mediterranean area and its resources, the fourth beast, under Antichrist, will extend its sway universally. See Appendix A. Yet the original ten-kingdom confederacy will remain intact, in government and territory, the dominant centre of the world ; for the fourth beast, *as such*, still distinct from the three, is destroyed by the Son of man from heaven, while the other three survive it for a time.   These again are distinct from the rest of the nations to be dealt with by the Lord later, according to many passages, for example, Isa. 66 : 19, or Matt. 25 : 31-46.

II. THE FAR EAST.   It cannot be stated too often or too plainly that, from the Bible point of view, Palestine is the geographical centre of the earth, and the terms north or south, east or west, apply in relation to that land as centre.   The limits of these terms in Bible usage seem to be : as to the north, Armenia and the Caucasus ; on the south, Egypt and Ethiopia (Abyssinia) ; on the west, the western end of the Mediterranean (Tarshish) ; toward the east, probably as far as western China (Sinim, Isa. 49 : 12).

The vast territories beyond this central area of the earth seem not to be noticed in Scripture—a sufficiently humbling thought for the proud peoples that occupy some of them.   Nor is this omission merely because the writers of the Bible may not have known of these regions.   The Divine Writer knew of them, and could have wrought into His Book references to them which would have become clear in due season.   That He did not do so can, it would seem, mean only that those outside regions will not materially influence the developments within the central region in the end days, which developments are a chief theme of prophecy. Had prophecy been a history in advance of those remoter areas the marked paucity of reference to them would be inexplicable.

This scarcity of reference is noticeable in relation to the Far East.   The recent aggression of Japan, first into China, and then further, makes reference to this matter opportune.   It is not to be expected that this people will attain influence as far as the Middle East, or, at least, not permanently or into the times of the end.*

There seems to be only the one passage above mentioned which relates certainly to a land eastward of Persia (Isa. 49 : 12), and this one place has to do, not with modern or even present history, but solely with the actual commencement of the reign of Messiah, when He will gather to Palestine the then still scattered remnant of Israel and comfort His people.   The singular number of the noun (" people " : in ver. 8 " the people," in ver. 13 " His people ") confines the thought to Israel, and the statement is that some of them shall come to Palestine " from the land of Sinim."   There is

* The above paragraph was written in July, 1942. The crushing defeat of Japan has so far justified the forecast.

general agreement that this name is the same as *Tsin*, a name of Western China at least as early as the time of Isaiah.

III. THE WESTERN POWERS. If it be asked, What place does this forecast leave for the present " Great Powers " ; it is to be asked in reply, What Great Powers are likely to remain to the era in view ? Three thus called, Germany, France and Italy, are already no longer great. And as to the other Great Powers, for all sober thinkers it must surely be a serious question how long these can remain Great if the present colossal peace-time expenditure should prove prolonged, or if by further war the wastage of men and material should become prodigious.

The closest scrutiny of prophetic Scripture yields, as far as we see, no hint of any power outside of the Middle East dominating that area in the period of the ten kings. On the contrary, as Assyria and Egypt maintain many wars with each other, and as Assyria and Palestine conclude a treaty, evidently these will be independent states, with no such overlordship at that time. It is conceivable that present world movements may result at last in the elimination from that central area of the remoter empires, so leaving the stage open for the arising of the more local powers which are to play the part foretold of them in the closing days of Gentile dominion.*

The remoter powers, though not mentioned specifically, are covered by certain general statements as to the world at large at the close of the age. Two such statements may be quoted as samples of the whole. Isa. 60 : 1–3 covers them both. (1) At the time of Israel's restoration to God " darkness shall cover the earth, and gross darkness the peoples." Spiritual and moral darkness will have settled upon the whole earth. (2) But when the Lord, at His return to the earth, shall have shone forth as the sun upon Israel, then to that people it is said, " the nations shall come to thy light, and kings to the brightness of thy rising " ; for the receiving again of Israel by God shall be life from the dead for the other nations (Rom. 11 : 15).

IV. THE BRITISH EMPIRE. If it be further asked, What then does Scripture predict as to the future of the British Empire in those last days of the age ? we answer (against all Anglo-Israelites), *Nothing !* We see no specific prophecies concerning the last days

---

* Note to this 1950 edition. The withdrawal of Britain from India and the Middle East, unannounced when the above suggestion was made, is manifestly in line therewith.

as to the political affairs of any kingdom outside of the area of the four beasts. And happy will it be for any peoples that are then remote from that vortex of Satanic rage and Divine wrath.

Already the pressure of mighty movements in Europe and the Far East has brought the British into close co-operation with their kinsfolk in the West. If it should please God that the Anglo-Saxon race, in its widespread branches and localities, shall continue to the end a political unity, this could be maintained by communications through the western hemisphere instead of the eastern. Only in that case the centre of gravity might come to be in the western continent, rather than in England. But this present trend of affairs being merely matter of human observation, not of Divine prediction, cannot be pursued in what is strictly a study of prophetic Scripture.

But the terrible possibilities latent in atomic energy may easily obliterate the *status quo*. The Chancellor of the University of Chicago has said that if two sufficiently powerful atomic bombs were detonated in Central California and Northern Oregon at a moment when steady winds were blowing towards the east, " the enemy would have a fair chance of making the United States uninhabitable " (*Daily Telegraph*, December 1st, 1947). If Western Europe and Western Russia were similarly destroyed the existing " Great Powers " would be no more a factor in the End Times.

V. It should be neither affirmed nor denied that the late strife in the Mediterranean is the commencement of the tempest of Daniel 7. But *on the pure assumption* that it *may* be this, then Italy, as the first Mediterranean power to enter the war, ought to be the first of the four beasts. And IF this is the case, then the meaning of the lion's wings being plucked may perhaps be seen in the late rapid crippling of Italy's fleet and air force. For this has effectually impeded its swiftness of action and left it largely crippled. Again writing IF this is the case, then the next phase should be a lifting up of the crippled beast and it becoming human, both in wisdom and conduct, instead of continuing the senseless savagery shown of late years, as in Abyssinia. And the next phase again should be the aggression in the Mediterranean sphere of a ponderous, ravenous, bear-like kingdom, that shall " devour much flesh." It will be no marvel should Russia prove to be this aggressor. Under all the changes brought by the 1917 Revolution there lies the same persistent ambition to be a Mediterranean power which has dominated

Russian policy for 250 years. See Fisher's *History of Europe,* one vol. ed., 724.

This persistency of Russian diplomacy was noted a century ago by the Hungarian patriot, Kossuth:

> Then Kossuth went on about Russian diplomacy, which he says is the most skilful—the deepest, most patient, most consistent and most successful—of any in Europe. "They are in no hurry, but they keep to one object, too far forward for anyone else to see it, and this they follow without a moment's relaxing . . . Russia makes fools of all others." (Emily Winkworth to her sister, 21st Nov., 1851. *Memorials of Two Sisters,* 81).

VI. A few words may be added upon the relationship of Islam to coming changes in its home sphere, the Middle East.

Mohammedanism as a religion has greatly lost its hold. The abolishment of the Caliphate by modern Turkey shows this relaxed grip. Modern education has compelled the present generation to recognize that the Koran, being plainly wrong in its astronomy and geography, cannot have come down direct from heaven to the prophet as he alleged. But as far as the system may survive the clash and confusion of races and politics, it will blend easily into the already rising philosophy and system that will reach its climax under Antichrist.

The set of Western philosophy in later times is toward pantheism.

In his most valuable treatise *Christianity and Antichristianity in their Final Conflict* S. J. Andrews showed this as far back as 1898. He said (p. viii):

> Philosophy and science in many eminent representatives agree in affirming that there is no personal God, only a universal, impersonal Spirit or Energy, of which everything that exists is a part. This, viewed on the material side, is atheism ; on the spiritual, is pantheism. If the transcendence of God in His acts of creation, as declared in the Scriptures, is given up, the ordinary mind—whatever some acute metaphysicians may say of themselves—can find no final resting-place but in the humbling negations of atheism, or the deifying affirmations of pantheism.

But abstract pantheism cannot hold the masses. For this it must be conjoined with hero worship. The abstract philosophy must be concentrated in a powerful personality which to them embodies the universal, impersonal Energy. Hence a Buddha, Emperor-worship, or a Mohammed. The essential fascination of pantheism is that man deifies himself, to his own self-satisfaction. Antichrist, at his height, will reign supreme because humanity will see in him itself personified and deified.

A perhaps temporary yet educatory and preparatory exemplification of this principle in Europe was Hitler and Germany. In the *Review of World Affairs* for November, 1941, p. 3, it was said :

Probably 40 to 50 per cent of the masses [of Germany] are still strongly National Socialist. Unhappily many are more than political supporters. They are raging fanatics who have no religion but National Socialism and no master but Hitler. They seem possessed by madness. This is how things are : we will quote from the report of an observer just back from the Continent. Discussing this matter he wrote : " If Germany wins this war Hitler will have achieved such a position in the hearts and minds of the German people, that it is not inconceivable that the new religion (already in its experimental stage in Germany) will attain permanency, and Hitler will become the new Messiah, and go down the ages as the supplanter of Christ. All this may sound fantastic, but . . . German youth is thoroughly permeated with these ideas, and they will create the legend. Paganism is rife among them."

Blasphemy indeed. We are striving with no second-rate politician, nor a clever gangster, but a kind of mad Mahdi—the leader of a fanatical sect, a false prophet with a sword in one hand and a book of black doctrine in the other. There is more in this business than mere reaction to the defeats of the last war—more in it than good organization and military preparedness. Few of those who know the true character of Hitler's Germany will deny this. These terrible forces can only be overcome by superior organization in every material sphere, and by a true—not nominal—devotion to a superior creed in the spiritual realm —a creed and a faith against which the evil can never prevail. We have not yet fully awoken to this—and consequently we are still floundering along in a half-sleep walk."

In the *Daily Telegraph* for November 7th, 1941, appeared what was confirmatory of the foregoing. It stated that a pre-war German Ambassador to Russia had a three-hours' interview with Hitler, from which he returned

" as pale as a sheet. ' When I had explained the reason of my call to Hitler,' he said later, ' he glared at me and then talked to me for two hours, in the course of which he said he had had a message from above that his mission was to destroy Russia. He finished up foaming at the mouth, threw up his arms, and cried, I am the Messiah ! ' "

The latent comparison, in the quotation from the *Review*, of Hitler to Mohammed is just. Mohammedanism on its philosophical side was styled by one deeply versed in its creed and practice, W. G. Palgrave, as the Pantheism of Force. See Dr. S. W. Zwemer's *The Moslem Doctrine of God*. And in practice hero worship has never been more luridly exhibited than in the flaming devotion of his satanically blinded followers to Mohammed. Thus the system may be expected to blend easily into that of Antichrist when he arises in its own native region, the Middle East. His early career of wide and ruthless desolation will resemble closely that of Mohammed, and his fierce alternative, Submit or perish ! will be precisely that of Islam, which very word itself means Submission.

Naziism helped to prepare for this pantheistic outcome. Thus Martin Borman, the head of the Nazi Party Organization, declared open war on every form of Christianity. He said : " If we National Socialists speak about ' faith in God ' we do not mean the same God as the naïve Christians. . . . The natural Force which maintains these innumerable planets in the universe we call the Almighty or God " (*Daily Telegraph*, February 21st, 1942). This theme I have treated at large in my recent book, *World Chaos*.

VII. The Roman Catholic Church must be mentioned as being another and powerful factor in the area of the four beasts. I have dealt with this in the separate discussion mentioned upon Babylon the Great (Rev. 17 and 18). Here it may suffice to offer the suggestions, (1) That the Church will some day remove its government from Italy to Palestine, and later to Babylon rebuilt. (2) That it may revert openly to the paganism which was its original form and which it has never more than thinly veiled. (3) That in the early stages of the ten-horned confederacy this religious system will dominate the fourth beast. (4) That shortly, however, the ten kings will destroy the Church, and Antichrist will succeed to her place and power, religious and political. This seems the meaning of Rev. 17 and Zech 5 : 5–10. See p. 33.

CHAPTER VIII

THE RAM, THE HE-GOAT, AND THE LITTLE HORN

FOR PERHAPS TWO YEARS DANIEL HAS PONDERED IN HIS HEART the vision of the four beasts and now further knowledge is imparted. God is patient as our Teacher, and we must be patient as pupils. He knows just when a former lesson has worked fully in us and we are prepared for the next lesson. It is wonderful how rashly some in our day, but lately brought out of darkness, write books on prophecy, as if they had walked in its light for long years and had pondered deeply the deep things of God ; whereas such writings usually show that they have learned from men, with little real research or reflection.

The time was critical. Great changes were in progress. The Babylonian empire had been subdued by Cyrus, and the city itself was besieged and its capture near. What shall be the end of this new world-power ? and in what way shall the further developments outlined in the former visions arise ?

I. In vision the prophet was taken from Babylon eastward to Persia. He did not go in body, for the city was invested, and he was there when it fell. But in spirit he was in the home region of the rising power. It was pictured to him as a ram with two horns, one higher than the other, and the higher rising after the shorter. This singular feature was itself an explanation. The Medes had previously dominated the Persians ; but Cyrus, the Persian, had reversed this, and made the Medes subordinate.

The ram was the national emblem of Persia, and this ram pushed its way westward, northward, and southward. Cyrus had already extended his dominions westward, and northward as far as Asia Minor, and his son would later conquer Egypt, to the south. For long the empire was irresistible (ver. 4).

But a he-goat with one notable horn rushed upon the ram with incredible swiftness and terrific fury, threw him down and trampled upon him, and there was none to deliver. The goat was the national emblem of Macedonia.   Here again the unusual arrests attention—a goat with only one horn, and that large, growing from the middle of its forehead.   This goat became exceptionally great; but shortly the horn was broken, and four lesser horns grew in its place and pointed in four different directions.   Lastly, out of one of these four a little horn grew, and became exceedingly great.

II. Daniel was not left to infer the significance of these things; nor was it revealed in a dream, as in ch. 2; nor opened to his mind by cogitation, as in 4 : 19; nor revealed to him directly, as in ch. 5 : 17; but, as with the vision of the four beasts, so now, an angel explained the matter.   Thus would it afterwards be with John when the closing prophetic revelations should be given (Rev. 1 : 1; etc.).

God has different ways of illuminating our minds.   But since Pentecost the chief of these is the direct instruction which the Holy Spirit gives by opening the meaning of Scripture to the humble, meditative, believing, obedient mind.

Yet there are students of that Word, such as listen dutifully and habitually to the Spirit, who know also that at rare times there come sudden revelations of what that Word means which are comparable to such plain explanations as Daniel now received through Gabriel, and whereby parts of Scripture long obscure become instantly plain and of extraordinary and unfading influence upon heart and life.

Such students of Scripture do not *say*, The Spirit told me, or, An angel spoke to me : they leave such remarks to the Swedenborgs, Joseph Smiths, and Mohammeds.   They are the more deeply aware of how illimitable are the spheres of truth, and that they still know but in part; yet in their secret heart they do *know* that God has spoken to them personally, while yet, like Daniel or Paul (II Cor. 12 : 7), they may be faint and sick and astonished, with no one of their brethren able to help them, as they rise up and do the king's business (27).   May the Lord in grace give to His church more such men.   They speak with steady conviction and convincing power, to the building up of their brethren.

Gabriel, then, said plainly that the ram was the Medo-Persian kingdom; the he-goat the first king of Greece; the four horns four kings that should divide his kingdom after his sudden death, but not to rule with his power.

It is no wonder that certain theological infidels of colleges and pulpits, who accept the views of earlier avowed sceptics that miracles, and therefore prophecy, are impossible, have laboured the demonstrably false proposition that the book of Daniel was written after the events.

In Daniel's time Greece was a mere collection of petty and contending states. Who could foresee and foretell (i) their union; (ii) the superb abilities and energies of the almost youthful first king; (iii) his audacious and wholly successful attack, with a comparative handful of troops, upon the mighty ram; (iv) that just when he had become strong his career should end (Alexander died at 33 years); and (v) end not by gradual decay, but abruptly, the horn being "broken"; and (vi) that four other rulers, but not of his calibre, should succeed to his realms?

No one but God could thus foretell the coming centuries: therefore, either the book was a divine prophecy, as it asserts itself to be, or it was a deliberate fraud, by pretending to be prophecy when it was actually history. In the latter case the writer was as fraudulent as those theologians and preachers who take their salaries from evangelical sources while spreading infidel and pagan philosophies. This the avowed sceptics, the Voltaires, Paines, and Bradlaughs would have scorned to do.

III. The commencement of the vision thus pointed to the immediate future, the supremacy of the ram, the Medo-Persian empire. Then it looked to a comparatively near future, the conquests of Alexander the Great (died 323 B.C.), and the division of his empire into four parts. The division was as follows:

Ptolemy had possession of Egypt, Cyrene, Coele-Syria, and some of the northern parts of Asia Minor.

Cassander, of Macedon and Greece.

Lysimachus, of Thrace, Western Bithynia, Lesser Phrygia, Mysia, and Lydia, with the Meander for a boundary.

Seleucus, of the remainder of Asia Minor, and the East.

But at this point the following statements by the heavenly interpreter must be noted and weighed :—

1. " The vision belongeth to the *time of the end*" (17).

2. " I will make thee know what shall be in *the latter time* of the indignation: for

3. " it belongeth to the *appointed time of the end*" (19).

4. " *in the latter time* of their kingdom, when

5. " transgressors are *come to the full*" (23).

6. " Shut thou up the vision, for *it belongeth to many days to come*" (26).

(i) From these statements it is clear that the essential burden of the vision has to do with the last days and the last world-ruler, the little horn.   Only in his days will the fulness of transgression arrive and judgment fall finally, as it always does when " the iniquity of the Amorites is full " (Gen. 15 : 13–16).

(ii) The repetition of the term " little horn " connects this ruler with the little horn of the fourth beast " (7 : 8).

(iii) He will be of " fierce countenance." It is through the eyes that this ferocity will blaze : " having eyes as the eyes of a man " (7 : 8).

(iv) He will " understand dark sentences." His penetrating mind has been before observed.   Again Pember's remarks are worth quoting at length, for the warning they contain for such as have ears to hear (*Great Prophecies*, pp. 125–127) :

> The clause, " understanding dark sentences," has been usually explained of diplomatic cunning and deceit, with a reference to the subsequent words : " And through his policy he shall cause craft to prosper in his hand."   But, in all probability, the meaning is to be sought in another direction.
>
> The Hebrew noun for " dark sentences " is used of Samson's *riddle* (Judg. 14 : 12), of the Queen of Sheba's *hard questions* (I Kings 10 : 1), and of the *dark sayings* of the wise (Prov. 1 : 6), which are too profound to be understood by the simple.   Again, God says of Moses : " He is faithful in all My house : with him will I speak mouth to mouth, even manifestly, and not in *dark speeches* " (Num. 12 : 8).   And two of the Psalms, the forty-ninth and the seventy-eighth, are declared to contain " *dark sayings* " (Ps. 49 : 4 ; 78 : 2).
>
> The former of these Psalms treats of the enigma of the present life ; and points out that its riches and honour are worthless, because they vanish for ever, like a dream, at the moment of death ; that the one thing for a man to desire is, that God may deliver him from the power of Hades, by taking him to Himself, as He took Enoch ; that those who are thus favoured, however lowly or oppressed they may have been during the earth-life, shall have dominion over the wicked in the morning of the Resurrection.   This was, indeed, a revelation of hidden things at the time when it was given.
>
> The seventy-eighth Psalm relates God's dealings with Israel, in such a manner that those to whom apprehension is vouchsafed may be enabled to perceive the golden thread of His love running through and connecting all His mysterious acts, His wondrous works, and His afflictive visitations ; and so to learn the secrets of the Almighty.

In other words, the narrative of facts is so arranged that it becomes a deep instruction from God, an unfolding of Divine mysteries. And in quoting from the introduction to this Psalm, an inspired evangelist translates the word which we are now discussing by τὰ κεκρυμμένα (Mat. 13 : 35)—that is, " the things that have been hidden "—and sets the Lord Jesus before us as the great Revealer of the secret things of God.   For in Christ, as Paul tells us, " are hid all the treasures of wisdom and knowledge " (Col. 2 : 3), and to Him we must turn, if we would know the mystery of God.

Since, therefore, it is said of the Antichrist, that he will understand dark sentences, we infer that he will be inspired of Satan to attempt rivalry of the Christ in His character of sole Hierophant or Revealer of secret things.   Now we know from daily experience how great an influence knowledge exercises over the men of the present day ; and especially that knowledge which seems to promise an insight into the awful problems of human life, into which so many powerful intellects are striving to peer, but with no more success than Charles Kingsley describes, when he speaks of such an investigation as the holding of a dim light over an unfathomable mine.   Hence, in the words " understanding dark sentences," we seem to detect one of the secrets of that fascination by which the Antichrist will bind the world.   He too will present himself as one in whom are hidden treasures of wisdom and knowledge ; and drawing from the vast, though limited, stores of his god—that is, Satan—will dazzle and bewitch men by his solutions of the enigmas of life, and, possibly, by his revelation of powers implanted in humanity but hitherto unsuspected, or of secrets and forces of nature as yet undiscovered.

The device of alluring men to destruction by the bait of knowledge is no new thing : it was first essayed, and with terrible success, in the garden of Eden.   For Satan had perceived, not merely that God had formed man to be an intellectual being, but also that through the intellect man's vanity could be raised and inordinately excited, to such a pitch, indeed, that he would even match himself with his Creator.   There is no limit to human folly : every common experience will justify the memorable words of the Preacher : " Yea, also, the heart of the sons of men is full of evil, and madness is in their heart while they live, and after that they go to the dead " (Eccl. 9 : 3).

In the legends of antiquity, there are numerous hints that the communication of knowledge was used by the Nephilim, or fallen angels, as a means of acquiring influence over the human race, and of establishing themselves as gods to the inhabitants of the world. Who can fail to perceive this, when he reads of the gifts said to have been conferred upon men by the Classic deities, or by the fallen angels of the Book of Enoch ?   What other interpretation can be given to the famous story of Prometheus the Titan, to his theft of

fire from heaven, and to his bestowal of other gifts and varied instruction upon mankind, in defiance of the will of the Supreme God ?
Occupying the first place among his teachings is the art of medicine,
in regard to which it is a remarkable fact, that another name for
Nephilim in Hebrew is Rephaim, which means " healers," and in
two passages of the Septuagint is actually rendered by ἰατροί—that
is, physicians (Ps. 88 : 10 ; Isa, 26 : 14). In other places, the
Septuagint gives Titans, or giants, as an equivalent for the same
word. Evidently, therefore, Procopius is justified in his remark,
that the Greeks term those beings giants or Titans whom the
Hebrews call " Rephaim."

From what has been said, it will be evident that modern Theoso-
phists, who are restoring the old Pagan philosophy, are perfectly
consistent when they boast that their lore was derived from supernatural beings, or angels. And the spread of their doctrines should
warn us, that we are nearing the time when Satan will repeat the
tactics of a pristine age, and again offer to the world deadly gifts
from his own stores of wisdom and knowledge ; first, through the
instrumentality of countless teachers, but finally, with supreme
fullness of power, through the mouth of his coming hierophant,
the Antichrist. Then, if it were possible, the very elect should be
deceived ; but it will not be possible, because God Himself will
keep them.

(v) " His power shall be mighty," for he will have at command
his personal abilities and the resources of the fourth beast ; but
pre-eminently

(vi) He will be energized by Satan. He will " be mighty, but
not by his own power " : that alone would not command such
universal success. In Rev. 13 : 2 it is said : " the dragon gave
him his power, and his throne, and great authority."

To one wholly dedicated to God the Holy Spirit can impart
supernatural strength—of body to labour, as to Samson ; or to
suffer, as to Paul (II Cor. 4 : 7–18) ; and of mind, as to the prophets ;
and of spirit, so that the man may be supernaturally holy and
heavenly (II Cor. 3 : 18). Similarly *Satan* can share *his* powers of
mind and body with those wholly devoted to him, and these
become supernaturally, diabolically wicked. " Satan entered into
him," and Judas did the foulest deed that ever will deface the
records of eternity (John 13 : 27). Liquid fire, poison gas, pestilence bombs—whence come *such* ideas into the mind of man ?

(vii) Thus empowered his path shall be one of vast destruction :
" he shall destroy wonderfully."

(viii) His conquests will extend mainly (*a*) toward " the south," that is, Egypt, North Africa, and Abyssinia (11 : 42, 43) : and (*b*) " eastward," which conquests may provoke the resentment and later reprisals mentioned in 11 : 44, " tidings out of the east and north shall trouble him " : and (*c*) " toward the glorious land," that land which God has justly described as " the glory of all lands " (Ezek. 20 : 6). This it truly will be when the blessing of Jehovah covers it, for, as the observant traveller can discern, it has all the natural features to make a land lovely and prosperous.

(ix) Energized by power and knowledge from another world, and commanding Satan's resources in that realm, for he has Satan's throne, and with an audacity that knows no bounds, he initiates a campaign in that upper region : " it waxed great even to the host of heaven ; and some of the host and of the stars it cast down to the ground and trampled upon them " (10), and thus it destroyed " the mighty ones " (24).

It has been suggested that it is the church, the people of the heavenly calling, that are here in view, called " the host and the stars " by way of anticipation of the heavenly place and glory that God, in His grace, has foreseen as their ultimate portion. But the meaning of these terms seems fixed by Rev. 12, which chapter, and the next, are so closely related to the visions of Daniel. In ver. 4 we read that " the dragon's tail draweth the third part of the stars of heaven, and did cast them to the earth " ; and, while that action may not be the same as this of the beast, it indicates that the terms before us mean angelic beings.

In truth, this sense of stars is of the earliest origin ; for those heavenly beings who already existed when the earth was founded, for they sang then for joy, are by God Himself called " morning stars " (Job. 38 : 4–7). Also Satan, by pre-eminence is styled the " day star, son of the morning " (Isa. 14 : 12) and is said to have " fallen from heaven."

The ancients spoke of a rebellion of the gods in the far-distant past, when the Titans sought to scale Olympus, the abode of the gods, and dethrone Jupiter ; but he hurled them back to destruction. The reality behind the myth is shown in this chapter 14 of Isaiah, for in ver. 13 we read of Lucifer that he said in his heart, " I will ascend into heaven, I will exalt my throne above the stars of God . . . I will be like the Most High."

The pride that conceived so bold and impious a scheme is revealed in Ezekiel 28. It was the project of the anointed cherub that had covered the glory of God, as the symbolic cherubim later did in the Tabernacle. But he had been destroyed from that chief post of service and honour in the universe and cast as profane out of that true Olympus, the holy mountain of God (Ezek. 28 : 11-19). Of this overthrow the Lord Jesus (Luke 10 : 18) seems to have spoken when he said : " I was watching (ἐθεώρουν) Satan [the Satan, the Adversary, τὸν Σατᾳνᾶν falling and] fallen (πεσόντα) out of heaven (ἐκ τοῦ οὐρανοῦ).

To that supreme summit of the universe the fallen one has now no access, though he *has* access to that lower heaven where Jehovah takes his place in that angel court we have considered (Job 1 and 2, etc.). But at the time of the end thence also he and his rebel hosts will be driven by Michael and his angels, and they will no more have place in any heavenly region (Rev. 12 : 7-12).

This expulsion will so enrage the Devil that he will precipitate the end of the age, and will bring up the beast as his great agent. In Isa. 14 and Ezek. 28 the descriptions of the heavenly being seem to descend and to merge into that of a human being. It will be no marvel if another attempt be made to recover that lost and wondrous realm on high by an attack upon the host above and its leaders. And as the former rebellion entangled many of those " stars " it cannot be beyond possibility that this may occur again and more " mighty ones " be overcome, especially as God has forewarned some of those angel rulers that their present ways will end in them also being cast down as earlier princes of that kingdom had been (Ps. 82 : 7).

And this may be the force of the R.V. margin (the reading adopted by Darby in ver. 25) that the beast shall " corrupt " the mighty ones. This would be impossible in the case of saints already glorified in resurrection or by rapture ; but thus had Satan before overcome the now fallen hosts of the heights, as he afterward corrupted our first parents and cast them down to trample upon them. At the end he may attempt a further such victory. There are angels whom God charges with folly (Job 4 : 18) : and if folly be not removed by accepting reproof and instruction it will easily run into danger, rebellion, and ruin, when adequate pressure of temptation assaults.

It is in line with this, and perhaps because of this, that a test of the fidelity of God of the angel hosts is to be made at that period : " When He [God] shall have brought in again the First Begotten into the inhabitable world He saith, ' And let all the angels of

God worship Him ' " (Heb. 1 : 6) ; and the chief proof of this fidelity will be seen in the chief heavenly angelic rulers giving up their age-long high offices to the Firstborn ; " they place their crowns " before the throne of the Ancient of Days (Rev. 4 : 10).

(x) It will therefore be small marvel that this daring rebel shall also seek to crush out of existence the earthly people of God, that " little remnant " of Israel, that " holy people " living at that last time (24). And the line of attack, as here given, will be a forcible suppression of the worship of God at Jerusalem. " The burnt offering will be taken away from Him, and the place of His sanctuary [=His holy place] will be cast down." And this will be permitted by God " because of the transgression " of His people. For worship from sinful hearts and offerings from unclean hands are an abomination to the Holy One (Isa. 1 : 10–17 ; Mal. 1 : etc.).

That there will be at Jerusalem at that time a temple and sacrifices is the consentient testimony of the prophets and the New Testament. See the following passages, all future : Ps. 66 : 13–15 ; 96 : 6–13 ; Isa. 19 : 21 ; 27 : 13 ; 66 : 20–23 ; Jer. 33 : 14–17 ; Ezek. chs. 40–48 ; Dan. 8 : 11–14 ; Hag. 2 : 6–9 ; Zech. 6 : 12, 13 ; 14 : 16–21 ; Mal. 3 : 2–4 ; Matt. 24 : 15 ; II Thess. 2 : 3, 4 ; Rev. 11 : 1, 2. Whatever explanation may be required as to the restoration of sacrifices in view of the abrogation thereof by the sacrifice of Christ at Calvary, or even if no explanation can be given by us, nothing can annul this uniform inspired testimony by prophets, by Christ, by apostles, that such restoration is to come. The difficulty arises from our lack of comprehension : the Scripture statements are plain.

(xi) A particular feature of this vision is that it adds the information that the little horn will rise out of one of the four parts into which the empire of Alexander was divided (8, 9, 23). Other passages show it will be the eastern portion.

1. In Isa. 10 : 5, 12, 24 he is called " the Assyrian," and the context is wholly of the last days, of the " consummation determined," of the return to Zion of the " little remnant," of the " Shoot out of the stock of Jesse " establishing His authority, destroying this Assyrian, relieving nature of the curse, and the earth being " full of the knowledge of the glory of Jehovah." It is the time when the Root of Jesse shall be the centre of the nations, when the remainder of Israel still dispersed will be gathered, and

they shall rejoice in the Holy One of Israel being in their midst (ch. 12).

As before mentioned (p. 18, *n*), in the time of Isaiah " Assyria " included Babylonia.

2. In other places Antichrist is styled " the king of the north " (Jer. 1 : 14 ; Ezek. 26 : 7), a term, as far as we see, regularly meaning in Scripture Assyria. To one in Palestine Assyria was the kingdom of the north, because its territory did in fact extend so far up the Euphrates valley as to be north of the Holy Land, but yet more because its armies, not being able to cross the wide deserts to the east of Palestine, went up north and turned southward to attack Palestine. The term is to be distinguished from " the uttermost parts of the north," as in Ezek. 38 : 6, 15 ; 39 : 2, a region then apparently indicating the countries north of Armenia between the Black and Caspian seas, or further north in Scythia ; regions so untraversed by the more southern races that they were to them among " the uttermost parts."

3. Again, Jeremiah (25 : 15–38) was ordered to send a symbolic cup of the wine of Jehovah's fury to various nations named until it should reach " all the kingdoms of the world which are upon the face of the earth " (26). In Rev. 14 : 10 the term " wine of God's wrath " finds its application to the period of Antichrist, and in Rev. 16 : 19 to the judgment of God upon his capital city, Babylon. After more than twenty lands have been named, and the " whole world " is stated to be affected, the prophecy of Jeremiah adds that " the king of Sheshach shall drink after them." This is a name of Babylon (see Jer. 51 : 41), and its king is to drink the wine of God's wrath *after* all the others, that is, last of all. This agrees exactly with the *Revelation* ; for the wide judgments of the end days have been detailed in the many visions, and in ch. 16 the final stages are depicted ; the seventh bowl completes the visitation upon Antichrist at the battle of Har Magedon (16 : 16, 17), and finally we read " that the cities of the nations fell, and Babylon the great was remembered in the sight of God, to give unto her the cup of the wine of the fierceness of His wrath " (16 : 19).

Therefore Antichrist will be the king of Assyria with Babylon as his capital, which of old was in the dominion of Seleucus, who gained the eastern area of the empire of Alexander.

Thus when Antichrist arises he will not come at Rome, or anywhere in the west. Had this been understood many vain and misleading speculations would have been avoided, such as that of the Pope, or the Papacy, or Napoleon, or others, being he. And when he comes his military efforts will be expended mainly upon Egypt and the south, the east, and Palestine.

(xii) Verse 13 is of peculiar interest. It tells of one heavenly being enquiring of another concerning the duration of one feature of the vision. (1) This illustrates Peter's words that angels desire to look into the ways of God (1 Peter 1 : 12). (2) Therefore there is no intuitive perception or general diffusion of such knowledge among the angels. They, as we, depend on revelation, or of inquiry of any of their number to whom the Most High may have explained any portion of the future and of His purposes. They, as we, learn by the slow development of affairs, especially by the ways of God with the church (Eph. 3 : 10). (3) And in consequence, they, as we, must serve in faith, each humbly and dutifully performing the particular service allotted. Thus that is simply, yet fully, true which one of them said to John when the latter, amazed at the vastness of the angel's knowledge, would have worshipped him : " See thou do it not : I am a *fellow*-servant with thee, and with thy brethren the prophets, and with them who keep the words of this book : worship God " (Rev. 22 : 8, 9).

How excellent therefore it is to be a humble doer of what is written in prophetic Scripture. In carrying out into life this instruction we, however unconsciously, are co-operating with the angel servants of our and their God : for " hearkening unto the voice of His words," and fulfilling what He bids is the exact principle of angelic service and strength, as of ours (Ps. 103 : 20, 21). Whereas they who neglect prophetic Scripture, or treat it as merely a theme for interesting speculation, their lives not being moulded by the plans of God, they fail of such holy co-operation. The Commander-in-Chief imparts various of his commissions to widely scattered sections of his forces, who never see each other ; and in carrying out these orders they effectually co-operate with him and with one another.

4. Further, the angelic enquiry shows upon what detail of the here-predicted events the angelic interest was concentrated. It was upon the desecrating and treading down of God's chosen earth-centre, the temple at Jerusalem. God's presence had once and again hallowed its precincts ; God's promises are indissolubly joined with its future. Even at that hour of desecration, and even though this is permitted because of the abominations practised

there by faithless Israel, it is still called by God " the holy city " (Rev. 11 : 2).

And surely those holy watchers feel yet more deeply concerned with that spot since the feet of the Son of God have trodden it, and near by His precious blood has reddened and redeemed the soil. How long, then, shall the desolation foretold last ? When shall that great redemption take effect as regards this sacred spot ?

The answer is that the desolation will cover " two thousand three hundred evening-mornings " (14) and then the sanctuary will be cleansed. Pember remarks that

The words of the angel in regard to the two thousand, three hundred days during which the Sanctuary and the Host are to be trodden under-foot, are, perhaps, not so mysterious as they seem. The literal Hebrew expression is not " days," but " evening-mornings " ; that is to say, two thousand, three hundred repetitions of the evening and morning sacrifices—which proves that actual days of twenty-four hours are intended. And we should note, that seven full prophetic years would contain two thousand five hundred and twenty days ; that is, that the time mentioned by the angel is two hundred and twenty days short of seven years.

Now, as we shall see when we consider the revelation of the Seventy Sevens, the Antichrist is to make a covenant with the majority of the Jewish nation for Seven Years, at the close of which period he will be destroyed by the appearing of the Lord, and the Sanctuary will be cleansed. It would seem, then, that he will not tamper with the Sanctuary, until the two hundred and twenty-first day from the date of the commencement of the covenant : indeed, it is possible that the building of the Temple may not be completed until that time. Perhaps, the two thousand three hundred days may represent the whole time of his personal connection with the City and Sanctuary. The actual suppression of the daily sacrifices will not take place, as we shall presently see, until three years and a half of the covenant-period have passed by. (*Great Prophecies*, 127, 128.)

For a chosen place as of a chosen people " the gifts and the calling of God are without change of mind " in Him (Rom. 11 : 29). He will " yet set His king upon His holy hill of Zion " (Ps. 2 : 6), and when Babylon, Satan's centre, lies in everlasting ruins (Isa. 13 : 19–22 ; Jer. 51 : 64 ; etc.), the city of the great King, beautiful in situation, shall be the joy of the whole earth (Ps. 48 : 2).

(xiii) God has provided and appointed only one Saviour, for private persons or public situations. Satan attacked and defeated every son of man until he stood up against the Son of man : then he was routed.   Antichrist will overrun the whole earth, over-whelm all opposition, wear out the saints, crush Israel, perhaps seduce angels, but when finally he shall " stand up against the Prince of princes " then " he shall be broken without hand " (25). The stone was hewed out of the mountain without hands (2 : 45) : the Word of God acts at last in direct judgment and the conflict is closed in complete victory (Rev. 19 : 11–21).   While God sees fit to employ angels and men the battle seems to hang in the balance, the issue of the whole campaign to be in doubt.   Thus are angels and men alike taught the insufficiency of the creature even when serving God.   But when the King takes the field in person the enemy is routed for ever.   " The sword that goeth forth out of His mouth " has an edge and point that no defence can turn : once again, as when at His word creation sprang into being out of nothing, " He speaks, and it is done."

CHAPTER IX

(A) PRAYER AND LIGHT

UCH HAD BEEN SHOWN TO GOD'S BELOVED SERVANT, AND we who read it in the light of later Scriptures may in measure co-ordinate the mysteries revealed. But as yet Daniel was perplexed : " the vision astonished him, but there was none to make it understood " (8 : 27).

What shall a saint do when the deep things of God baffle him ? Some neglect them, as impracticable and unpractical. Some force and distort them by human fancies. Some smite their brethren whose understanding of divine mysteries differs from their own. Daniel shows the true course.

1. He turned to scriptures already in his hand and studied these, and " by means of the books " he gained further knowledge and was prepared for yet further instruction.

The present is rooted in the past, and the future will grow out of the past through the present. Hence the true method for study of the book of Revelation is to begin with Genesis, gradually to accumulate the predictions given by God through Moses and all the prophets, and thus to bring the mind to the measure of knowledge which the apostles had when the Lord Jesus began to teach them. To know what the Old Testament *says* is prerequisite to learning what it *means*.

The Lord added much knowledge to the apostles, and we should add His teachings to what has been learned from the Old Testament. Neglect of the Gospels is a fruitful source of misunderstanding of the Epistles and the Revelation. But Christ had told the disciples that there was more to be revealed (John 16 : 12, 13). It was with all preceding instruction in their minds that their education was taken up by the Spirit and completed. No one will master trigonometry who does not approach it progressively, beginning with twice two make four. Much confusing, albeit very positive, talking and writing about the Epistles and the Revelation does but show that the would-be teachers have a meagre knowledge of the prophets and the Gospels.

So Daniel studied what was already given of the Word of God, and it was made clear to him that the affairs of his people had reached a turning-point, when it was to be expected that God would act, definitely and with power. This had not been opened up to him earlier, for there was no need. The time for action had not before arrived. Divine predictions are given for practical purposes. " I have told you before it come to pass, that, when it is come to pass, *ye may believe* " (John 14 : 29). While events are far distant prophecy remains sealed (Dan. 12 : 4) : when the time has drawn near the book is not to be sealed (Rev. 22 : 10). Hence the need of humility and caution in treating of the remote future : but God will make clear to the true Daniels what they will need to know with definiteness for practical ends, and especially that they may co-operate with Him intelligently in His affairs.

Deut. 32 : 8, 9, states a fundamental feature of matters international :

> When the Most High gave to the nations their inheritance,
> When He separated the children of men,
> He set the bounds of the peoples
> According to the number of the children of Israel.
> For Jehovah's portion is His people ;
> Jacob is the lot of His inheritance.

So when the foretold moral condition of Israel had arisen, and chastisement, with removal from their land and loss of sovereignty, could no longer be deferred, at that very juncture a world-power (Babylon) had arisen that could be God's servant thus to deal with Israel. And now again that the determined period of chastisement had passed, and a limited restoration of their land must take place, a second world-power (Persia) had arisen that could be used of God for His then present purpose.

Thus are mighty world changes caused to coincide with God's thoughts as to the children of Abraham His friend, for they are loved evermore for the sake of their fathers, though often so unlovable in themselves.

2. But when Daniel saw that the seventy years of the then captivity were elapsed he gave himself to special supplication. He was no fatalist, nor did he so conceive of his God. That Jehovah could and would fulfil His purpose and promise did not exclude the correlative truth that it is a part, an essential part of those

purposes that they shall be fulfilled in answer to the prayers of men. So Daniel prayed. For when predicting such a chastisement and captivity as Daniel had experienced, and a restoration, Moses had said : " And they shall confess their iniquity, and the iniquity of their fathers," and this should be a condition of recovery from their captivity (Lev. 26 : 40).

3. *A Model Prayer.* When the apostles asked the Lord to teach them to pray He gave them sample petitions to guide their hearts in approaching God, and added an illustrative case upon the matter of urging petitions (Luke 11 : 1–13). He had formerly (Matt. 6 : 5–15) given similar instruction ; but it is noticeable that upon repeating the lesson He greatly varied the phrases and the wording (see the proper text in the R.V.). This shows that He did not give a *form* for prayer, or He would have repeated the form on the second occasion ; but it was a sample prayer : " *after this manner pray ye.*" Yet naturally we must keep the pattern before us, and study it, or we cannot be guided by it.

But in Scripture there are many other examples of prayer that proved acceptable to God and were answered. Each of these also is worthy of study, so that we may master this holy service of supplication. The prayer before us teaches the spirit, manner, and language of prayer for general forgiveness. It shows how a man on earth may prevail to affect powerfully both the heavenly world and thereby vast and critical affairs on earth.

It is a moving spectacle, this secret dealing of a man with his Maker. Daniel is very old. If he was fifteen when Jerusalem was captured he is now eighty-five, for seventy years have passed. What a period of change, of danger, of great service it has been, and now he is again the chief Minister of State in a world-empire. Wealth, luxury, splendour, authority have not hurt his soul. How marvellous, how exceptional ! The things of his God are the concern of his heart ; the people of God are dear to him because they are *that* ; the city he had left in his youth, because it is the city of his God, is precious to his soul. By such devotion to the affairs of his God Daniel was saved from the subtle perils of a palace, as Paul was from the opposite dangers of imprisonment, as witness his prison epistles. And both these great men here reveal a prime secret of power in prayer—absorption with God and the things of God. And a far Greater than they said in His youth, " Wist ye not that I must be [occupied] in the things of my Father ? ", and He so continued unto life's latest hour, and is so occupied for ever, the divine Meditator and Intercessor.

Daniel's prayer is marked by :

(i) *Determination.* " I set my face unto the Lord God." This phrase expresses a resolute purpose and will. In II Kings 12 : 17 the face of a soldier is set for battle : " Hazael set his face to go up to Jerusalem." It reminds of the saying of Cromwell's men that their leader had on his battle face. This determination of heart the Christian warrior greatly needs. The Lord " steadfastly set His face to go to Jerusalem " (Luke 9 : 51) to accomplish all the will of God, though the path was to be so rough. Isa. 50 : 7 foretold this holy determination, and the faith that imparted such vigour of soul, by the words : " For the Lord, Jehovah, will help me ; therefore have I not been confounded : therefore have I set my face like a flint, and I know that I shall not be ashamed." On a later occasion Daniel " set his face toward the ground and was dumb " so as to hearken with utmost attention (10 : 15) ; and in our passage this concentration of mind is applied to seeking God in prayer.

Nor will any less resolute effort suffice, particularly in so mighty a crisis as had been reached. For the deep sense of unworthiness he felt could have hindered faith counting upon God ; the knowledge that his people as a whole were little the better for the seventy years of discipline could have weakened hope of God helping ; that the Persians, newly come to world-authority, and with such vast and widespread affairs to regulate and consolidate, would concern themselves with this small captive race must have seemed most improbable ; and then behind all of these mundane difficulties there was that array of powerful wicked angel princes, and their numberless subordinates, of whom Daniel knew so well, " the principalities, the world-rulers of this [age of] darkness, the spiritual hosts of wickedness in the heavenly places." These were his foes, as they are ours, and against these all other proper measures will prove ineffective unless guided and invigorated by that all-embracing prayer and supplication which Paul the Warrior urges upon us as he closes his words on the foes, the armour, and the battle (Eph. 6 : 10–20).

So Daniel set his face towards God.

(ii) The sense he had of his God produced *humiliation.* He had known and walked with God for seventy years. He had served Him faithfully ; had been honoured by Him with high duties, special deliverances, unusual visions ; but this had not puffed him up. A later saint of seventy years' knowledge of God and great service, George Müller, was known to pray that God would keep him from becoming a wicked old man. Such deep sense of unworthiness is hallowing. Combined with a due knowledge of God it does not diminish the co-existing sense of His grace and goodness, but it preserves from the subtle abuse thereof which vitiates prayer.

(iii) This humility of heart led to *intensity of spirit*. He who *feels* that he has no personal claim (not merely admits it theoretically, as a matter of doctrine) will the more earnestly beg for help. One who believes he has a right, a claim, goes to his bank with quietness, with a sense of title. He takes for granted that he will receive without trouble what is his own. Not so the *suppliant*, as Jacob to the angel to whom he made *supplication* (Gen. 32 : 26 ; Hos. 12 : 4) ; not so the beggar, the leper, the demon-possessed who cried aloud and oft, " Thou Son of David have mercy on us. . . . Have mercy upon me, O Lord ; my daughter is grievously vexed with a demon ! "

Such humility and intensity expressed itself in oriental garb, with " fasting and sackcloth and ashes " (3). Perhaps to the modern westerner this would be so unnatural as to be formal, and therefore vain. But let him ask himself if he has ever felt in his soul such deep and desperate need of divine intervention, and such utter unworthiness of divine help, that he would readily and naturally have so debased himself in person had it been his instinctive way of acting ?

Let the scene be visualized. Daniel is old, dignified, a Prime Minister ; he is usually clothed in almost royal attire ; his hospitable table commands all the luxury that belongs to his office : now in secret he is lying in coarse sackcloth, his head smeared with ashes, his appetite curbed, denied, while he humbles himself before God.

If the reader knows little or nothing of such a state of heart, so that this picture is strange, a mere oriental extravagance, let him reflect whether this want of sympathy may not be one cause why his prayers prove ineffective ; let him ask his Master to repeat to his heart and conscience, as with His own voice, what He said to the first disciples concerning almsgiving, prayer, and fasting (Matt. 6 : 1–18). And let him beware of silencing His Lord's voice by the paralysing assertion that Matthew's Gospel is for Jews, not Christians !

(iv) Daniel's prayer was saturated with *confession of sins and sinfulness.* Yet he had not himself been guilty of what he confesses. Quite the contrary : his is one of the very few lives told at any length in the Bible against which no failure is recorded. But the people of God are an unity. Quickened individually, passing from death into life personally, they are forthwith united by that common life into one family, and the sin and shame of any members is unavoidably the sorrow and reproach of all.

The Spirit of Christ wrought in Daniel this feature of his Lord as the Priest who would take up the burden of this world's sin as if it were His own. Thus still earlier had Moses interceded for sinning Israel : " Yet now, if Thou wilt forgive their sin— ; and if not, blot me, I pray Thee, out of Thy book which Thou has written " (Exod. 32 : 32). Thus also centuries later Paul wrote of his bitterest persecutors : " My heart's desire and my supplication to God is for them [not against them, as would have been natural to the carnal man], that they may be saved. . . . I have great sorrow and unceasing pain in my heart. For I was wishing [if it were practicable] I myself to be anathema from Christ for my brethren's sake, my kinsmen according to the flesh " (Rom. 10 : 1 ; 9 : 2, 3 ; see Liddon, Moule).

He who brings before God the needs of others as his own will bear away from God the mercies they need. This is a chief point in our Lord's instruction as to the man who pertinaciously disturbed his friend at midnight. He pleaded as his own the requirements of the friend who had turned in to him. " Every one that [so] asketh receiveth ; and he that [so] seeketh findeth ; and to him that [thus] knocketh it shall be opened " (Luke 11 : 5, 10). It was thus that Daniel had asked, sought, and knocked, and had obtained his great request.

(v) But the chief strength of Daniel's faith lay in his intimate knowledge of the One whose help he sought : " they that know Thy name will put their trust in Thee ; for Thou, Jehovah, hast not forsaken them that seek Thee " (Ps. 9 : 10). Daniel had long walked humbly with his God, and knew Him well. To him God was : 1. Adonay Elohim, the mighty, covenant-keeping possessor of all things (3) ; 2. Jehovah, my Elohim, the self-existing, unchanging, faithful, covenant God, known to Daniel personally (4); 3. Adonay, as the Lord who is great and dreadful, yet faithful and merciful (4, 7, 17, 19).

It is a great loss that in translation these majestic names of God are obscured, for so *we* do *not* " know His name " as they did to whom these were *names*, not general titles only.   These names reminded the Jew of distinct attributes of God, such as awed the soul and yet inspired confidence.

It is a most hopeful thing to appeal to One so kind, just, merciful, faithful, rich, and powerful as these names show their Owner to be. And Daniel turned this knowledge to good account as he prayed. He owns God's righteousness in His treatment of sinful Israel (7) ; but he reminds Him that He has also a prerogative of mercy and pardon (9, 18) ; and he urges that God's own glory is involved in the state of Israel, Jerusalem, and the temple, seeing that His name is connected with them (16, 19).   This is perhaps the most powerful plea that faith can urge in prayer.   God owns its force, as when speaking of the future and final restoration of Israel to His favour He says : " I do not this for your sake, O house of Israel, but for My holy name " (Ezek. 36 : 22).

How bold was Daniel to associate that Name with Israel dispersed under the holy indignation of God, with Jerusalem utterly laid waste, with the sanctuary no longer existing.   But to faith they were still " *Thy* people, *Thy* holy mountain, *Thy* city, *Thy* sanctuary." Thus they were to Paul also, though Christ had rejected them. Faith knew that God had not finally and for ever cast off His people , Israel shall all be saved (Rom. 11 : 1, 11, 26, 27).   The temple remains the temple of God, though Antichrist sits in it for a time (II Thess. 2 : 4), even as the church at Thyatira was the *church* there, though Jezebel sat there and taught and worked iniquity (Rev. 2 : 20).

Thus in a right spirit Daniel prayed, urging cogent and appropriate grounds of appeal, and was heard because of his piety. " Lord, teach us to pray."

4. Such praying sets the heavens in motion.   Gabriel was caused to fly swiftly : to come into direct contact with the man of prayer (" he touched me ') ; to do this upon the basis of a sacrifice not then being offered, yet still available for faith (" he touched me about the time of the evening oblation ") ; and to give to the man greatly beloved by God and angels the instruction, wisdom, understanding that should relieve his heart of the perplexities not yet resolved.

May this become our own experience and blessing.   But for this we, like Daniel, must study to be such men of God as he was, to walk before God as he had walked, so as ourselves to be of those loved by that holy world; and then also we with him must

" consider the matter." For no special illumination from above ever relieves of the duty to ponder, to meditate, to consider.

Here all too many sincere but fanatical minds have been deceived. Sudden illuminations have been received, and forthwith the prophet pours them out upon mankind without having first, with angels and with Daniels, searched, pondered, examined, and watched to see the source, the nature, the moral tendencies of the vision or inspiration. God does indeed give such special enlightenment, but He distinctly calls upon us to *consider* what He says. And thus Paul, who claimed authority in the churches as given to him by the Lord, says also, " I speak as to wise men ; judge ye what I say," and to Timothy, " Consider what I say ; for the Lord shall give thee understanding in all things " (I Cor. 10 : 15 ; II Tim. 2 : 7). Whereas wicked spirits, speaking in His name, declare it sinful to test their utterances, asserting that it is to sin against the Holy Spirit. This leads ever to confusion and awful darkness ; whereas humble and prayerful consideration brings understanding of the vision.

(B) THE SEVENTY SEVENS

O F RECENT YEARS ATTEMPT HAS BEEN MADE TO REVIVE THE idea that the predictions now before us were *fulfilled* in the beginning of this Christian era. We think this unfounded and misleading. It would put the prophecy out of harmony with the general method and burden of prophetic Scriptures, both those of Daniel and the rest of God's Word, which is to throw the weight of prediction upon the consummation of the age, first in Antichrist and finally in Christ. See Preliminary Dissertation III (" The Latter Days are the Chief Period of Prophecy ") in my *The Revelation of Jesus Christ.*

It may help the student to see four careful renderings of the prophecy. The clauses in brackets in the first column are the marginal renderings of the R.V. (*See pages* 128, 129.)

For the critical reasons which determined the particular translations the reader must consult the works of the scholars cited. Darby's translation is in close conformity. It is to be observed what large agreement they reveal. Our part is only to indicate how we ourselves understand the prophecy.

1. *Seventy Sevens* means of *years.* The expression itself may mean hours, days, weeks, months, or years. The context must determine. This period was to commence at a decree to rebuild the holy city and was to conclude with the abomination of desolation and the afore-determined consummation. Neither hours, days, weeks, nor months can cover that period, however it might be calculated. Four hundred and ninety *months* (about forty years) would not stretch from Artaxerxes to Antiochus and his abomination, while 490 *years* stretch far beyond his period. Thus is he, at any rate, shut out of this prophecy. If we read with the R.V. (but wrongly) that the city shall be built again for 62 sevens, and should take the sense as months, it is wrong, for the city remained built far longer. *Years* is the only possible sense.

2. *Decreed* means divided or severed off from the whole period of world-empire in the hands of Gentiles, as to which Daniel was already well informed. It points to a fixed and limited period, of definite duration, forming part of a longer period the duration of which is not fixed, or at least not declared.

REVISED VERSION

Ver. 24. Seventy weeks are decreed upon thy people and upon thy holy city, to finish (restrain) transgression (the transgressor), and to make an end of sins (seal up sins), and to make reconciliation for (purge away) iniquity, and to bring in everlasting righteousness, and to seal up vision and prophecy (Heb. prophet), and to anoint the most holy (a most holy place).

25. Know therefore and discern, that from the going forth of the commandment to restore and to build Jerusalem unto the anointed one, the prince (Messiah, the prince). Or an anointed one, a prince), shall be seven weeks : and threescore and two weeks, it shall be built again, with street and moat, even in troublous times (seven weeks, and threescore and two weeks : it shall, etc.).

26. And after the three-score and two weeks shall the anointed one be cut off, and shall have nothing (there shall be none belonging to him) : and the people of the prince that shall come shall destroy the city and the sanctuary ; and his end (the end thereof) shall be with a flood, and even unto the end shall be war ; desolations are determined.

27. And he shall make a firm covenant with many for one week : and for the half of (in the midst of) the week he shall cause the sacrifice and the oblation (meal offering) to cease ; and upon the wing of abominations *shall come* (upon the pinnacle of abominations *shall be*) one that maketh desolate ; and even unto the consummation, and that determined, shall *wrath* be poured out upon the desolator (*or* desolate).

S. P. TREGELLES

Seventy weeks have been determined (more strictly " divided ") upon thy people and thy holy city, to finish the transgression, and to make an end of sins, and to make reconciliation for iniquity, and to bring in everlasting righteousness, and to seal vision and prophet, and to anoint the holy of holies.

Know then and understand, from the issuing of the decree to restore and to build Jerusalem unto Messiah the prince (shall be) seven weeks, and threescore and two weeks : the street shall be again built, and the trench (or scarped rampart), even in pressure of times (i.e. in times of straitness or pressure).

And after the threescore and two weeks shall Messiah be cut off, and there shall be nothing for Him ; and the city and the sanctuary shall the people destroy of a prince who shall come ; and his end shall be in the overflowing ; and until the end (there is) war (even) that which is determined for desolations.

And he (the prince who shall come) shall confirm a covenant with the many (or with the multitude) for one week ; and at half the week he shall cause sacrifice and offering to cease ; and upon the wing (or pinnacle) of abominations (shall be) that which causeth desolation, even until the consummation and that determined shall be poured upon the causer of desolation.

B. W. NEWTON

Seventy hebdomads are severed (or divided off) upon thy people and thy holy city, to shut up transgression, and to bring under atonement iniquity, and to bring in everlasting righteousness, and to ratify (lit. to seal) vision and prophet, and to anoint the most Holy Place.

Know therefore, and understand, from the going forth of the commandment to restore and to build Jerusalem unto the Messiah, the Prince, are seven hebdomads, and sixty and two hebdomads; the street shall be built again, and the wall, even in pressure of times (i.e. in times of straitness or pressure).

And after sixty and two hebdomads, Messiah shall be cut off, and there shall be nothing to him; and the city and the sanctuary shall the people destroy of the prince that cometh; and his end shall be in the overflowing, and until the end there is war, even that which is determined for desolations.

And he (the prince that cometh) shall confirm a covenant with the many (i.e. with the multitude) for one hebdomad; and at half the hebdomad he shall cause sacrifice and oblation to cease, and upon the pinnacle of abominations (i.e. the idolatrous pinnacle) shall be that which causeth desolation, even until the consummation, and that determined shall be poured upon the causer of desolation.

G. H. PEMBER

Seventy Sevens have been severed off upon thy people and upon Thy Holy City, to shut up the transgression, and to seal up sins, and to cover iniquity, and to bring in everlasting righteousness, and to seal up vision and prophet, and to anoint a Holy of Holies.

Know, therefore, and understand :—From the going forth of a commandment to restore and to build Jerusalem unto an Anointed One, a Prince, there shall be Seven Sevens and Sixty and Two Sevens : it shall be built again with street and moated wall, even under pressure of the times.

And after the Sixty and Two Sevens an Anointed One shall be cut off, and there shall be nothing for Him. And the City and the Sanctuary shall the people destroy of a Prince that shall come : and his end shall be in the flood ; and until the end, there shall be war, a decree of desolations.

And he shall confirm a covenant with the many for one Seven: and during half of the Seven he shall cause sacrifice and offering to cease, and upon a wing of abominations he shall come desolating, even until the consumption and that that is determined, which shall be poured upon the desolated.

3. *Upon thy people and thy holy city.*   The limited period is that portion of the times of the Gentiles within which the divine dealings with Israel and Jerusalem will be carried on and completed.   During the remainder of the times of the Gentiles, however extended, Israel and Jerusalem will not be the immediate objects of God's working, though indirectly affected.   But inasmuch as the whole period of Gentile supremacy has been so much longer than 490 years there must of necessity be a break somewhere in the direct dealings of God with Israel and Jerusalem ; for those direct dealings commenced with the decree to rebuild the city and are even yet not completed : they must therefore have suffered interruption.

It is affecting to the heart, and important for the understanding, that, in the view of heaven, Jerusalem even in desolation remains " the holy city " : " the gifts and calling of God are without change of mind " in Him.   The endeavour to apply this prophecy, in general or in detail, to others than Daniel's people, Israel, and Daniel's city, Jerusalem, is an outrage upon exegesis, being forbidden in advance by the express terms used.   It was concerning Israel and Jerusalem, in the only sense that Daniel could possibly mean those terms, that he had been praying (16–19) ; it was specifically to answer that prayer that Gabriel was sent (23) ; and to Daniel the terms the angel used could mean nothing other than he himself had meant, the literal Israel and Jerusalem.

" But there is also a second deduction of great moment to be drawn from the same words. The Seventy Sevens are separated, off, not only upon the people, but also upon the City—that is, upon the people in connection with the City. Therefore, during the whole course of the Sevens the Jews must be dwelling in their own country " (Pember, Ed. 1941, p. 134).

4. Pember continues :

We may, then, sum up the meaning of the words which we have thus far considered as follows. Seventy Sevens—that is to say, 490 years—would be taken by God out of the protracted Times of the Gentiles for special dealings with the Jews in their own land, apart from the discipline to which they would also be subjected in the Dispersion, when, according to the prophecy of Moses, they would be dwelling in the lands of their enemies.

And the pleadings of God with them during these 490 years should be made to yield six results, which are given as follows :

    (i) To shut up transgression.
    (ii) To seal up sins.

(iii) To cover iniquity.
(iv) To bring in everlasting righteousness.
(v) To seal up vision and prophet.
(vi) To anoint a Holy of Holies.

Now we may divide these six consequences into two classes : for the first three are concerned with the removal of sin, and the last three with the bringing in of righteousness. And the latter will be found to correspond, each to each, to the former.

"*To shut up the transgression.*" That is, to arrest and restrain it, so that it can no longer work and spread. The article, probably, indicates the whole course of Israel's transgression, or "breaking away" from God.

"*To seal up sins.*" The sins are the symptoms or proofs of the revolt, and the figure of sealing is connected with that of shutting up in prison, or restraining. So Darius seals the stone, which is put at the mouth of the lion's den, with his own signet and with that of his lords (Dan. 6 : 17). And in the Book of Job, God is said to seal up the stars, so that they do not shine (Job 9 : 7) ; and is also described as sealing up the hand of every man, when, by the frost and rain of winter, He prevents the continuance of daily labour in the fields (Job 37 : 7). The sealing up of sins, consequently, signifies their restraint under safe custody.

There is a good illustration of both figures, and, probably, a clue to the interpretation of the passage, in the twentieth chapter of the Revelation, where an angel, after binding Satan and casting him into the Abyss, shuts him up and sets a seal upon him, that he may deceive the nations no more.

"*To cover iniquity.*" That is, according to the well-known Scriptural figure, to make reconciliation or atonement for it, to expiate it by sacrifice. While the previous clauses refer to the members of the Jewish nation which will perish during the refining process, these words speak of another way of removing sin, and point to the Holy Seed that will be saved.

Of course, the reference to expiation is not to be understood directly of what Christ did upon the Cross, but of the application of it to the Jewish people, which will not take place until the close of the age. For Jews as a people there is no expiation in this dispensation : if an individual would have the benefit of the Saviour's death in this time, he must resign his nationality, and become a member of Christ, in Whom there is neither Jew nor Greek. But when the Body of Christ has been completed, then the Jewish *nation* shall look on Him Whom they have pierced, and mourn for Him ; "and in that day there shall be a fountain opened to the House of David, and to the inhabitants of Jerusalem "—that is, to Jews as Jews—" for sin and for uncleanness " (Zech. 13 : 1).

We now come to the second group of results:

"*To bring in everlasting righteousness.*"   When the transgression is shut up and sins are sealed, then everlasting righteousness shall be brought in.   This will be done by the introduction of the new covenant, in accordance with which God will no longer write upon tables of stone, but put His law in the inward part of His people, and write it in their hearts (Jer. 31 : 33–40).

"*To seal up vision and prophet.*"   When sins are sealed up, vision and prophecy shall also be laid aside, as being no longer needed.   For it was only after sin had come into the world that prophecy was introduced as a great instrument of God in the war against it ; and so, when sin is put away, prophecies also shall fail.   [See ver. 34 of Jer. 31 cited.]

"*To anoint a Holy of Holies.*"   Lastly, in the place of the Tabernacle and former Temples, in which the covering, or propitiation, was wont to be typified, a new Holy of Holies shall be anointed.   There is great significance in this announcement ; for, although the Tabernacle of Moses was anointed, there is no mention of such a ceremony in the consecration of the Temple of Solomon, the latter being regarded as a mere continuation of the former.   And it is, doubtless, for a similar reason, that we hear nothing of an anointing in the case of the Temple of Zerubbabel.

But the Holy of Holies of this prophecy, the innermost shrine of the grand Temple described by Ezekiel, will be no mere continuation of former Sanctuaries.

The fact that the great Sacrifice has already been offered once for all, and that sin—as regards Israel at least—will then be shut up and sealed, will, doubtless, cause great changes in the ordinances and service. Moreover, the Ark of the Covenant will not be found in the future Holy of Holies, neither shall it be any more remembered (Jer. 3 : 16) ; but in its place will stand the Royal Throne on which the Messiah will sit as Priest (Jer. 3 : 17 ; Zech. 6 : 13).   And it is, probably, this last change more than all others which will involve the necessity for a fresh anointing and consecration.

Such, then, will be the results of God's dealings with the Jews, at the close of the 490 years.   Their transgression will be restrained and their sins sealed up, so as no longer to affect them—for the stumbling-blocks will then have been consumed with the wicked (Zeph. 1 : 3) : their iniquity will be expiated, and the new covenant of their God will confer everlasting righteousness upon them : all the promises will then be fulfilled : the law of God will be written upon the heart of every Israelite, so that there will be no further need of the exhortations, rebukes, warnings, and threatenings, of the prophets : and Mount Zion will be crowned with a Temple, of which the building of Solomon was but a very faint type, and to which, as we are elsewhere told, the Cherubim and the

Glory will return (Ezek. 43 : 1–7), to be a cloud of smoke by day, and the shining of a flaming fire by night (Isa. 4 : 5). So will the words of Haggai be fulfilled : " The latter glory of this house shall be greater than the former, saith the Lord of Hosts : and in this place will I give peace, saith the Lord of Hosts " (Hag. 2 : 9).

We have now before us an outline of the whole prophecy. And, after considering the statement of results which are to follow God's disciplinary dealings, we cannot but conclude that the close of the Seventy Sevens must coincide with the end of the present order of things and the beginning of the Coming or Millennial Age.

5. The " *Commandment to Restore and to Build Jerusalem* " was that of Artaxerxes Longimanus given to Nehemiah in answer to his request that he might be sent unto Jerusalem to build it and its wall (Neh. 2 : 3, 5, 8). Tregelles and Newton give the year as 454 or 455 B.C. ; Sir R. Anderson as 445 B.C. (*The Coming Prince*, p. 127) ; Anstey (*Bib. Chron.*, I, p. 282) adopts the Cyrus decree and dates this 536 B.C. He concludes (II 34) that the decree that Nehemiah should rebuild the city was issued by Darius Hystaspes in 502 B.C. He owns that in this he stood alone, and quotes *Athanasius contra mundum*. His calculations and reasonings are difficult, but he demands a deduction of 82 years for an alleged mistake in the common reckoning. This brings his actual date for Cyrus to 454 B.C., thus agreeing with the first-named scholars as to the year, but not as to the decree in question.

The earlier decree of Cyrus spoke only of building the temple (II Chron. 36 : 22, 23 ; Ezra 1 : 2–4 ; 6 : 1–5). That of Darius Hystaspes did but confirm the former decree as to the temple (Ezra 6 : 1–12). That of Artaxerxes to Ezra (7 : 11–26) dealt only with the temple services and the magisterial and judicial arrangements required in the land. When some years later Nehemiah went to Jerusalem the walls were still broken down, the gates burned with fire, and the city lying waste (Neh. 1 : 3 ; 2 : 3, 13, 17).

6. From this decree unto Messiah the Prince there were to pass two periods of Sevens : one of seven Sevens, the other of sixty-two Sevens, that is, 483 years in all. We are not told why these periods were distinguished. Possibly the former was that during which the city was completely rebuilt. Under what pressure of the times the work was carried on may be seen in the histories of Ezra and Nehemiah. Enemies of various races and ranks perseveringly, and at times violently, hindered.

There is no suggestion of any interval between these two periods, nor reason to suppose any.

7. In the life of our Lord there was only one occasion when He presented himself openly as Messiah the Prince, which was when He rode into Jerusalem on the ass, fulfilling the prophecy of Zechariah, " Tell ye the daughter of Zion, Behold, thy King cometh unto thee ; He is just and having salvation ; lowly, and riding upon an ass " (Zech. 9 : 9 ; Matt. 21 : 5). On former occasions He had refused to be made king, or to act as judge (John 6 : 15 ; 8 : 1–11 ; Luke 12 : 13, 14). He had charged the disciples not to proclaim Him as the Messiah (Matt. 16 : 20). But on this occasion the crowds vociferously acclaimed Him as the Son of David, the king that should come in the name of Jehovah, and when the Pharisees complained of this He justified the people (Luke 19 : 37–40). It was unto this occasion that the sixty-nine Sevens extended.

Sir Robert Anderson believed that secular chronology establishes that the interval from the decree of Artaxerxes unto the entry into Jerusalem was exactly 483 years to the very day (*The Coming Prince*, p. 127). Anstey reaches the same essential conclusion though working from the different data mentioned above. The calculations are complicated. But Pember's remarks and attitude will be sufficient for the believer : " Both starting-point and goal are so clearly indicated in Scripture that, as believers, we have no need to trouble ourselves with the uncertainties of human computation, but may at once assume that the interval was exactly four hundred and eighty-three years. . . . For our own researches have almost convinced us, that, in much of ancient chronology, we must be content with approximate results, and cannot hope for absolute accuracy." In a footnote he adds : " But the reader will find it worth while to consult Dr. Anderson's interesting book *The Coming Prince*."

8. "*After the Sixty-two Sevens Messiah shall be cut off, and shall have nothing.*" It was in the month Nisan that Artaxerxes issued the decree : it was in the same month of the year that Christ our passover was sacrificed. The 483 years had barely closed when, after but a few days, the Lord was crucified, and was banished from the world with nothing. His career had commenced in a borrowed manger, it closed in a borrowed grave. " Ye know the grace of our Lord Jesus Christ, that, though He was rich, yet for your sakes He became poor, that ye through His poverty might become rich " (II Cor. 8 : 9).

9. *The Interval.* There remains one Seven, that is, seven years, of the whole period, yet to be detailed. The angel intimates that

their course brings matters to " the end " (26), to " the consummation " (27). Events are included that never yet have happened
since Messiah was cut off. Therefore it is here that the interval
in the Seventy Sevens must fall. This is not a matter of interference,
but of fact. Messiah was cut off, and the remaining events still
wait fulfilment, with the possible exception of the destruction of
the city and the sanctuary.

10. *The Destruction of the City.* The usual explanation of this
clause runs thus : (i) " The coming prince " is the Antichrist.
(ii) He will be the last sovereign of the fourth empire. (iii) This
commenced at Rome, whose armies may therefore be called " the
people of the coming prince." (iv) These armies, under Titus,
destroyed the city and the sanctuary, A.D. 70, which was thus the
fulfilment of this prediction.

This explanation is possible. As the sixty-ninth Seven was just
about to end the Lord solemnly announced that coming overthrow
and the dispersion of the people, to result from their rejection of
Himself (Luke 19 : 41–44 ; Matt. 24 : 1, 2).

But we are not satisfied with this application to the year 70.
It brings in an event not to take place within the period of 490
years which is the sole subject of this prophecy. This is wholly
exceptional, and ought to be plainly justifiable from the terms of
the prophecy itself, which, however, it is not. Nor is the introduction of this event necessary, because there is to be a destruction
of Jerusalem within the final Seven of Years, to be effected by the
very armies of Antichrist himself, which gives a more natural force
to the term " the people of the coming prince."

This yet future destruction of Jerusalem is described in Zechariah
14 : 1, 2 :

" Behold a day of Jehovah cometh, when thy spoil shall be
divided in the midst of thee. For I will gather all nations against
Jerusalem to battle ; and the city shall be taken, and the houses
rifled, and the women ravished : and half of the city shall go
forth into captivity, and the residue of the people shall not be cut
off from the city." Now this was not the capture in A.D. 70,
because then no residue was left in the city, indeed, no city was
left. But this destruction is immediately to precede the personal
intervention of Jehovah, for the next verse (3) adds : " *Then* shall
Jehovah go forth, and fight against those nations . . . and His
feet shall stand in that day upon the mount of Olives."

It is to this dread time that Rev. 11 : 1, 2 points : " And there was given to me a reed like unto a rod : and one said, Rise, and measure the temple of God, and the altar, and them that worship therein.   And the court which is without the temple cast without, and measure it not ; for it was given unto [that is, into the power of] the nations : and the holy city shall they tread under foot forty and two months." The past tense " it *was* given " ($\dot{\epsilon}\delta\dot{o}\theta\eta$) is to be noted.   It puts the handing over of the city to the oppression of the nations into an indefinite past, and can refer back as far as to this prophecy in Daniel.

Now John was writing after A.D. 70, and therefore foretells some destruction of the city future to his day.   Nor can this verb *to tread under foot* refer to any peaceable holding of a city, as Jerusalem was held by the Turks for centuries, or as lately by the British.   To the former as Moslems the city was most scared, being the spot where Abraham offered up Ishmael (as they say), and there they built the great mosque that is still standing.   To the latter the city is sacred in a Christian sense, and they laboured to extend and beautify it. But *to tread down* ($\pi\alpha\tau\epsilon\omega$) means as a man stamps violently on a serpent (Luke 10 : 19), or as grapes are crushed to pulp in the press (Rev. 14 : 20 ; 19 : 15), both actions being fierce and destructive.

It was to *this* destruction of Jerusalem, not to A.D. 70, that the Lord pointed when speaking on Olivet of the end times and of His coming in glory (Luke 21).   He first warned the apostles that the end was not to be soon : " the end is not immediately " (9). Having thus carried their minds far forward He spoke of the international wars that would usher in the end, and of accompanying disturbances on earth and in heaven (10, 11).   He mentioned also a *universal* persecution of His followers : " ye shall be hated of all men for My name's sake " (12-19).   This is to take place *before* any other events He predicted (12).   With this compare Rev. 17, a picture of the end times, when the " harlot " shall dominate the " beast " and will use the power to make herself drunken with the blood of the saints.

There is no ground to turn back at this point in the prophecy to A.D. 70.   The Lord passes at once to that invasion of Palestine by Antichrist which had been before detailed by Isaiah (10 : 28-32), to culminate at Zion in the horrors shown in Zech. 14 : 1, 2 above considered.   He said : " When ye shall see Jerusalem being encompassed ($\kappa\upsilon\kappa\lambda o\upsilon\mu\epsilon\nu\eta\nu$) with armies . . . then . . . flee unto the mountains."   This has been generally, but wrongly, applied to

A.D. 70. It is said that the Christians then in Jerusalem acted upon this verse and fled from the city before Titus invested it, and went to Pella beyond the Jordan. Eusebius asserted that they did so flee, but he wrote from tradition some two and a half centuries later. It is not otherwise known. But even if they did so flee, it is a mistake to say that they did so because of the Lord's words in question. Eusebius does not suggest this, but, quite to the contrary, says distinctly that they acted upon divine counsel given to certain godly men at the time (*Eccl. Hist.*, Book III, c. 5).

His words are : " The whole body, however, of the church at Jerusalem, having been commanded by a divine revelation, given to men of approved piety there before the war, removed from the city, and dwelt at a certain town beyond the Jordan, called Pella." The " men of approved piety " were not the apostles, for he has just before stated that these had been already " driven from the land of Judea " and " had gone forth to preach the gospel to all nations." That he does not suggest that this removal was actuated by any word of Christ is clear ; for, whereas in c. 7 he has shown that he thought the Lord referred to A.D. 70, in this place, on the contrary, he says the Christians acted upon a revelation given "before the war," which could hardly mean nearly forty years before.

But if the words of Christ are considered strictly they suffice of themselves to forbid application to A.D. 70. For He said : " These are days of vengeance, that *all* things that are *written* may be fulfilled" (Luke 21 : 22). Now (i) nothing specific as to A.D. 70 was written in the Old Testament ; and (ii) very many other things *are* written there about Jerusalem which were *not* fulfilled in A.D. 70 but still remain to be fulfilled. Such passages as Isaiah 10 and Zechariah 14 are among these.

Moreover, speaking of the " great distress " and " wrath " and slaughter, and the sending into captivity of the people, He added, " Jerusalem shall be trodden down of the nations, until the times of the nations be fulfilled " (Luke 21 : 23, 24). This is the same verb *to tread down* that comes in Rev. 11 : 2 as above, and the Lord shows that when this treading down takes place it will continue to the very conclusion of Gentile world power, that is, to the destruction of Antichrist shown in Isa, 10 and Zech. 14 cited. For when Isaiah's description of his advance has brought him to Zion the thought then passes to the Lord cutting him down (33) ; and when Zechariah has described the horrors of the siege, capture and captivity (as repeated by Christ in Luke 21 : 24), then in verse 3 he too at once speaks of the Lord appearing to deliver Zion.   Thus also Rev. 11 similarly contains both the " treading down " (between trumpets 6 and 7) and the Lord taking over the kingdom of the world (trumpet 7).

We therefore prefer to regard the destruction of the city foretold in Daniel 9 : 26 as pointing to this final overthrow, thus bringing all the matters of the prediction within the period of the Seventy Sevens.   This harmonizes with the feature of our passage that it connects the destruction of the city with the "end " : " the people of the coming prince shall destroy the city and the sanctuary ; and his *end* (or, the end thereof, that is, of the destruction) shall be in the flood."   Now Titus did not come to his end in that war, nor did the flood of desolations for Jerusalem then end.

11. *The Flood*.   This expressive figure for an invading army is used in Isaiah 28 : 2 of Antichrist as the Lord's agent for destroying the wicked of Israel : " Behold, the Lord hath a mighty and strong one ; as a tempest of hail, a destroying storm, as a tempest of mighty waters overflowing, shall he cast down to the earth [cp. Dan. 8 : 10, 12] with the hand " (with violence, *Variorum* and R.V. margin).   This must refer to a final overwhelming of the ungodly of Israel, because " *in that day* shall Jehovah of hosts be for a crown of glory, and a diadem of beauty, unto the residue of His people " (ver. 5).   It is therefore of the agreement of these apostates with Antichrist that the chapter afterward speaks (15) : " Because ye have said we have made a covenant with death, and with Sheol [Greek *Hades*] are we at agreement ; when the overflowing scourge shall pass through, it shall not come unto us ; for we have made lies our refuge, and under falsehood have we hid ourselves."   Then immediately Messiah is mentioned as the only security and safety, the foundation stone in Zion, and apart from trust in Him only destruction shall befall them.   This destruction is again pictured as a flood, so that the very flood they had hoped to escape shall destroy them.

For this same figure see Jer. 46 : 7, 8 and Nahum 1 : 8.

12. Thus " *unto the end shall be war* " ; the city, once this destruction has commenced, shall know no respite until the time of Gentile rule shall cease for ever at the coming of the King.

13. " *Even the desolations determined*."   Israel's chastisements are not left to chance, or to the malice of those whom God uses to inflict them.   He loves them for their fathers' sake, and yet more for the sake of Him who, after the flesh, was born in their race.

The length and severity of His dealings are " determined," and will end when their end is served. But not until then. This expression of the angel referred Daniel to the great passage of Isaiah mentioned, uttered some two centuries earlier : " A remnant shall return, even the remnant of Jacob, unto the mighty God. Foʳ though thy people, Israel, be as the sand of the sea, only a remnant of them shall return : a consumption is determined, overflowing with righteousness. " For a consummation, and that determined, shall the Lord, Jehovah of hosts, make in the midst of all the earth " (Isa. 10 : 21–23). Thus Antichrist himself will destroy their trust in himself, and the small remnant shall trust in their God, whereupon the desolation shall immediately give place to restoration.

14. *The Covenant with the Prince* is that already predicted in Isaiah 28 above cited. " The many " means the multitude, the great majority. It means Israel, because they are the theme of the prophecy (Dan. 9 : 27), and because the interruption of their public worship is at once mentioned.

The prophets show distinctly that, at that time, the vast majority of the people of Israel will be ungodly. Zephaniah 1 : 1–6 distinguishes four classes : (i) Rejectors of Jehovah, open idolators, worshippers of Baal and the stars ; an organized idolatry with its priesthood. What has been can be. There was such a section in the days of Antiochus Epiphanes. In the middle ages many Jews espoused the idolatry of the Roman church to escape persecution. This will occur again, in hope of escaping the final flood of persecution. (ii) Compromisers, who will seek to conjoin idolatry with some respect for the name of Jehovah. (iii) Apostates, who had turned back from following Jehovah as they formerly had done. (iv) Those indifferent to religion, who neither seek, nor even inquire after the God of their fathers. The vast majority of the Jews now in Palestine, as far as we observed in two sojourns there of late years, belong to the two last classes. Zephaniah's prophecy has to do with " the great day of Jehovah " (1 : 14).

Zechariah 13 : 8, 9 announces the cutting off and death of two-thirds then in the land, and the third part having to go through the fire to be purified. So will be reached the condition foretold in Isaiah 1 : 9, that only a " very small remnant " will survive. It is out of this remnant that the new national life will be built up (Mic. 4 : 6, 7).

It has been of late the policy of Israel to seek aid from Gentile powers. First Dr. Herzl sought the Sultan. Then visits followed to this and that government. Until recently the British were in question. This policy will lead finally to an agreement with Antichrist, in hope of his protection during the floods of distress then submerging the nations. It will be an agreement with death and Hades because it will be known that he is being resuscitated from that world of the dead, and having alliance with him who has the power of death, the devil (Rev. 13 : 2–4 ; 17 : 8). Thus extreme can become the apostasy of those privileged with divine revelation. But they will be bitterly deceived. His aim being to attract all worship to himself he will forcibly suppress their religion, set up his own image in their holy place, and command its adoration under penalty of death. Thus will burst the final persecution, unparalleled and, God be praised, never to be repeated (Matt. 24 : 21), " the tribulation, the great " of Rev. 7 : 14.

When this agreement shall have been confirmed the wise will know that the final Seven of years has commenced, that the end days are present, that the consummation of the age has arrived. They will expect the violation of the covenant after three years and a half, and will not be overwhelmed with surprise, having been told beforehand by this prophecy. Then will it be seen in fulness that the knowledge of prophetic Scripture is simply priceless.

This desolation will be that " consumption that is determined, overflowing with righteousness," that " consummation strictly decided upon, which Jehovah of hosts shall make in all the earth " (Isa. 10 : 20–23). And being the *consummation* it will be the conclusion ; the flood shall reach its highest point, shall perfect the dreadful but so indispensable work of purging the sinners out of Zion, and then subside. And after both the desolated and their desolator have been thus dealt with in judgment, the tempest shall cease, the clouds break, and the Sun of righteousness shall shine forth with healing in His wings for them that feared Jehovah and thought upon His name when it was very treason to mention that name (Mal. 4 : 2). They will have been " hidden in the day of Jehovah's anger " (Zeph. 2 : 3 ; Isa. 26 : 20), and, with all the meek, shall shine forth as the sun in the kingdom of their Father, and inherit the earth (Matt. 13 : 43 ; 5 : 5). Then at last shall all men discern clearly between the righteous and the wicked, between him that serveth God and him that serveth Him not (Mal. 3 : 18), " so that men shall say, Verily there is a reward for the righteous ; Verily there is a God that judgeth in the earth " (Ps. 58 : 11).

CHAPTER X

A WORLD UNSEEN BUT NEAR

BY THE THIRD YEAR OF CYRUS DANIEL WAS ABOUT NINETY years of age, an example of Solomon's saying, " The hoary head is a crown of glory, It shall be (or, it is) found in the way of righteousness " (Prov. 16 : 31). A man who for eighty years has walked on that road is a noble and encouraging sight. His life had been strenuous and exacting : few statesmen live so long : yet his faculties retain such vigour that he can see and understand the great and long and elaborate vision that completes the revelation that God will give to and through him.

I. Repetition gives emphasis. In verse 1 the vision is three times termed a " thing " : " a thing was revealed . . . the thing was true . . . he understood the thing." This emphatic use of the singular number indicates the unity, the oneness of the whole vision. Though including a considerable number of " things " (12 : 7, 8) they are all but one thing, not a series of disconnected events or interrupted groups of events.

II. Early habits persist, whether good or bad. How important therefore that they be formed with care. Our first view of Daniel is of a youth of noble rank who has mastery over his eating and drinking : that mastery he held to the close of his long life, though having full opportunity for self-gratification. Extreme age induces weakness and craves indulgence, yet Daniel can deny himself all pleasant food, and abstain from flesh and wine and the refinement of ointments. He is still master of his appetites.

But this abstinence was not asceticism or formality. It was the outward expression of inward distress. His soul was so sorrowful that he had no heart for luxuries or even usual and proper enjoyments. This is true fasting : " I was mourning three whole weeks " (2). Why ? Was it at the meagre response of his people to the royal permission that they might return to their own land ? Some two years had passed since the decree of Cyrus, and only some 50,000 had shown love enough to the holy land and the city of their God to go back (Ezra. 2 : 64, 65). The majority were content to remain elsewhere, though in banishment, and with deprivation of the privileges of freedom, of national unity, of worship. Well might the aged saint mourn that though God had opened His door the people cared not to enter it. Well may such as have the mind of God to-day mourn that many to whom access to the heavenly places and heavenly privileges is open " mind earthly things."

From the carnally minded the face of God is averted : upon such the Sun of righteousness does not arise with healing in His wings : but " thus saith Jehovah : To this man will I look, even to him that is poor and of a contrite spirit, and that trembleth at My word " (Isa. 66 : 2). Of this promise Daniel found fulfilment, as do all of his spirit. Still are the eyes of such enlightened to know the hope of God's calling and to learn His purposes (Eph. 1 : 18) ; whereas those whose minds are set on earthly things see only earthly things, and these in a fog of human ideas in which objects are seen distorted and take fantastic or fearsome forms.

III. To the materialist the world of heavenly beings is unreal. To the spiritist it is real but deceptive. To the majority of believers it is a land admitted to exist, yet known only by hearsay. But Daniel was familiar with its inhabitants. The histories of his race told of many visitants therefrom and he himself had conversed with such and been instructed by them. And now he meets and hears another and mighty prince of that world, and so deep was the impression that the day and month when it occurred were duly noted, and the place. Such rare hours are never forgotten. Would that we all knew more of them ; then should we use with truth the smoothly sung, but little experienced lines :

> " There, there on eagle wings we soar,
> And time and sense seem all no more,
> And heaven comes down the soul to greet,
> And glory crowns the mercy seat."

The appearance of this heavenly being is given in eight particulars.

1. His form was human : " behold, a man." This is so frequently the case in Scripture as to raise the inquiry whether Adam's form was the first of its order, or whether it was not rather moulded after an already existing type, illustrated in a higher form in the angels in heaven, and of which the ultimate standard is God himself, even as it is written that God said : " Let us make man in *our image*, after our likeness. And God created man in *His own image*, in the *image of God* created He him " (Gen. 1 : 26, 27). Here again the

triple statement gives emphasis. The term " image " naturally implies external resemblance, and it seems only what might be expected that a being in whose nature the Son of God should at last and for ever sit on the throne of God should from his creation have a human counterpart of the form of God, such as when glorified should suit that high place. May it not be rather in attributes and accompaniments that the " form of God," in which the Son was originally, differed from the " form of man " which He in grace assumed, even as it is in majesty that the " form " of the sovereign differs mainly from that of his subjects ?

2. This angelic being was clothed in linen, that is, in the flowing oriental garb, or a girdle were needless. Linen is in Scripture the garment pre-eminently of priestly service, of access to the holy place, the presence of God.

3. The girdle was of pure gold. Gold is the accompaniment of princely rank and office (Dan. 5 : 16, 29).

4. His body was like the beryl, probably suggesting that lovely tinted white which tells of perfect health. No element of sin had tarnished the pristine beauty of this heavenly form.

5. His face shone like the lightning, as in the case of Moses a reflection of the glory of God who is light, into Whose face they both had looked.

6. His eyes were as blazing lamps, flashing with intelligence and penetrating discernment.

7. His arms and feet were as burnished brass, as of one who walked up and down amidst the stones of fire that pave the path to the throne of the God who is a consuming fire (Ezek. 28 : 14 ; Heb. 12 : 29).

8. His voice was full and mighty as the roar of a vast crowd, a voice to awe, subdue, alarm, command, as occasion might require.

These particulars are so closely parallel to the description of the Son of man glorified, as seen by John (Rev. 1), as to prompt the suggestion that it was He whom Daniel saw. But this seems excluded by Daniel's narrative. If verse 10, the first sentence of 16, and verse 18 be put in brackets the narrative is seen to be a continuous interview with the one being described in the vision, and he speaks of himself simply as one " sent " (11), a messenger, and he shows that he was not able alone to overcome the opposition of a rebel angel, the prince of Persia, but required the aid of another angel. Thus he was not the Lord of all angels, but only one of these.

Others have thought that Michael, also here mentioned, and in ch. 12 : 1, and called in Jude 9 " the archangel," is the Son of God in angelic guise.   But this is excluded by what the former angel here says of him, that " he is *one* of the chief princes," and that one who stands in the interests of the people of Israel.   The special interests of the Son of God are not thus limited to Israel. Moreover, in Rev. 12 : 7–10 Michael is distinguished from God and from Christ, and is seen as one who serves in the establishing of Christ's sovereignty by overthrowing Satan.

The true lesson from the correspondence marked is not that this angel is the Son of God, but that the glory given to such is akin to that put now in fulness upon the glorified Son of man, and that the attributes and powers of the higher angels are a reflection of His.   For all in the whole creation that is good, pure, glorious is but a display in the creature of that which the Son is ; in it derived, in Him original.   Of these powers and glories He voluntarily emptied Himself to become man, and now as man is reinvested by the Father, as a reward for His fidelity here, with that glory which He had originally with the Father before creation (Phil. 2 : 5–11 ; John 17 : 5).   It is out of His fulness that the creature ever did and still does receive.

IV.   It is healthy for man to remember that he is *not* the most glorious or powerful being in the universe.   Whatever hides pride from man is salutary.   If so advanced and true a saint as Daniel was prostrated by the glory of the angel, and felt corrupt, how much more must the rest of us need humbling into the dust !   May the contemplation of these mighty messengers of the Most High as they are revealed in Scripture prove a sanctifying influence. Though we see them not, by sight or in vision, they are near, and are sent forth to serve us (Heb. 1 : 14).   They find their delight, and show their real dignity, by serving us who as yet are their inferiors.   Thus are they partakers of the moral glory of their Lord who was in the midst of His servants as their servant (Luke 22 : 27), and Who, in the very day of His enthronement, shall again " come forth and serve them," that is, those who have served Him by serving *their* fellow-servants, and thus have now manifested His spirit (Luke 12 : 35–48).

How searching is the work of God in the soul.   The aged saint faced with the glory of a heavenly being, feels his very " comeliness," the very elements in him upon which complacency might have feasted, turn to corruption (8).   Thus does heaven abase earth, strip the best of his best, exhaust the strength of the strong, till he limps for the rest of his days, so that there shall be *no* confidence in the flesh, but the Lord alone be exalted.

Only he who is willing to be thus abased in his own estimate of himself will ever be conscious of or understand what Daniel describes, even that " a hand touched me . . . one touched my lips . . . there touched me again one . . . and strengthened me " (10 : 16, 18). And this one had " the similitude of the sons of men," and was, we think, that Son of man whom Daniel had long before seen in the clouds of heaven, the same One who afterward laid His hand upon His prostrate servant John and strengthened him to receive yet fuller and more awful visions than Daniel saw (Rev. 1 : 17).

When such sacred seasons, or anything like them, however inferior, are granted to ourselves, and the soul feels shattered and undone, then let us take courage and say to that grand yet blessed One :

> " Thy touch has still its ancient power,
>   No word from Thee can fruitless fall,
>   Hear in this solemn, searching hour,
>   And in Thy mercy heal us all " ;

and the humble shall find in truth that He is indeed " the same yesterday, and to-day, and forever." For such a soul is " greatly beloved " by that Lord and His heavenly servants, nor need they tremble with fear ; rather for these are strength and peace provided (10 : 19).

Yet must that soul not be surprised if restoration from such inward and outward collapse be wrought but gradually. It is safer so. The first touch of that hand raised the prostrate prophet so far as to lean totteringly upon his hands and knees (10). Then the angel encouraged him to stand upright, but still his frame trembled, his face was set downward, and his lips remained dumb (15). Then that same hand touched his lips, and power of speech returned (16). Again that life-imparting touch, and vigour revived to see, to hear, to understand (18).

All this has its counterpart in deep soul experience, known doubtless to few, by them seldom mentioned, but the secret of that humility, that sense of God, which others discern in them and covet, but which will not, cannot be attained until they be ready like Daniel to seek God with the whole heart, at every cost of time and self-pleasing. A theological professor said to one of his students who was marked by great grace and power, " I would give *all I possess* to get what you have ! " and was answered, " Then, sir, you may have it, for *that is just what it cost me* ! "

When the price has been paid, and the Daniel experience has been in some measure known, both its exhaustion and its touch of power, there may remain still a " tottering and trembling," even as Paul said, " I was with you in weakness and in fear and in much trembling " (I Cor. 2 : 3). But He who has begun the recovery will perfect it. Presently the soul will stand upright ; then the eyes will be lifted to the One that has so effectually and tenderly touched us ; the lips will hold communion with heaven, and strength will be infused. Then the soul will have inward sympathy with him who wrote :

> " For Thy heart my heart has a language ;
> For other hearts it has none."

To one so renewed into the image of Him who created him the word will come, " Fear not, I have much people in this city," and henceforth service rendered in conscious weakness will never fail of blessed effect (Acts 18 : 10). The words of Daniel and of Paul are still bearing fruit.

V. In ancient times it was a common conviction that each king and kingdom was under the protection of a particular god. Thus Isaiah mentions that Sennacherib of Nineveh " was worshipping in the house of Nisroch *his* god " when his sons murdered him (Isa. 37 : 38) ; and Nebuchadnezzar said of Daniel that his " name was Belteshazzar, according to the name of *my* god," that is, Bel (Dan. 4 : 8).

So profound was this belief that a defeated king (Ahaz) was known to transfer his religious devotion to the gods of his conqueror in hope of obtaining their help (II Chron. 28 : 23). The record adds the instructive comment : " But they were the ruin of him and of all Israel," suggesting that the " gods " were not the blocks of stone or metal that represented them, but were real and malevolent beings who, by permission of God, could effect the ruin of apostates like Ahaz and his people.

Such worship and devotion both gratified the demons who desired and attracted it and enslaved the devotees to Satan and his kingdom. Thus was it true that men " sacrificed to demons " (Deut. 32 : 17 ; Ps. 106 : 37 ; I Cor. 10 : 20). And that these demon princes were wicked is clear from the wickedness that developed the more in their subjects and worshippers the more they honoured these gods.

Satan's dear delight being the ruin of man, it served well his interests that these unseen princes should incite and assist nations to destroy one another. That the reputation of now this god, now that, should suffer from his subjects being defeated in war mattered little, for one god gained influence as another lost it, and the carnage went on.

Our chapter unveils this dread and powerful situation. It speaks of three of these angel princes, one by name. There was a prince of the kingdom of Persia (13, 20) then operating; another of Greece, who should later begin to act in the realm of Persia (" the prince of Greece shall come," ver. 20); and a third, " Michael your prince " (21) ". . . the great prince who standeth for the children of thy people " (12 : 1). If the Variorum Bible rendering of ver. 13 is correct Michael is " the *first* of the chief princes." This would agree with his title " the archangel," and with the facts that it is he who is powerful enough to enter into personal conflict with Satan, who had overcome such a host of lesser " stars of heaven," and that it is he who will command the army that will eject Satan and his angels from heaven (Rev. 12 : 7).

That this prince of Persia is an angel, and a rebel angel, is shown by the fact that he withstood God's heavenly messenger : that he was a mighty spirit is seen by the length of time he was able to obstruct him, even three weeks, and in that his opposition was only overcome when Michael threw his weight into the scale on the side of his fellow-soldier (13). Thus reinforced the latter prevailed (Darby : whose German translation reads, " I carried off the victory "—*ich trug den Sieg*); he was no longer needed there with the kings of Persia and could fulfil his mission to Daniel.

The positions and actions of these angel princes is part of the scheme of administration of the universe. Other details of the organization in the unseen world are that certain angels (of great honour before God, for they have unrestricted access to His presence) are in charge of little children (Matt. 18 : 10; comp. Esther 1 : 14), and that over each Christian assembly there is an angel guardian and protector (Rev. 2 and 3). This need occasion no surprise, since such an one cares for even the earthly people of God, and the churches being the special object of attack from Satan's forces greatly need heavenly protectors,

Surely all this throws light upon obscure and startling happenings in affairs international. What else but just such a universal spirit activity can reasonably explain the universal upheaval of our time ? Colossal and simultaneous disturbances have caused all over the world vast changes such as were neither foreseen nor even desired by men, nor could have been produced by men in so short a time or on so world-wide a scale.

Again, of late, men of whom the world had scarcely heard rose suddenly out of obscurity to power, men who simply *dominated* millions of their fellows, fascinating them with a perfectly preternatural influence, such as extremely few ever exercise. These quickly showed a genius in solving ancient disputes—as between Church and State ; they bluffed or tricked objecting and more powerful nations and their statesmen ; repudiated treaties and solemn promises as they pleased, and those aggrieved, though mightier, could not redress the wrongs ; they easily overwhelmed and appropriated whole countries ; and in all respects displayed an astuteness and energy that manifestly had come upon them almost suddenly and without premonition from anything seen in their past.

Portentous is the situation that has been thus produced. Well may the hearts of men fail for fear as to what may develop therefrom. Nevertheless let the God-fearing be still. The experience of Crœsus before mentioned (p. 59) has been often repeated, as formerly, in Alexander the Great and Napoleon, and recently in Mussolini and Hitler, and there will be other fulfilments yet. Let the righteous be still, and walk before God in a perfect way.

> Wait on Jehovah, and keep his way,
> And he shall exalt thee to inherit the land :
> When the wicked are cut off, thou shalt see it.
> I have seen the wicked in great power,
> And spreading himself like a green tree in its native soil.
> But one passed by, and lo, he was not :
> Yea, I sought him, but he could not be found.
> Mark the perfect man, and behold the upright :
> For there is a reward for the man of peace.
>
> Ps. 37 : 34–37.

VI. How great is the influence that the holy and prayerful exert that these so powerful demon princes dread them, as this prince of Persia dreaded Daniel. What endeavours they had made to destroy or seduce him. And now that he set his face to seek

God, and a messenger from the throne of heaven is despatched to bring the answer to his prayers, this evil prince fights hard to obstruct this true Mercury, the messenger of the Most High and succeeds in this for three weeks. Here is one explanation of delay in the answering of prayer. The very first day that Daniel had prayed his prayer had been heard and the Divine answer had been sent forth, but the messenger had been intercepted and obstructed. Let the man of prayer pray on. His prayers, if guided by the Word, are accepted by God through Jesus Christ, and are, indeed, part of the appointed process to effect the purposes of God for the fulfilment of that which he asks. And though mighty foes may provoke conflict and commotion in that unseen world, all the resources of heaven, up to the greatest prince before the throne of God, shall be set in motion to accomplish the promises of Jehovah. How powerful is persevering prayer! It is the mightiest force that man can wield. " The supplication of a righteous man availeth much in its working " (Jas. 5 : 16).

CHAPTER XI

THE WRITING OF TRUTH

" I WILL TELL THEE THAT WHICH IS INSCRIBED IN THE WRITING of truth. . . . Now will I show thee the truth " (10 : 21 ; 11 : 2).

I. There is, then, in the heavenly realm that which corresponds to writing. Indeed, it is called plainly a " writing." God's " book " is mentioned frequently. The first passage is Ex. 32 : 32, where the way it is mentioned by Moses shows that he was already aware of that book and knew that a name written therein might be erased (see also Rev. 3 : 5). The last place is Rev. 21 : 27, which speaks of " the Lamb's book of life." The passages last preceding this are Rev. 20, 12–15, where the book of life determines destiny, and where other " books " are mentioned. This implies various writings, in this place obviously the records of the works of men.

But the " writing of truth " is a statement in advance of events foreseen as to take place on earth, and it is of these that the angel informed Daniel and us. Writing and reading are, therefore, not a human invention, but a power that associates men with angels and with God. With God, for it was with His own finger that the ten words were written upon the tables of stone at Sinai. That the angel had read this " writing of truth " is evident. And that angels quote Scripture so freely shows that they can read human records. Satan quoted from a psalm when tempting Christ.

Thus angels are instructed by the written page. Those of them to whom these books may be accessible have therein proof of the foreknowledge of God, are made acquainted with His purposes, and can co-operate intelligently in furthering them. If these writings are open to Satan and his angels, or any of them, these also can learn what God has in mind and has foretold, what He will allow to be done or will disallow, and can utilize this knowledge by furthering or opposing what is written. Certainly that knowledge from the writing of truth which is found in Daniel 11 and 12 can be known and used by them, as also what is in other scriptures.

But we must beware of attaching to these writings a fatalistic element. Scripture forbids this. Names written therein in grace may be expunged for sin (Ex. 32 : 33). Covenants may be revoked (Num. 14 : 34). Blessings promised and judgments denounced may both be cancelled (Ezek. 18 and 33). God acts on moral grounds for moral ends. Foreknowledge does not of necessity involve foreordination, or the Holy One would be responsible for the sins of angels and men. One may get to know that a burglar intends to raid his premises, but he does not foreordain it.

This heavenly writing is *truth*. It is not the shrewd speculations of men or of angels as to what is probable or desirable. It is not conjecture based on long observation of the ways of angels, demons, and men. It is a faithful transcript of what the foreknowledge of God sees as to take place in the realm international of men. Thus for faith, in angels and men, it becomes a priceless preparation and guide, a light shining in a truly dark region.

II. How thought-provoking is Scripture. The angel must say that of all the hosts on high " there is none that strengtheneth himself with me against these [rebel princes ; or perhaps, concerning these matters, that is, for their furtherance] but Michael your prince " (10 : 21). Why is this ? Are the others too engaged in other high affairs of the kingdom of the heavens ? or does each wait for specific divine direction before acting ? or is it that Israel being the pivot of earth's national affairs it is specially the business of Israel's heavenly prince to co-operate in the matters mentioned and to be mentioned ?

III. As it appeared to men Darius the Mede reached the throne of Babylon by the will of Cyrus the Persian. From history we learn that Cyrus had dethroned his grandfather, king of the Medes, had reversed the ancient subordination of the Persians to the Medes, and had made the former the superior partner. From him Darius " *received* the kingdom " (5 : 31); not " *took* it," as A.V. here, though at 9 : 1 it says rightly that he " was made " king. In the former place, as so often, being inexact as to detail translating, the A.V. is historically erroneous and leaves itself open to criticism, besides hiding what the correct rendering (as R.V.) hints.

It would seem that Darius at this first stage of the conquest of Babylonia was made king over that newly-acquired territory, styled in 9 : 1 " the realm of the Chaldeans," while Cyrus exercised the sovereignty over the whole of his far vaster empire (10 : 1), to which at his death his son Cambyses succeeded. Now what enabled Darius to maintain this new and onerous position in face of all

the intrigue and difficulty that must have beset him, as they ever
do one thus exalted, and especially ruling a conquered people, ever
ready to give trouble and to revolt, and who did actually rebel
against a later Darius? Is not the real, though unseen, cause
given in the angel's words "And as for me [my part has been that]
in the first year of Darius the Mede I stood up to confirm and
strengthen him" (ver. 1)? God purposed that this new power
should befriend Israel, and so both Cyrus and Darius received
heavenly support and direction (II Chron. 36 : 22, 23). By the
knowledge of this Daniel would be encouraged to expect the fulfilment of the promises of God, however unlikely and forbidding
might be the prospects humanly considered.

IV. *The Revelation Imparted. The Near Future.*

The vision of ch. 7 was connected with the image of ch. 2 by
the mention of ten horns that should arise on the head of the fourth
beast. Then the scene passed to the final ruler who should be
destroyed to make way for the kingdom of God.

Ch. 8 showed the same features of just enough reference to
the development of world affairs to connect the present and near
future with the final things, whereupon the scene passed at once
to that same little horn and his destruction at the end of days
by the Prince of princes.

Our present chapter (11) follows the same order. Verses 2
and 4 show the then near future, and again, as we understand,
the scene passes straight to the last time, with yet fuller details
of the days preceding the last emperor and of his doings and his
destruction.

1. There were to be four more Persian kings. They proved to
be Cambyses, the son of Cyrus (Ahasuerus, Ezra 4 : 6), Smerdis,
the usurper (Artaxerxes, Ezra 4 : 7), Darius Hystaspes (Ezra 4 : 24),
and Xerxes (Ahasuerus, Esther 1 : 1). The last did indeed grow
rich, and did employ, and lose, vast riches and power in the celebrated attack on Greece, where he was defeated in the naval battle
of Salamis, 480 B.C. (2).

On the ground of revenging this invasion Alexander the Great,
the "mighty king" of ver. 3, invaded Persia and destroyed that
empire (333 B.C.), died early (323 B.C.), and his kingdom was divided
into four parts, as before mentioned. But none of his family
succeeded to his authority, nor did any of the generals who divided
the empire rule with his supreme power ; and in due time the whole

Grecian empire was " plucked up," and passed to " others besides these " generals, that is, at last, to the Romans.

2. This succinct and exact outline of the near future contains some seventeen details to occur during a period of some two centuries. These are (i, ii, iii) three Perisan monarchs would yet rule, no more, no less, before (iv) a fourth. (v) He should be richer than them all, and (vi) should grow gradually strong (" waxed ") through riches that is, rather than by military or other means. (vii) He should employ his whole resources in an attack on Greece. (viii) Later there should rise a monarch of great power, who (ix) should exert vast dominion, (x) so as to rule autocratically, and do exactly as his own will determined. (xi) But he would have but a brief career, for " when," that is, almost as soon as, he should stand up, (xii) his kingdom should be broken, and (xiii) be divided into four parts, no more, no less. Yet (xiv) none of his family should inherit any part, an unnatural circumstance ; nor (xv) should those who took power, singly or together, have such authority as his. (xvi) In the sequel his empire should be done away, be " plucked up," and (xvii) it should pass away entirely from his successors.

The student of history knows that all this had literal fulfilment, though none of the persons concerned had the least idea of fulfilling Hebrew prophecy or probably knew a word of the predictions. Again the issue must be pressed that this was either a shameless literary fraud, if written after the events, or else it was what it purports to be, a divine prophecy, a statement of what the angel knew was in the writing of truth on high. Had it been the former it was indeed a *blasphemous* fraud, by claiming the authority of heaven so as to foist the deceit on men, and no pious Jew would have thus invoked the wrath of Jehovah under the third commandment of the law (Ex. 20 : 7).

The strict fulfilment of the angel's words thus far is rational ground for faith to await the exact fulfilment of the remainder of his forecast.

V. *The Approach of the End.*

Thus far devout students are agreed as to the application of this prophecy, but here difference of judgment enters. Of the expositions offered only two will be here considered.

(i) It is suggested that from ver. 5 to ver. 33 is a detailed prophecy of the conflicts between Egypt and Syria which followed the division of Alexander's empire, extending to the reign of Antiochus Epiphanes of Syria, with his oppression of the Jews and desecration of the temple, and the heroic resistance of the Maccabees. Then at verses 34, 35 the prediction passes on to the time of the end and the last emperor, the Antichrist. This view was set forth by B. W. Newton in *The Prospects of the Ten Kingdoms*, and a full, lucid, and learned exposition of it is in Pember's *The Great Prophecies of the Centuries concerning Israel and the Gentiles*.

(ii) The other interpretation may be studied in Dr. S. P. Tregelles' very valuable *Remarks on the Prophetic Visions in the Book of Daniel*. This devout scholar considered (*a*) that the unnoticed interval is found between verses 4 and 5, not between verses 33 and 34. (*b*) That at ver. 5 the thought passes direct from the days of the ancient Grecian empire to the end days. (*c*) That verses 5 to 20 foretell the political events that will lead up directly to Antichrist, and (*d*) that verses 21 to the end give his career.

It is to be observed :

1. That both views agree (*a*) as to the *commencement* of the prophecy : it is the Persian and Grecian period that immediately followed the time of Daniel ; and (*b*) as to the *close* of the prophecy : it is the time and career of Antichrist. The difference is (*c*) whether verses 5 to 33 apply to the period extending from the division of Alexander's empire to the days of the Maccabees (cents. 3 and 2 B.C.), or (*d*) to the years immediately to precede the rule of Antichrist in days still future.

2. (*a*) Upon the former view it is conceivable that the Jews of that earlier period drew light, strength, comfort from this portion of the prophecy as they went through the trials of those years. But then the direct application and value of the portion ended. (*b*) On the second view the section of the chapter will yield instruction and vigour to saints who will go through the closing period of this age. They will be able to follow with exactness the political disturbances of the Near East, to recognize the advent of Antichrist, to observe his rise and progress, and thus seeing these things coming to pass men of faith will lift up their heads knowing that their redemption has drawn nigh (Luke 21 : 28). In view of the wholly unparalleled severity and spiritual danger of that period, and the vast need believers will then have of comfort and guidance, the latter seems the more needful and likely purpose of the predictions. Nor is there any other scripture that will afford them the detail knowledge here given.

3. On the former view this final passage of *Daniel* differs in form from those preceding ; on the latter view it exactly corresponds thereto.

(*a*) In ch. 2 the interpretation dwelt but briefly upon the lengthy period of Gentile dominion from the head of gold to the period of the feet, only 17 lines sufficing for this, and then 30 lines being given to the closing days of the age.

(*b*) In ch. 7 the whole of the long chapter is occupied with the end days and especially with Antichrist, the little horn.

(*c*) In ch. 8 six verses (3–8) suffice for the near future ; then the vision passes from Alexander's successors direct to the end days and the same little horn, whose affairs occupy 17 verses.

(*d*) In the prophecy of the Seventy Sevens in ch. 9 the rebuilding of the city in troublous times, under the kings of Persia, was mentioned, then the predictions once more passed over the Syrian period, touched briefly on the cutting off of Messiah when sixty-nine sevens should have passed, and went on, as had the former visions, direct to the Antichrist and the consummation (27). This habit of touching quite briefly the present and the near future and then passing to the close of this age characterizes prophecy from first to last. Bitter as were the times of the Syrian kings yet were they not so essentially different as to require separate and detail fore-telling. This remark applies to the political events and persecutions during the general course of this Christian period also.

(*e*) This suggests how to read ch. 11. Verses 2, 3, 4 lead down to the same point as ch. 8 1–8, the division of Alexander's empire, and then in ver. 5 the scene goes to the end of the age. There seems no good reason for regarding this closing vision as varying from the plan and form of those it completes.

4. The angel himself virtually settled the question as to the burden of what he would communicate. Anticipating that which he would impart he said : " I am come to make thee understand what shall befall thy people in *the latter days* [or, with Darby, *at the end* of the days], for the vision is yet for many [Darby, those] days " (10 : 14). This seems to preclude that three-fourths of the prophecy would be concerned with the then near future.

5. If the abomination of ver. 31 refers to the image that Anti-ochus set up in the temple then of necessity the " people who know their God " of the next verse, and who do exploits, must be the godly of that time, the Maccabees and their helpers, and the period in which they " fall by the sword " must be that period B.C.

But their "fall" is referred to again in ver. 34 "now when they shall fall," and again in ver. 35 "some of them that be wise shall fall," these "wise among the people" having been before mentioned in ver. 33. Thus, according to the grammar of the passage, verses 32–35 all refer to the same people and persons and these live under the persecution of ver. 31 when the abomination is set up. Now the period of ver. 35 is to continue "even to the time of *the end* because it is yet for the *time appointed*," and then, as all agree, the next verse (36) speaks of the great king of the end, Antichrist. It would therefore seem that the Antiochean period cannot be in view, however much it may have anticipated the time and events which are the direct subject of the prophecy. But if Antiochus be not the last figure in the predictions as far as ver. 33, then the kings of the south and the north previously detailed will not be the kings who preceded and led up to him, but those who will lead up to Antichrist, the king of ver. 36.

6. Ch. 12 : 1 begins, "And at that time," which shows that this chapter is part of the preceding vision. Indeed, there should be no chapter division here. Now ver. 11 says that "from the time that the continual burnt offering shall be taken away, and the abomination that maketh desolate shall be set up," there shall be so many days, and the whole context is of "the time of *the end*" (4, 9), the time for "*the end* of these wonders" (6). The Lord Jesus also places this "abomination of desolation" in the days shortly before His return (Matt. 24 : 15–31). But the words of 12 : 11 are plainly a repetition of those of 11 : 31 : "they shall take away the continual burnt offering, and they shall set up the abomination that maketh desolate." Save as referring back to the former place ch. 12 : 11 would be without explanation and beyond understanding, and also the definite article used twice, "*the* burnt offering" and "*the* abomination" imply that former mention. Therefore the abomination of 11 : 31 and 12 : 11 being the same, and the latter being future, in the days of Antichrist, so must the former be. Antiochus and his doings were a foreshadowing of this prophecy, but Antichrist and his doings will be its fulfilment. It is a weakness in the other view that it must avoid this plain grammatical connection of these two passages.

This conclusion is confirmed by the fact that the prophecy of the little horn in ch. 8 includes this taking away of the continual burnt offering and the desolating of the sanctuary (11, 12, 13); but *this* horn cannot be Antiochus, and must be Antichrist because he is to stand up against the Prince of princes and be broken without hand (8 : 25). Ch. 9 : 27 is to the same effect ; when " the sacrifice and oblation are caused to cease, and upon the wing of abominations one shall come that maketh desolate," then will be the time of the " consummation," not a time preceding the consummation by more than two thousand years, as Antiochus did.

Pusey says justly : " The image of the Antichrist of the Old Testament melts into the lineaments of the Antichrist himself. . . . One trait only of the anti-religious character of the Antichrist was true of Antiochus also : ' he shall speak marvellous things against the God of gods.' Blasphemy against God is an essential feature of any God-opposed power or individual. It belongs to Voltaire as much as to Antiochus. All besides has no place in him. . . . The characteristics of this infidel king are (1) self-exaltation above every god ; ' he shall magnify himself above every god ' ; (2) contempt of all religion ; (3) blasphemy against the true God ; (4) apostasy from the god of his fathers ; (5) disregarding the desire of women ; (6) the honouring of a god whom his fathers knew not. Of all these six marks, one only, in the least, agrees with Antiochus." Upon this Anderson comments : " The entire passage is valuable, and the arguments conclusive " (Pusey, *Daniel*, p. 93 ; *The Coming Prince*, p. 195).

We therefore follow Tregelles in regarding verse 5 and onward as applying to days yet to come, and which are almost a century nearer than when he wrote.

VI. *The Middle East.*

By the time intended in this prophecy

(a) The four empires of ch. 2 have neared their end, in a ten-kingdomed form.

(b) The fourth beast of ch. 7 has become supreme in the Mediterranean area and has formed that ten kingdom confederacy.

(c) The little horn of ch. 8 has yet to appear in the middle east, and

(d) as the Coming Prince of ch. 9 to complete the chastisement of Israel.

The chapter before us (11) enlarges upon his rise and doings, being thus marked by the feature of all the former visions, that each amplifies what has preceded.

Six sections in this account can be distinguished.

1, His connection with the past, with the Grecian empire of

Alexander, in verses 2–4, above considered. He is not to rise in the west, but in one of the areas into which Alexander's empire was divided (8 : 9). We saw ground to expect it to be the eastern, the Syrian, portion (see p. 114).

2. Verses 5–20 detail certain preceding conflicts to take place in that Middle Eastern region.

3. Verses 21–30 give his appearing and his opening activities.

4. Verses 30–35 enlarge upon that covenant with the Jews mentioned in the Seventy Sevens (9 : 27) and which he will violate.

5. Verses 36–39 show his supreme power and the inner explanation thereof.

6. Verses 40–45 describe the closing stages of his career.

We shall examine these sections in order.

1. As Antichrist is to rise in the Syrian area the prophecy naturally takes us to that country (the king of the north) and to its rival, Egypt (the king of the south). At the time of Daniel, and long after, Syria (the term now limited to the small country immediately north of Palestine) and what is now termed Assyria were one kingdom of Syria, ruling for a time to the frontiers of India.

2. From the conflicts now detailed it seems that at this stage of affairs neither Syria nor Egypt form part of the fourth, the ten-horned beast. That kingdom is everywhere presented as a unity, its ten kings being in alliance, all horns of one beast, not with internal conflicts, as is the case with these two kings now in question.

In the ancient times these two powers fought long for world supremacy, and " Syria," under Nebuchadnezzar, and later under Cambyses, gained and held it. This rivalry, like other features of the ancient world, will revive, and again cause vast miseries, especially to Palestine, which, as of old, both antàgonists must traverse. And again Syria will become master.

Thus it was foretold that at the end of the age Egypt and Syria would become independent sovereign states. After almost 2,000 years this has lately come to pass in measure. It implies that outside tutelage will cease, for Syria, Egypt, and Palestine are to be in a position to make treaties and wars. Political conditions move to-day in this direction. Let the thoughtful ponder the bearing of this as regards Britain's recent surrender of overlordship of the Middle East, or the power that other rulers would fain gain in that area. When Mandatory Powers have fulfilled Gods' will they will recede, and will find, as ever, that all their

endeavours to solve problems have but created new and greater
difficulties.

These new problems form the theme of the present unfolding
of the future.   Dr. Tregelles so well elucidates these verses that
we quote him at length, save at a few points.   Remarks in square
brackets are our own.   He says (p. 135 ff.) :

> I now take the former part of the chapter, in order to follow
> closely the persons and events brought before us ; this requires
> attention, but I believe it will be found that this anticipative history
> is just as definite (with the single exception of the *names* not being
> mentioned) as is God's record of the past.   I take the words of the
> chapter, introducing what I consider suitable explanation, and
> affixing, for distinction's sake, numbers to the kings of the north
> and south who are spoken of ; by these numbers I simply mean
> the first, second, etc., who are *here* mentioned.
>
> Verse 5 :   " And the (first) king of the south (i.e. Egypt, see verses
> 7, 8) shall be strong, and one of his princes (shall also be strong) ;
> and he (the prince) shall be strong above him (the first king of the
> south), and have dominion ; his dominion shall be a great dominion."
> Thus a great dominion is possessed by a prince who had previously
> belonged to the first king of Egypt here mentioned [it is easy to
> conceive that a king of Egypt will think to strengthen his own
> position by securing a neighbouring region for one of his own
> servants or family] :   the prince is spoken of immediately after as
> "king of the north."   This seems to occasion a rupture between
> them, and an attempt to accommodate this appears to be the
> purport of the beginning of the next verse.
>
> Verse 6 :   " And in the end of years they (i.e. the first king of the
> south, and the prince) shall join themselves together ; for the
> (first) king's daughter [i.e. rather, the daughter of the (first) king]
> of the south shall come to the (prince now become the first) king
> of the north to make an agreement :   but she shall not retain the
> power of the arm :   neither shall he (i.e. the first king of the south)
> stand, nor his arm ;   but she shall be given up, and they that brought
> her, and he that begat her, and he that strengthened her in these
> times."
>
> Thus this attempt to form an alliance by marriage becomes wholly
> fruitless, and only ends in the destruction of the first king of the
> south.
>
> Verse 7 :   " But out of a branch of her roots (i.e. out of the same
> family from which she sprang) shall one stand up in his estate "
> (this means, I believe, rather, *on his own basis*, and not, *in his stead*,
> which would be here inapplicable, as a woman has been spoken of),

" which shall come with an army, and shall enter into the fortress of the (first) king of the north, and shall deal against them and shall prevail : (ver. 8) and shall also carry captives into Egypt their gods, with their princes, and with their precious vessels of silver and gold ; and he " (i.e. the branch out of her roots, now become the second king of the south) " shall continue more years than the (first) king of the north. So the (second) king of the south shall come into his kingdom " (i.e. Egypt, as shown in the preceding verse), " and shall return into his own land." [It is open to construction whether the last clause does not require that the ' his kingdom ' of the last clause but one should mean that of the king of the north, not the south. And perhaps the R.V. is still more lucid : " and he [the second king of the south] shall refrain some years from the king of the north. And he [the king of the north] shall come into the realm of the king of the south, but he shall return into his own land : " [that is, the expedition shall be abortive.]

In order to understand to whom the pronouns in the next sentence refer, the whole passage must be read, and then it becomes clear that they relate to the king of the north. Verse 10 : " But his sons " (those of the first king of the north) " shall be stirred up, and shall assemble a multitude of forces : and one shall certainly come, and overflow, and pass through ; then shall he " (i.e. one of the sons of the first king of the north, who is himself presently spoken of as becoming king) " return and be stirred up even to his fortress."

Verse 11 : [These hostile acts stir up reprisals,] " And the (second) king of the south shall be moved with choler, and shall come forth and fight with him, even with the (second) king of the north : and he (the second king of the north) shall set forth a great multitude : but the multitude shall be given into his (the second king of the south's) hand.

Verse 12 : " And when he (the second king of the south) hath taken away the multitude, his heart shall be lifted up ; and he shall cast down many ten thousands : but he shall not be strengthened by it.

Verse 13 : " For the (second) king of the north shall return, and shall set forth a multitude greater than the former, and shall certainly come after certain years with a great army and with much riches.

Verse 14 : " And in those times there shall many stand up against the (second) king of the south ; also the children of the robbers (see margin) of thy people shall exalt themselves to establish the vision, but they shall fall."

It will be well to repeat Dr. Tregelles' warning that the kings mentioned are not the first or second *of his time*, for there were then no kings of Syria or Egypt; nor the kings of our time; but the first and second of the days when the predictions begin to be fulfilled. It can be understood that the success of his campaign, as well as the ferocity with which he will slaughter tens of thousands, may make others jealous and afraid of the king of Egypt, and thus a combination against him will be provoked. As regards that last clause Tregelles supposes it to point to Gentile powers, who have been robbers of Israel the centuries through; but it is better to read as R.V., " The children of the violent among thy people," or with the *Variorum*, " the robbers among thy people "; that is, certain of the Jews themselves shall seek to establish the vision, for Gentiles are not likely to attempt to do this. But this carnal effort of violent men of Israel will fail and they themselves will be killed. Not by their own power shall the people be saved, but by the faith in God that will come only when their own power shall have been wholly exhausted (Deut. 32 : 36 ff. : Isa 63 : 1–6 ; Joel 2 : 15–17).

From the fact that it is only certain of the people that make this attempt it may be inferred that the vision has not yet reached the point when the nation as a whole will make the covenant foretold in 9 : 27. Yet that period is nearing, for in verse 13 it has been said that " *the end of the times* " has come; and though this is not strictly the same as " *the time of the end* " (ver. 35) it leads on to it. Both phrases stand in the way of applying this chapter to days long past.

Tregelles continues :

> Verse 15 : " So the (second) king of the north shall come, and cast up a mount, and take the most fenced cities ; and the arms of the south shall not withstand, neither his chosen people, neither shall there be any strength to withstand." Verse 16 : " But he (the second king of the north) that cometh against him (the second king of the south) shall do according to his will, and none shall stand before him : and he shall stand in the glorious land " (i.e. the land of Israel) " which by his hand shall be consumed." Thus frustrating the efforts spoken of in verse 14, and making the Holy Land the particular scene of his military operations.

We are grateful for Tregelles' help in simplifying this somewhat intricate passage, and now return to our own comments, following in the main the R.V. Verse 17 : " And he [the second king of the north] shall set his face to come with the strength of his whole kingdom, and shall make equitable conditions with him [or, as Pember, ' having an agreement in intention '] ; and he shall do his pleasure [or, Tregelles, ' thus shall he do '] : and he shall give him [the second king of the south] the daughter of women [meaning, a still youthful maiden], corrupting her ; but she shall not stand [on his side], neither be for him."

Having thus concluded affairs with Egypt, " after this he [the second king of the north] shall turn his face unto the coastlands [that is, of the Mediterranean], and shall take many : but a prince shall cause the reproach offered by him to cease ; yea, moreover, he shall cause his reproach to return upon him." His hands being free as regards the south he shall repeat the ancient attempt of Xerxes, and attack the countries bordering upon the eastern Mediterranean and will seize many. This will bring him into collision with the ten-horned confederacy, now, as we suppose, existing ; and one of its princes will repel the invasion and relieve those coast-lands of the reproach of defeat by the Syrian king. But the prince will not leave matters there. Again, as of old, the now successful western power will " return the reproach " upon the late invader, that is, will in turn invade and subdue his territory, whereupon (ver. 19) the second king of the north, retreating to his own fortified cities, shall stumble, fall, and disappear, and his land will pass under the control of the ten-kingdomed confederacy.

Ver. 20. In place of the fallen king one shall have power who, it should be noted, is not called a king. Of the ruler next again mentioned (ver. 21) it is said that " *they* had not given him the honour of the *kingdom.*" This seems to imply a contrast from the ruler just before mentioned and suggests that the latter (20) had not been made king, but had been appointed as governor by the " they," whom we suppose to be the ten kings of the " beast," one of whom had conquered Syria and attached it to the united empire. It will be but the common course of affairs that this nominee be charged to tax heavily the annexed regions, for which purpose he will " cause an exactor to pass through the glory of the kingdom." " But within few days he shall be broken, neither in anger [by sudden, unpremeditated violence] nor in battle." The alternative seems to be death by deliberate plotting and assassination. Natural death or suicide seem scarcely to fit the word " be broken."

3. Ver 21. *The Antichrist—His Appearing and Opening Activities.*

In conquered and discontented areas such a sudden vacancy is often followed by disturbances or by attacks by designing neighbours. But measures will be taken that will produce a " time of security," a further hint that some sufficiently strong overlordship is upon the land. In place of the governor thus suddenly broken there shall " stand up a contemptible person to whom they had not given the honour of the kingdom " but who shall obtain it by flatteries. The subsequent actings and successes of this new king show that he was in no way contemptible as regards courage, skill, and ability ; the term will therefore mean as to his rank in society. He was, as we say, a nobody.

We agree with Tregelles (followed by Anderson, *The Coming Prince,* p. 195) in regarding this as the advent of the Antichrist, and that his doings occupy the rest of the chapter. Through all the following verses to 35 at least he remains the only antecedent to the " he," " his," " him " constantly recurring, no other person to whom the pronouns can apply being introduced. But before that verse is reached the setting up of the abomination is mentioned (31), which is the work of Antichrist, and also by that verse (35) the vision has arrived at " the appointed time of the end," leaving no space for any other so great monarch to arise.

The details given in other passages concerning the Antichrist confirm this identification.

(i) He is to commence as an insignificant ruler, a " little horn," agreeing with the feature that he is at first held in contempt, that is, by the " great powers " of the period, one whom they had passed over and to whom they had not given the kingdom. So also is he shown as starting his career with a " small people " (23).

(ii) His powers of speech have been noticed : here he is shown as a mastery of flattery.

(iii) Having gained a footing among the ten kings he is to pluck up three of them by the roots (7 : 8). Here, after having gained a kingdom, we now, at once (22) read of military operations with vigour. " With the arms of a flood shall they be swept away before him, and shall be broken "—victory the first. But also " the prince of the covenant," or, as Darby, the " allied prince," is broken before him, because (ver. 23), after having made this league, he shall work deceitfully, and grow strong though having but a small following—victory the second. Then, having gained adherents by the unusual course of scattering, " prey, spoil, and substance " (ver. 24), he succeeds in reducing further strongholds —conquest the third. All this agrees with the statement of 8 : 25 that his policy will be to prosper both by craft and force.

In ch. 8 : 9 it is said that the little horn shall wax exceeding great and operate especially " toward the south, and toward the east, and toward the glorious land." The repetition of the pre-position marks that these operations will be distinct, not conjoined. Now in ver. 25 of our chapter (ch. 11) he is shown conducting a great campaign against the king of the south. The latter is defeated by military strategy : " they devise devices against him " ; and also (26) because some of his own friends " that eat of his dainties " prove treacherous ; so that he is broken, and there is vast slaughter of his army.

Ver. 27. These kings of the north and of the south now sit at table together and confer, but in heart each is plotting mischief and lying to the other. How fearfully common is this in worldly diplomacy. At the time of a celebrated post-war conference a few years later than 1918, when statesmen of two enemy countries had entered into a much belauded covenant, a discerning man of one of those lands said to me, " It is all lies," and so it proved. But as with all lying, so with this of these two kings, it shall not prosper. Neither shall secure permanent supremacy ; for " yet the end shall be at the time appointed," and that end is the lordship of Christ, not of Antichrist.

Ver. 28. Having thus triumphed in Egypt and made this false agreement, the king of the north returns towards Syria, greatly enriched ; and now there rises in his heart that hostility to the holy covenant which shall bear such evil fruit for Israel and himself. In furtherance of this he will take certain preliminary steps : " he shall act," in ways not here detailed, and then shall return home. This is the first appearing of the dark cloud that shall blacken Israel's sky into deepest night, the first muttering of that final tempest that shall sweep away every refuge of lies.

Ver. 29. But " at the set time " (Darby) : for his times are not left to his own ordering, astute and determined and Satan-helped though he is. Of this there is a notable and comforting hint in our Lord's counsel to believers of that very epoch : " Pray that your flight be not in the winter, neither on a sabbath " (Matt. 24 : 20). For the prayer of faith can affect the period of the year in which Antichrist shall attack, yea, the very day of the week when flight shall become imperative. How little will the proud and God-defying monarch conceive that these puny believers in the God he scorns can thus influence by their prayers his impious and elaborate military undertakings. God is verily a refuge and strength for the man of prayer.

So at the set time Antichrist, in violation of the agreement with the king of the south, shall again attack him. But it will be to find that the latter has been equally deceitful, and has applied to a western power for help against him ; and so " it shall not be with him in the latter time as it was in the former," when he conquered Egypt, for (ver. 30) " ships of Kittim shall come against him." This term can have a fairly wide application to the Mediterranean countries, and is somewhat indefinite. But in the first Book of Maccabees (1 : 1 and 8 : 5) it is used of Alexander's expedition against Persia, from which it would seem that the Jews of that period applied it to Greece. But perhaps here it has its original meaning of Cyprus, become a maritime base.

Thus far it has been rather assumed that the ten-horned beast is in existence. But it seems to be demanded by the fact that this king is the one who attacks Israel in their land and sets up the abomination in their sanctuary. Now since the " little horn " who does this is to arise " among " the ten horns (7 : 8), the ten-horned beast must be present and must have absorbed the Near East.

It can be easily understood that this confederacy will be indignant at the uprooting of three of their number, and alarmed at the power this gives to the one they had held in contempt and had tolerated only through him having deceived them with his flatteries. Thus they will be very ready to respond to the appeal of Egypt and move a fleet against the aggressor.

In ch. 7, section V, 2 (pp. 86, 87), it has been suggested that at this stage of his career the events arrive which are depicted in seals 2 and 4 of Rev. 6 ; but in Dan. 11 his relations with the West are not pursued because the matter has been opened suffi-ciently in the vision of the fourth beast (ch. 7), and because here it is his covenant with the Jews that is the immediate subject and only events that bear on this are introduced. His contact with Daniel's " people in the latter days " is that which regulates this whole vision (10 : 14). Thus his wars with the king of the south occupy very much space because Palestine must be traversed and Israel must be sadly distressed by these vast armies and operations.

4. *Seven Years' Covenant.*

Ver. 30.   It is, of course, implied that he had not yet reached his goal of universal supremacy as Satan's viceregent, but he is hacking his bloody and deceitful way to that height.   At the moment in view he is disappointed of his objective in Egypt and bitter against the West for their opposition : " he shall be grieved, and shall return " toward his own land.   In this furious state of mind he fans the malice of his heart against the " holy covenant," that is, the worship of the true God by the godly of Israel who fear Him and obey His exhortation through Malachi, directed to this same era, " Remember the law of Moses My servant, which I commanded unto him in Horeb for all Israel, even statutes and judgments " (Mal. 4 : 4).

This malice now bursts into open " indignation against the holy covenant " ; he vents his rage at being thwarted in the south in sundry acts against it, and now makes overtures " unto them that forsake the holy covenant."   It can be well understood that at this serious juncture he will find their help in men and money of particular value, and also they will be a useful barrier against retaliatory measures from the king of the south.

Ver. 31.   Thus " arms shall stand on his part," meaning here, not weapons, but human arms, that is of the apostates of Israel, who will, as we know, be the vast majority (9 : 27).   With these he will make the covenant before considered, to run for what we see to be the final Seven of years.   Of the first three and a half years no details seem to be distinctly given, but we suppose it will be during this time that he will be recognized by the ten kings as overlord, and that he and they, having thus " come to one mind " (Rev. 17 : 17), will first destroy the apostate religious system, the " harlot " of that chapter, and then will compel the rest of the world to own his authority.   Thus supreme politically, and having exterminated bastard Christianity, he will be at last in a position to attain his real and deeply cherished ambition of being the world's god as well as its king.   In callous disregard of this as of former covenants he will " profane the sanctuary " of Jehovah, " even the fortress "—for the temple and city will have been again fortified against attack, but in vain ; and he will suppress the sacrifices of the true God, and will establish the worship of himself.

Ver. 32.   Religious persecution has always two effects.

(i) The wicked side with the persecutors.   They become their zealous tools, and in their fanatical zeal will go to the most unnatural lengths. Of this very time our Lord has warned us His disciples that " ye shall be delivered up even by parents, and kins-folk, and friends " (Luke 21 : 16) ; yea, " brother shall deliver up brother to death, and the father his child ; and children shall rise up against their parents, and cause them to be put to death ; and ye shall be hated by all men for My name's sake " (Mark 13 : 12). And as to Israel it shall be again as in Jeremiah's days : " take ye heed every one of his neighbour, and trust ye not in any brother . . . Thine habitation is in the midst of deceit ; through deceit they refuse to know me, saith Jehovah " (Jer. 9 : 4–6).

This gives the inner secret of such heartlessness and depravity : " they *refuse* to know Me " ; they have a determined and perverted heart ; they " do *wickedly* against the covenant," and thus become easily the dupes of their diabolical foe ; deceiving they are deceived, for he " perverts them with flatteries."

(ii) But, on the other hand, such fiery trials prove and reveal the gold, yea, they make it pure, and " the people that know their God shall be strong." How crucially important, therefore, it is to know God, to be ever " increasing in the knowledge of God " (Col. 1 : 10).

For the warning of the wicked and the strengthening of the godly, at this fearful juncture an angelic message, loudly proclaimed, will denounce inescapable and unending perdition upon each that shall succumb to flattery or to force and worship the Beast or his image (Rev. 14 : 9–12). The pious, both believers in Jesus and also God-fearing Jews, will know what to do " and shall act " ; they will take an active stand against the idolatry and refuse submission at all costs. The fiery furnace will glow, the lions will roar for their prey ; but what is such transitory agony to everlasting torment ? And the angelic summons to fidelity to God will be reinforced by that of the Two Witnesses of Rev. 11 : 3.

Ver. 33. At severe junctures especially God displays His care and His resources. He now gives to His suffering servants wise men, teachers, as the word means, to instruct, console, inspire the faithful : " the teachers among the people shall instruct many." So grace is still at work, the grace that instructs (Tit. 2 : 11–13), that instructs us to deny ungodliness, to live righteously, in even so evil a time as that in question, and to expect the appearing of our great God and Saviour Jesus Christ. Seasonable as such in-struction has ever been, it will be simply priceless in that closing era of this age, when it will be both given and followed at such fearful peril.

But grace will not prevent persecution. That would frustrate the double and needful end of removing the wicked and of preparing the godly for the kingdom of their Father : " Yet they [here the people of Israel in particular] shall fall by the sword, and by flame, and by captivity and by spoil—days," that is, the days appointed, three and a half years. Thus shall Zechariah 14 : 1, 2 be fulfilled : the sword slaughters, houses and cities go up in flames, some are dragged into a wretched slavery, all are despoiled and beggared.

Ver. 34. But " God has not cast off His people whom He foreknew." Though He will chasten them severely for their humbling and restoration, yet He will keep His oft-repeated promise not to make a full end of them (Jer. 30 : 11 ; etc.). He watches over the crucible and tempers its heat, and so " when they shall fall, they shall be helped with a little help." It is not said who will help them, or by what measures ; but it is added that at this moment there will be false and deadly foes : " many shall join themselves to them with flatteries," yet only to secure their confidence and abuse it to their hurt. They must learn deeply the lesson that only God can save, that trust must be set on Him undividedly, that Jehovah alone must be exalted.

Ver. 35. Nor are the valiant and wise teachers exempt from the testing ; rather will they be, as always, the special objects of malice. They will understand Paul's words, " I think God hath set forth us the apostles last of all [that is, set us in the lowest rank of hardship], as men doomed to death ; for we are made a spectacle unto the world, both to angels and to men " (I Cor. 4 : 9). As in war officers are picked out by enemy sharpshooters, so by persecutors are faithful elders and teachers specially hunted to destruction. And there is a needs be why the faithful John the Baptist shall languish in prison. Even his faith needs testing and refining. The bravest teacher or preacher is not yet perfected, not yet *only* gold, not yet so resplendent in character as to be a vessel only unto praise and glory and honour at the King's banquet. So " some of them that be wise [the teachers] shall fall [by the persecution] to refine them, and to purify and to make them white," and this feature shall continue " even to the time of the end," and then shall be wondrously fulfilled the promise," He that endureth unto the end, this one shall be saved " (Mat. 24 : 13 ; Mark 13 : 13).

The Deliverer who will effect this salvation is not the especial subject of this prophecy, but rather the Desolator and the desolated. But we know that at this blackest hour of Israel's night the day will break with sudden blaze as the Son of man, like a flash of lightning, bursts forth in the triple glory of Himself, His Father, and of all the holy angels (Luke 9 : 26).

> " Let that day come, O Lord,
> And other days pass by :
> Night is far spent, and dawning tells
> That Thou art drawing nigh."

5. *Antichrist's Supremacy : its Nature and Explanation.*

I. *His Supremacy.* As ver. 35 brought the thought down to " the time of the end . . . the appointed time," it is plain that ver. 36 must turn back somewhat, for it speaks of the supremacy of the king. " And the king shall do according to his will." In the days when we thought that in this vision Antichrist is first mentioned here, we often felt that this abrupt mention of him was peculiar. On that view he enters into the vision quite suddenly, unannounced and unexplained. This abruptness disappears on the view here given.

Now he stands forth as " the king," that is, the king before-mentioned who had " obtained the kingdom by flatteries " (21). And truly, for his little hour, he is indeed *the king*, another Nebuchadnezzar who consults no will but his own (5 : 19). And his will is to " exalt himself " ; not only above his fellow-mortals, but " above every god " ; not merely above those that by men are called gods, but especially shall " he speak marvellous things against the God of gods." No bolt from heaven shall strike him, nor lightning blast him ; this is the permitted climax of the hour and power of darkness, and the great God is silent. So the king " shall prosper," and still the feet of the pure of heart shall almost slip as they see this unexampled prosperity of the wicked (Ps. 73 : 2, 3). But it shall be only till " the indignation " against Israels' apostates and all the lawless of mankind " shall have been accomplished ; for that that is determined [strictly decreed] shall be done."

Ver. 37. The suppression of all other religion, that he alone may be worshipped, will be thorough. It has been a changeless feature of heathendom that men have worshipped the same deities as their fathers though millenniums pass by. But custom and precedent are shattered by him and swept away ; the whole system of things mundane shall be new, designed only to his exaltation : " Neither shall he regard the gods of his fathers, nor the desire of women "—that is, that most ancient female deity, the Queen of Heaven, Ishtar, Isis, Venus, Astarte, Diana, " Mary," who has ever attracted the devotion of women, and of licentious men; nor shall he pay the least regard to any other god, " for he shall magnify himself above all."

II.   *The Nature of His Supremacy.*   It is not matter of speculation that is before us, but of certainty.   The language of the angel is not figurative but literal.   It is no question of some system of religion that is idolatrous in fact hough owning the triune God in creed. There is no sense in which it could be said of a religious *system,* that it does not " regard the god of *his* fathers."   The New Testament speaks of this man of lawlessness and his doings as a concrete person and concrete realities that are to be expected as definitely as is the coming of our Lord Jesus Christ, and directly before this last event.   Nothing can be more explicit or more confirmatory than the apostle's testimony in II Thess. 2 : 1–4 :

> Now we beseech you, brethren, touching the coming of our Lord Jesus Christ, and our gathering together unto Him ; to the end that ye be not quickly shaken from your mind, nor yet be troubled, either by spirit, or by word, or by epistle as from us, as that day of the Lord is now present [already beginning, *Variorum*] ; let no one beguile you in any wise ; for it will not be except the apostasy come first, and the man of lawlessness be revealed, the son of perdition, he that opposeth and exalteth himself against all that is called God, or that is an object of worship ; so that he sitteth in the sanctuary of God, setting himself forth as God.

It is a moral certainty that neither Daniel nor the Thessalonians could by any possibility have extracted from the words they heard or read any such notion as that what we know as Pope and Papacy were here meant.   The only sense they could have seen in the language is its natural sense of a literal individual and a literal sanctuary.

It is of such urgency that Christians should understand this feature that the Enemy of truth will stop at nothing to confuse Christians about these things.   False spirits, false messages, false letters from an apostle would be employed to this end.   And altogether apart from such nefarious means, right well has this end been served by many good men.   For instance, to some the Papacy is at once the harlot, the beast, and the Antichrist; and thus is the whole subject inextricably confused.

Again, to others the Lord will descend from heaven for His church before Antichrist will appear, though II Thess. 2 seems most definitely to assert the contrary. Thus is II Thess. 2, as we think, set aside, while I Thess. 4 is retained and misused; and by consequence the prophecies in the Gospels and the most of the Revelation cease to apply directly to Christians. And the result? We do no more than mention the moral loss to believers from practical inattention to the commands of the Lord to disciples. In addition, the many who name the Name refuse to consider the Great Hope because of the diversities and disputes which have partly elucidated, but partly obscured, the theme.

Yet the subject as divinely set forth must be plain, not confused, for Paul instructed newly converted heathen, babes in Christ, in these practical and powerful themes : " Remember ye not that when I was yet with you I was wont to tell you these things ? " (II Thess. 2 : 5). And it is most helpful, for in Antichrist all the subtle, powerful, dominating principles of sin-cursed human history reach their full embodiment : " the secret lawlessness doth already work," and will do so until " the Lawless One be revealed " (II Thess. 2 : 7, 8), and then its working shall be arrested, as leaven by fire, when he is blasted by the outshining of the glory of the Lord.

By studying the awful final Product of the principle we can discern its hidden and corrupting nature, can detect its subtle working betimes, and in unlikely spheres, and so can preserve ourselves from its depraving and defiling influence. The essential principle of all lawlessness is self-exaltation : " he shall magnify himself " ; the essential principle of all godliness is : " the Lord alone shall be exalted." Let each apply this infallible touchstone to each detail of life, yea, to each thought and feeling and purpose of his heart.

This lawlessness, this self-exaltation, this vainglory of life is the indispensable quality by which supremacy is attained in this world, the kingdom of darkness ; and the King of Glory, the Sovereign of the world of light, lived and died on this earth to display the moral grandeur of the exactly opposite principle of living, and in order that, in great grace, He might " rescue us out of this present evil age, according to the will of our God and Father," with the final object that to the Father might " be the glory for ever and ever," and to Him alone (Gal. 1 : 4, 5). Is this object distinctly and steadfastly before my heart ?

III. *The Energizing Secret.* For a season " the whole earth will wonder after and worship the Beast " (Rev. 13 : 3–7). His resuscitation from death and Hades will become known, and this, with his incomparable abilities, successes, and splendour, will cause men to cry, " Who is like unto the Beast ? " That he is a *beast*, and a *wild* beast (θηρίον), will be ignored, or will cow men into submission. His brilliant victories, his overwhelming military and economic strength, will dazzle and awe. Men will ask, " Who is able to make war with him ? " and for a time none will attempt it.

And so " all that dwell on the earth " will give him the worship demanded, *except* those whose names have been written from the foundation of the world in the book of life of the Lamb that hath been slain (Rev. 13 : 8). Let me then examine this point with diligence, with minute scrutiny, with personal application, and decide whether I have associated myself with the *Lamb*, with the One who came into this world armed in His mind with the resolution to suffer in the flesh (I Peter 4 : 1), and Whose principle of life, in this very world of sin where I still live, was that He would be *slain* rather than not do the will of His God.

Ver. 38. Now there is a sufficient secret of Antichrist's unparalleled success : " *The Dragon* gave him *his* power, and his throne, and great authority " (Rev. 13 : 2, 4). The whole world is Satan's sphere (I John 5 : 19) : all the kingdoms of the world, with their authority and glory, are committed to him, as he asserted fearlessly to the One he knew could deny if it it were not so, and Who did not deny it, but Who three times thereafter called Satan the " prince of the world " (Luke 4 : 5–7 ; John 12 : 31 ; 14 : 30 ; 16 : 11). And he will readily bestow all on the one who will make him his *god* : " If Thou therefore wilt *worship* before me it shall all be Thine." And Antichrist will accept what Christ rejected.

Where and when is this awful compact made ? Was it concluded during the former life on earth of this devil-bound man ? or is it to be made in Hades when Satan is to be permitted to bring him back from the Abyss ? (Rev. 17 : 8–11). We *know* not : but if the explanation we should offer of II Thess. 2 : 6–8 be correct, he is already fretting against the bars of the prison, already straining at the leash, and were he allowed, would rush into this world's chaos before his time, and make its confusion to be worse confounded (see p 31.).

Satan, then, is the " god of fortresses," those stern proofs of the cruelty of man and the danger in which he is from his brother. He is the god whom the ancestors of Antichrist knew not in person, but whom he will know right intimately, and upon the honouring of whom he shall lavish " gold, silver, precious stones, and pleasant things." Not that Satan personally needs or uses such trifles ; to him the external and material glory of the kingdoms is nothing in itself, and he will easily let some duped tool enjoy these baubles ; but he covets the honour and worship which the giving of these displays. Satan is that " foreign god by whose help he shall deal with the strongest fortresses," through whose superhuman cunning, driving force, and demonic influence he shall prove invincible—for a short space. (Ver. 39)

From Satan's treatment of himself he shall learn to " increase with glory whosoever acknowledgeth him : and he shall cause them to rule over many, and shall divide the land [or *earth*] to them as a reward " (Darby). But the righteous will say of him and his retinue and rewards : " O my soul, come not thou into their counsel ; unto their assembly, my glory, be not thou united " (Gen. 49 : 6).

6. *His End.*

Ver. 40. " And at the time of the end." Thus this narrative-in-advance has once more reached " the end," and it shall prove the end of this brilliant but monstrous agent of the Devil. He is at the pinnacle of prosperity : his plans have materialized, his ambition is fully gratified ; but now the price of the evil, Satan-bestowed prosperity must be paid in full. Daring as he is he remains subject to the fundamental moral law of the universe that " whatsoever one shall sow *that* shall he also reap." The king of the south had been crushed and reduced to acquiescence in the new order : indeed, he too had wondered at and worshipped this Emperor, his conqueror ; he also had hoped that under so powerful a central authority his kingdom, among the others, might have rest. But he had been deceived bitterly and treated brutally ; resentment revives, and ambition with it ; and seizing some seemingly favourable hour, he daringly " pushes at " the tyrant. The reaction is terrific in its swiftness and fury : " the king of the north shall come against him like a whirlwind, with chariots, with horsemen, and with many ships." One result of his control of the ten kings is that the western navies that once attacked him are now at his disposal. Land and sea forces combine to crush the rebellion : like a flood " he shall enter into the countries, and overflow and pass through," on his way from the north to the south.

Ver. 41. Of necessity " he shall enter into the glorious land, and many countries [or, peoples] shall be overthrown : but these shall be delivered out of his hand, Edom, and Moab, and the chief of the children of Ammon."

Now why do these escape his fury ? and why is this specified ? Let it be observed that the preceding prophets of God everywhere assert and presuppose that these lands east of the Jordan will be re-peopled in the latter days.   For many centuries they have been desolate, which also had been foretold ; but if and when the pro-jected Palestine to Baghdad railway shall be running it will follow naturally that all adjacent lands will become valuable and inhabited, and the sons of Esau, Lot, and Ishmael will occupy them.   This, not the partitioning of Palestine formerly proposed, is the course afore-announced by God.   The Jews will have their land, and the Arab races their lands.

Yet the prophets show that at the end of the times the ancient, vindictive, covetous spirit of the races named will persist and be virulent.   They will hate the Jew, for he will have crowded them out of Palestine, and they will be greedy again to enjoy his land, made rich by his skill and toil.   Psalm 83 foretells a deliberate and concerted endeavour " to cut off Israel from being a nation : that the name of Israel be no more in remembrance " (4).   And those who have thus consulted together and made a covenant do this avowedly against the God of Israel, not against that people only : " Against *Thee* do they make a covenant."   Of the races that will join in this league Edom, Moab, and Ammon are mentioned, with some smaller surrounding peoples, and perhaps Edom is mentioned first as being possibly the instigator of the scheme, even as of old they were the fiercest of all these enemies of Israel, and therefore when other lands near them pass under the benign rule of Messiah theirs shall lie desolate in perpetuity (Ezek. 35 : 9, 14).

But behind these smaller and nearer peoples looms the sinister power of Assyria, that is, the king of the north, Antichrist : " Assyria also is joined with them.   They have been an arm to the children of Lot " (Ps. 83 : 6–8).   Now history has no record of a combination of all these nations here named for a hoped-for final destruction of Israel.   It therefore waits development ; and as the purpose will coincide exactly with the desires of Antichrist it can be understood why his forces do not ravage these lands on his march to Egypt.   Yet their judgment is but deferred, as the prophets show in many places, such as this Psalm 83, Isaiah 11 : 14, and elsewhere.

Ver. 42. But the fierce conqueror will lay his hand heavily on other countries, " and the land of Egypt shall not escape."

Ver. 43. But he shall have power " over the treasures of gold and of silver, and over all the precious things of Egypt : and the Libyans and the Ethiopians shall be at his steps." Thus shall black races, as well as others, be under his sway. It will seem as though his triumph is complete, his position in the universe unassailable.

Ver. 44. But his tyranny, cruelty, rapacity, deceit, and pride will bring their just recompense of reward. While he is thus away from his centre, with his hands full and his forces occupied, " tidings out of the east and out of the north shall trouble him." Resentment and rebellion are not confined to Egypt. The ancient enemies of Babylon, the Medes, shall at the end of the age destroy the city (Isa. 13 : 17 ; Jer. 51 : 11, 28). These passages cannot refer to Cyrus for three reasons : (i) He was king of *Persia*, and had made the Medes subordinate ; but these passages specify the Medes as acting, and do not mention the Persians. (ii) It is *kings* of the Medes that are to effect this destruction, a combination, not one monarch. (iii) As a fact Cyrus did not at all destroy the city when he took it. We have before cited the explicit testimony of Herodotus to this effect, and he tells that, after a later siege, Darius pulled down the walls and gates. But not even then was the city itself destroyed (see p. 34).

Faced with this new combination against himself and his empire " he shall go forth with great fury to destroy and utterly to make away many." Again will the Near and Middle East be deluged with blood as this mightier monster than a Jenghiz Khan or a Tamerlane rages around.

Ver. 45. Excited now to the full passion of his devil-driven nature he will decide to execute utterly at this time his rage against the people of Jehovah. " And he shall plant the tents of his palace [that is, his royal pavilion] between the seas [the Mediterranean and the Dead Seas] at the glorious holy mountain." Again the heart will linger as the angel so describes the guilty, yet by heaven the ever-beloved centre of the earth. Now is seen the last mustering of his devastating hordes. All is in readiness for the final extirpation of this hated race, and final obliteration of this devoted city. But " he shall come to his end, and none shall help him," not even the Dragon who had beguiled, bedizened, and blasted him.

Accounts of this collapse of Satan's schemes and sovereignty, and the end of his viceroy's pride and glory, with the destruction of the myriads of his sin-loving, God-hating followers, can be read in Isa. 10 : 33, 34 ; Ezek. 38, 39 ; Joel 3 : 9–16 ; Zech. 14 : 12–16 ; Rev. 14 : 17–20 ; 19 : 11–21.

Of him shall these famous stanzas of Byron be as true as of Sennacherib, his early predecessor on the throne of Assyria :

> The Assyrian came down like a wolf on the fold,
>   And his cohorts were streaming with purple and gold,
> And the sheen of their spears was like stars on the sea
>   When the blue wave rolls nightly on deep Galilee.
>
> Like the leaves of the forest when summer is green
>   That host, with their banners, at sunset was seen ;
> Like the leaves of the forest when autumn hath blown
>   That host on the morrow lay withered and strown.
>
> For the Angel of Death spread his wings on the blast,
>   And breathed in the face of the foe as he passed,
> And the eyes of the sleepers waxed deadly and chill,
>   And their hearts but once heaved, and for ever grew still.
>
> And the widows of Asshur are loud in their wail,
>   And the idols are broke in the temples of Baal,
> And the might of the Gentile, unsmote by the sword,
>   Hath melted like snow in the glance of the Lord.

" So let all Thine enemies perish, O Jehovah : but let them that love Him be as the sun when he goeth forth in his might." (Judges 5 : 31).

CHAPTER XII

THE END

THIS LAST CHAPTER IS A PART OF THE WHOLE VISION THAT occupies the two preceding chapters. It contains the closing scenes and instruction, and must be read as one with the whole.

It has been pointed out that the visions of this book follow a general feature of prophetic scriptures by connecting each with the foregoing and then passing to the end of this age. Another literary feature is important. Each vision ends at the same point, the destruction of world-empire and the setting up of the kingdom of God, but each in succession commences by turning back to some earlier point, covering part of the ground of the visions that had preceded, introducing new features, and finally reaching the one goal. Thus :

(i) Ch. 2 opens with the start of Gentile world power and ends at the Stone filling the whole earth.

(ii) Ch. 7 begins near the close of the image of ch. 2 and ends with the kingdom being given to the Son of man and the saints.

(iii) Ch. 8 shows the connection of the last Emperor that will rule with the early Grecian empire, and ends with him being broken by the Prince of princes.

(iv) Ch. 9 starts with the decree to rebuild Jerusalem and ends with the completion of the judgments upon both Antichrist and Israel.

(v) Ch. 11 starts again from the Persian and Grecian days, passes on to the rise of Antichrist and carries the mind at ver. 35 to the " appointed end " of the tribulation for Israel. It then turns back to some further details of the career of the Persecutor, and at ver. 45 reaches the same terminus, his end.

(vi) We shall see that in ch. 12 the vision again turns back somewhat, but again ends at the triumph of the righteous, at the first resurrection.

This gives an important clue to the complementary prophecy, the *Revelation*.

(i) The Introduction takes the mind to the coming of the Lord in clouds of glory (1 : 7).

(ii) The letters to the Seven Churches carry the picture, *not* to an imagined coming of Christ prior to the end days, but right on to the overcomers in the churches sitting down with Christ upon His throne, that is, the beginning of the kingdom (chs. 2 and 3).

(iii) The Seven Seals go beyond the Tribulation (comp. 6 : 12–14 with Matt. 24 : 29) to the same public intervention of the Lord (8 : 1), after the great multitude who come out of the great Tribulation have been taken to the heavenly world (7 : 14).

(iv) The Trumpets end with the kingdom of the world having become the kingdom of God (11 : 15).

(v) Ch. 12 begins with the birth of a " man-child " who is to rule the nations (that is, the same overcomers in the churches ; comp. 2 : 26, 27). He is caught away to the *throne* of God (not, as in I Thess. 4, to the clouds near the earth), and thereupon Satan is cast out of heaven and brings on the end days and brings up the beast to persecute (ch. 13). This series of chapters ends with the destruction of that beast (ch. 14 : 19, 20 ; and see 19 : 15).

(vi) Ch. 15 begins in the period of the last trumpet (11 : 19) and ch. 16 ends with the battle of Har-Magedon and the destruction of the city Babylon. Ch. 11 : 19 is a condensation of, a sort of chapter heading to, chs. 15 and 16. Chs. 12–14 are a parenthesis.

(vii) Ch. 17 pictures the extinguishing of bastard Christianity *before* the Beast reigns supreme : ch. 18 details the same destruction of his city, Babylon, at the *close* of his career.

(viii) Ch. 19 to 20 : 6 again carries the scenes on to the destruction of the Beast and the saints taking the kingdom.

Each of this series starts at a different point, traverses parts of the same period, giving different and supplementary information, and ends at the one grand climax.

Ch. 12 : 1. " At that time," a general expression, equivalent to " during that period," the period which will close this age.

This " standing up of Michael, the great prince that standeth for the children of thy people," is the same event as in Rev. 12 : 7–9 " And there came war in heaven : Michael and his angels going forth to war with the dragon ; and the dragon warred and his angels ; and they prevailed not, neither was their place found any more in heaven. And the great dragon was cast down, the old serpent, he that is called the Devil and Satan, the deceiver of the whole world ; he was cast down to the earth, and his angels were cast down with him." The effect of this ejection was greatly to enrage the Devil, and to precipitate a woeful time on earth (ver. 12). He persecutes the " woman," as a system (the church of God), and makes war with her children individually, " the rest of her seed," therefore the brethren of the " man child," that is, those of the family of God who had not " prevailed to escape all these things that shall come to pass " at that time (Luke 21 : 36). For this warfare he brings up the Beast, and the last persecution follows (Rev. 13 : at verse 1 read as R.V., " he—the dragon—stood . . . and I saw a beast," etc.).

Similarly, in Daniel 12 : 1 the standing up of Michael precipitates " a time of trouble, such as never was since there was a nation, even to that same time." Since there cannot be two utterly unequalled events this must be the same as that of which our Lord said (Matt. 24 : 21) that " there shall be great tribulation, such as hath not been from the beginning of the world until now," but God be thanked for the words added, " no, nor ever shall be." It is the same event as that which Rev. 7 : 14 describes as " the tribulation, the great one."

" At that time thy people shall be delivered, every one that shall be found written in the book." Not because men belong to a privileged family with which God is in covenant, do they escape temporal judgment, even unto death. For it is written, " Whosoever sinned against Me, him will I blot out of My book " (Ex. 32 : 33 ; cf. Ps. 69 : 28 ; I Cor. 11 : 30 ; Rev. 3 : 5). The theme is profound ; but it looks as if all names are there, giving a right to life on earth until the name is blotted out. " The *Lamb's* book of life " (Rev. 13 : 8) we suppose to be another, a different record, in which His redemptive work has effect, and which book therefore affects destiny. This whole theme needs further elucidation, but not by that type of person who speaks with dogmatic positiveness about all matters, known and unknown. " We know in part " only, said Paul, and it is blessed to be of his company and those of like humility.

Ver. 2. " And many of them that sleep in the dust of the earth shall awake, some to everalsting life, and some to shame and everlasting contempt." Revelation 20 : 1–6 shows distinctly that there is to be a resurrection before the millennial kingdom and another thereafter, and in the former believers only take part, and of these such believers (i) as are adjudged worthy to sit on thrones and exercise judgment, that is, the overcomers; see Rev. 2 : 26–28 ; 3 : 21 : " He that overcometh, I will give *to him* to sit down with Me in My throne " ; (ii) such as at any time suffered death for Christ's sake ; and (iii) in particular those who defied the Beast and worshipped him not (ver. 4).   Then it is added explicitly (ver. 5) that " the rest of the dead lived not until the thousand years should be finished.   This is the first resurrection.   Blessed and holy is he that hath part in the first resurrection."

This must govern the passage before us in Daniel, which therefore cannot mean that those who are to suffer " everlasting contempt " will rise *at the same time* as those who are blessed and holy and who awake to " everlasting life."   Dr. Tregelles translates : " And many from among the sleepers of the dust shall awake ; these shall be unto everlasting life ; but those [the rest of the sleepers] shall be unto shame and everlasting contempt."   Thus Pember also : " ' And many of them that sleep in the dust-formed ground shall awake : these '—that is to say, those who awake— ' shall be for eternal life ; but those '—that is, the remainder of the sleepers, who do not awake—' for shame and eternal contempt.' "

As this whole vision concerns Israel firstly and directly the conclusion is certain that godly Israelites will share in the first resurrection :

> But by no means all.   For it appears that of Israelites also, as well as of Christians, there will be a first or select resurrection, before the establishment of the Millennial Kingdom.
>
> To this fact the well-known words of the First Psalm refer :
>
> " Therefore, the wicked shall not rise in the judgment,
>   Nor sinners in the congregation of the righteous."
>
> There can be no doubt that the word " rise " is here used in its primal meaning, and that it means resurrection, just as it does in Isaiah 26 : 19.   Both the Septuagint and the Vulgate understand it in this sense, the former rendering it by ἀναστήσονται the latter by *resurgent*. (Pember, *The Great Prophecies of the Centuries concerning Israel and the Gentiles*, 463.)

Ver. 3.   The teachers of the people before-mentioned will have especial honour in the kingdom, as reward for their special service and its perils.   " And the teachers shall shine as the brightness of the firmament, and they that turn many to righteousness as the stars for ever and ever."   They diffused the light of truth in the time of thick darkness, and hereafter shall radiate brightness as the atmosphere disseminates and tempers the brilliant sunlight, dispersing the direct and scorching rays into every nook and cranny, but softened and cooled so as to benefit and not to injure. Is not this a striking hint of the priestly, intermediate function of the glorified saints, in fellowship with the Son of God, even the diffusing in their persons something of the presence and glory of God so as to be a blessing to those who could not themselves endure the direct blaze of His unveiled glory? These shall themselves " see His face "; others will see Him in them as in a " tabernacle " (Rev. 22 : 4 ; 21 : 3).

In the midnight gloom these teachers had been as stars to cheer and to guide the wayfaring and the mariner that they lost not their perilous ways; in the future they shall shine brightly for ever and ever. Coming glory results from present service, and " one star differeth from another star in glory " in correspondence with faithfulness and usefulness in this life. For this principle compare Matt. 25 : 21, 23 ; Luke 19 : 17, 19 ; Rev. 3 : 4, 5 ; 6 : 11 ; 19 : 7, 8.

> " O happy band of pilgrims,
> Look upward to the skies,
> Where such a light affliction
> Shall win so great a prize."

Ver. 4. The prophecies of Daniel were to be " sealed," that is, to remain a closed book, but little understood, " even to the time of the end," but then, say the Versions, " many shall run to and fro," a non-consequential idea, disconnected from anything in the vision, and that has given rise to such an irrelevant notion as that the angel pointed to trains, motor-cars, and aeroplanes which would bring about the modern half-insane, restless rushing hither and thither. The real sense, however, is : " Many shall peruse the book " (*Variorum*) ; " many shall diligently investigate " (Darby) : " many shall read and review the book " (Pierson) : " many shall scrutinize the book from end to end " (Tregelles) : " many shall search it through and through " (Pember), and so " knowledge [of it] shall be increased."

That this process of enquiry, and this result, to come at the time of the end, have been seen during the past hundred years beyond any former time is certain. And such search is now legitimate, for Christ has, as it were, broken the seal from this prophecy by saying concerning the "abomination" here mentioned, "let him that readeth understand" (Matt. 24 : 15).

Ver. 5 6, 7. Two other heavenly beings are now seen. They again reveal the deep interest their order take in the affairs of earth. What they have heard their fellow narrate has provoked deep concern. To them such things are "wonders," and they desire to know how long it shall be to their end. The answer is given with the most impressive solemnity. The angel takes oath in the name of the Ever Living ; and the more solemnly in that he raises to heaven both hands, instead of the right hand only as is customary in taking an oath (comp. Rev. 10 : 5–7). He declares two things ; one a temporal and the other a moral sign of the end : the period of trouble shall endure "a time, times and half a time," three and a half years ; and the goal to be reached with Israel, the holy people (holy by calling, in spite of being as yet unholy in state), is that their power shall be completely broken to pieces ; and then "all these things shall be finished." Yes, finished because man's extremity is God's opportunity, and when He looks and there is *none* to help, then His own arm will bring salvation (Isa. 63 : 5).

Ver. 8, 9, 10. But Daniel desired to know something more, even what should be the ultimate issue from all these developments. But it was not needful that he should know : it would suffice that the exact and full result should be made clear in God's time and way. What is vital, however, is *moral state*. All Satanic effort is directed to the wicked doing wickedly ; all divine working is to the end that men shall "purify themselves." Oh, let the stress of this bear upon our conscience and will. In one sense it is only God who can purify the defiled. Without His prior grace we had gained neither desire nor power for purity. But God works by providing all needful means and powers, but *we must be diligent in the use of these*. And thus it is written : "Having therefore these promises, beloved, let us *cleanse ourselves* from all defilement of flesh and spirit, perfecting holiness in the fear of God" (II Cor. 7 : 1) ; and again : "seeing that His divine power hath granted unto us all things that pertain unto life and godliness . . . for this very cause adding on your part all diligence . . . give the more diligence to make your calling and election sure" (11 Peter 1 : 3–11); the "calling" here in question being, not salvation from wrath, but "unto God's eternal glory" (I Peter 5 : 10). And yet again : "Every one that hath this hope set on Him purifieth himself, even as He is pure" (I John 3 : 3).

At that time of the end many shall heed these exhortations, and
" shall purify themselves, and make themselves white, and be
refined." But that they needed to do this implies that they had not
done so at all adequately. From Rev. 3 : 4, 5 we learn that there
are saints who keep their garments undefiled; from 7 : 14 we learn
that there are those whose garments need washing, and which were,
therefore, in measure defiled. The latter stand at last before
the throne of the King in bliss, but the former are His personal
companions who walk about in His company. Rev. 7 applies to
that same time of the end as Daniel 12.

The inevitable effect of persistence in wickedness is to blind the
understanding, and " none of the wicked shall understand " ; they
have shut their eyes, and shall not see when good cometh. But
the God-sent teachers shall understand, and shall instruct others.

The last prophetic scripture closes with a similar most solemn
passage as to the perpetuity of state which men can reach in this
life for evil or for good. And when the Lord comes suddenly
at that time each shall receive his wages according to his work
(Rev. 22 : 11, 12).

Ver, 11, 12. Another, and double, note of time is added :
" And from the time that the continual burnt offering shall be
taken away, and the abomination that maketh desolate set up,
there shall be 1,290 days. Blessed is he that waiteth, and cometh
to the 1,335 days." There is no definite instruction as to these
periods, nor have we yet gained light upon them from other scriptures. The one runs on a month beyond the three and a half years ;
the other extends forty-five days further again. The distinctive
features of these weeks will be seen at the time, of course ; but
apparently it is not what will go on during the weeks, but what
will be reached at the close of each in succession that will be important. It is clear that after the destruction of the Beast and his
armies much will remain to be done in the introducing of God's
order for Israel and the world. But those who are then alive will
quickly learn the work to be done of both judgment and renewal,
and by patience in well-doing will reach the special blessing to
attend the full period named.

Ver. 13. In view of all made known, what now is to be Daniel's
path ? Thus does this chief prophecy turn to a practical question,
even as that of the *Revelation*. His path was what our path is to
be ; " Go thy way," that is, the way, the work, the walk appointed
by God for each. Keep on in that path and task, whether exalted

as was Daniel's, or humble; keep on if aged, as he was, and the rest of the way be short; keep on if in youth, perseveringly, stead-fastly, faithfully, with patience under thickening trials.   "Go thy way *till the end*"; for, when life's course is over, "thou shalt rest" —a summary of the state of the godly between death and resurrec-tion, at least in relation to the toils and sorrows of earth; and when the day shall break, and the shadows flee away for ever, then, in resurrection, "thou shalt arise into thy lot at the end of the days."

"Wherefore girding up the loins of your mind, be sober, and set your hope perfectly upon the favour that is being brought unto you at the revelation of Jesus Christ" (I Peter 1 : 13).

CONCLUDING REFLECTIONS

Some general observations may now complete our detail studies.

1. *How Unchangeable is Fallen Human Nature.*   The principles that ruled men and nations of old rule to-day, and will do until Christ has returned and the Spirit from on high be poured upon all men (Isa. 32 : 15 ; Joel 2 : 28).   The same principles produce the same practices.   The same root of selfishness produces the same fruit of pride, deceit, cruelty, war, and destruction.   "Ye *must* be born again," from above.   Regeneration alone can change man, for in itself his nature is irremediable, unimprovable.

2. *The Gospel of Faith in Christ* changes those individuals that rely upon and obey Him, but prophetic scripture most uniformly, distinctly, and solemnly shatters the dream that the world in general will slowly improve until the kingdom of God shall at last dominate the earth.   On the contrary, the world's most impious Ruler is its last, and his end is that he will be "broken," not perfected.

3. *The Hope of Permanent World Peace* before the return of the Prince of peace, with power and great glory, is vain.   By all means let right-minded rulers promote peace with all diligence.   While men talk and plan and argue they are not fighting ; and may God prosper every upright statesman who sincerely seeks righteousness and peace.   But the Word declares plainly that "unto the end shall be wars, the desolations strictly decreed" (Dan. 9 : 26).   It is not leagues of nations but the King of nations who alone can make wars to cease unto the ends of the earth (Ps. 46 : 9).

4. During the whole mighty epoch of world-empire in the hands of man the Son of man is seen but once, and then He is in heaven,

not on earth ; and the point of development at which He is seen is not till the very close of the epoch. Only then does He begin active intervention in affairs governmental (7 : 13). All through the age of Gentile rule, except the thirty years of His humiliation, He is absent from the earth, nor is sharing its rule. That is in the hands of the Ancient of Days, Who overrules by His great angel princes and hosts.

In this age the disciple of Christ is " called into the fellowship of God's Son, Jesus Christ our Lord " (I Cor. 1 : 9). He, too, is of heaven (Eph. 2 : 5, 6) ; in heart he is to live there (Col. 3 : 3, 4) ; that is his political sphere (Phil. 3 : 20). Christ is not ruling nor restraining the " wild beasts " ; He never will : when He deals with them at all it will be but to destroy them as thoroughly and suddenly as the Stone crushed the image. Then neither is this the present business of those in fellowship with Him ; though when at length He judges men and angels, so will they (I Cor. 6 : 2, 3). They who dwell in Babylon will too easily partake of her sins, and, if there, must risk receiving of her plagues. Let them remember Lot and his wife, and rather walk with Abraham in a fellowship with the Lord that kept him apart from the inhabitants of the land, than sit with Lot in the seat of the scornful, even though he did his best (but quite in vain) to judge and to remedy their evils.

> Strangers and pilgrims here below
>   This earth we know is not our place ;
> But hasten through the vale of woe,
>   And, restless to behold Thy face,
> Swift to our heavenly country move,
>   Our everlasting home above.
>   WESLEY.

5. Certain prominent conditions which in acme are to mark the End Days seem to have set in.

I. In *Christendom*—(i) A vast apostasy among Protestants from the apostolic faith ; (ii) A consequent immense turning to spiritism in its various guises ; (iii) A powerful movement toward reunion of denominations that may well develop into " Mystery Babylon the Great " (Rev. 17).

II. In *Jewry*—(i) The lapse of multitudes from any acknowledgement of the God of Israel ; (ii) A steady resettlement in their own land in this unbelief ; (iii) The establishment of a Jewish State, which can make treaties.

III.   In the *world*—(i) The re-opening of the Middle East, and the tendency of world politics to centre there; (ii) The intense and sinister nationalism which precipitates international strife; (iii) Yet the effort after co-operation which may issue in the " ten horns "; (iv) The fermenting and awakening in the Far East, in preparation for its part at the end time.

IV.   Among *true Christians*—(i) The searching into prophecy; (ii) The longing after practical holiness, the indispensable condition for meeting the Lord in peace when He comes; (iii) The zeal in spreading the gospel among all nations.

But in spite of this cumulating ground of hope that the End nears, the past teaches caution, more caution, yea, much more caution than many writers and speakers show.   Quotations enough could be given from good men who long since thought that conditions would culminate very speedily and the Lord return.   Events have often moved strikingly and rapidly, but then there have as often come periods of slowing down.   It may be so again.   And it at least remains uncertain whether the vast wars in the Mediterranean and Near East outlined in Daniel 7 and 11 as to usher in the End, have yet come and therefore whether the End Time has yet commenced.

6. The final and chief practical lesson is, that the personal return and reign of the Lord Jesus Christ is God's solution for earth's misery.   Let us be ever looking for and hastening the coming of the day of God (II Peter 3 : 12); let us, with John and Christ, James and Jude, Peter and Paul preach persistently the good news of the kingdom of God, and not merely that part of it which announces the forgiveness of sins.   It is the only message of salvation for the individual; it is equally the needed and blessed message of hope for the race corporate.

" Ye therefore, beloved, knowing these things beforehand, beware lest, being carried away with the error of the wicked, ye fall from your own steadfastness.   But grow in the grace and knowledge of our Lord and Saviour Jesus Christ.   TO HIM BE THE GLORY BOTH NOW AND FOR EVER, AMEN " (II Peter 3 : 17, 18).

APPENDIX A

(To Chapter II)

THE UNIVERSALITY OF THE RULE OF THE ANTICHRIST

THE extent of the sovereignty of Antichrist is a subject of deep interest and much importance. Will it be universal or restricted? It has been held by many that he will rule only the " Roman " world, and then it is suggested that it will be in territories outside his area that persecuted saints will find refuge. Even so, that form of escape would afford no fulfilment of the promise that, consequent thereupon, they that escape shall " stand before the Son of Man " (Luke 21 : 36), for He will not then be yet on earth.

1. The rapid unifying of the world in this generation is surely significant. Steam, electricity, aerial transport, and wireless telephony have contributed to international commerce, and have made the interests and intercourse of nations common and universal. Politics have inevitably followed the trend. No nation can longer maintain a " splendid isolation." Combination and centralization are unavoidable. The two Great Wars have revealed that the action of one power now involves all nations. The trend towards world unification is marked. Cæsar could conveniently leave conquered tribes to starve and perish : now the victors find it economically necessary to feed and rehabilitate the vanquished. Formerly if a criminal succeeded in leaving his country he was seldom brought to justice : to-day, messages arrive at other countries before the fugitive, and he is sent back. Extradition treaties are right and good as against criminals ; but how ready an instrument of persecution they will be once the law declares again that to be Christian is to be a criminal !

2. That the territories of the ten kings of the fourth Beast will not embrace the whole globe is doubtless true, but neither will they be limited to what the Roman Empire was at any point in the past. Their dependencies and confederated states, *as they will exist at the time of Antichrist*, will be part of his dominion. And can it be questioned that when such a masterly Satan-inspired ruler has at his absolute command such an empire, the preponderance of power will be so vastly in his favour that all other nations will be bound to fall into line, willingly or unwillingly, and so in effect his dominion will be universal ?

It would have been a great gain to the study of Daniel and the Revelation if the term " Roman " empire had never been employed.   It is not Scriptural.   In the Word of God, the first three empires are named from the countries of their origin, Babylon, Persia, Greece (Dan. 1 : 1 ; 2 : 48 ; 8 : 20, 21), but the next is not named, it is simply the " fourth Beast." Of its rise and career little is said.   It, like the others, would be adjacent to " the great sea," the Meditrreanan : it would be strong and merciless and triumphant.

Beyond this, its course is unnoticed until the final stage, when ten kings should arise out of it, and then an eleventh, who should be its last head, and should be destroyed by the Son of Man, Whose kingdom should supersede his.   The interest and detail centre upon this concluding stage and final Emperor, and there is no ground for supposing him to be emperor of *Rome*, but, on the contrary, to have his centre at Babylon (Isa. 14 : 4 ; etc.).

It is to be noticed further that the Babylonian kingdom did not become the first empire of prophecy until the time when Nebuchadnezzar had made his city, Babylon, the capital of the world.   The century and a half during which the kingdom had existed, and the changes that it had undergone, were not of moment prophetically ; but at the same time that a king of Babylon had gained world-wide dominion, the hour had come when Israel no longer could he held worthy of that dominion, and the sovereignty was for a time transferred by God to the Gentiles, whereupon commenced " the times [that is, opportunity of world-authority] of the Gentiles," and the first empire of prophecy emerged.

The assumption (as in Dr. Grattan Guinness's *Light for the Last Days*, with which pure assumption all his calculations start) that the period of one hundred and forty years of the Babylonian kingdom prior to Nebuchadnezzar is included in the head of gold is, in view of Daniel 2, unfounded.   It is contrary to the inspired, double, and emphatic statement to that king, "*Thou*" (not thy predecessors, or their kingdom), "*Thou*, O king, art king of kings . . . *thou* art the head of gold* " : and contrary also to the reason expressly given why he was this, namely, that universal dominion had been granted to him by God ; for this grant his predecessors never had, and therefore the reason for him being the head of gold cannot apply to them.

If it be asked if Nebuchadnezzar actually dominated the whole of mankind, the answer will be that, as far as we know, he did not, but this does not alter the fact that not even the grant of such dominion was made to his predecessors, and that therefore they cannot be the head of gold.   Doubtless Mr. Darby's rendering, " God hath made thee *ruler* over them all " is to be preferred to the usual translation, " God hath made thee to *rule* over them all."   Nebuchadnezzar was granted that dignity as to position even though he never completely developed its possibilities.

But it is to be noted that the gold, silver, and brass portions of the image are viewed as still existing with the iron and clay when the stone falls, for they are expressly specified as being " broken in pieces together " (Dan. 2 : 35). Antichrist will incorporate into himself and his kingdom all that pertained to all four empires and will accomplish fully all that is foretold of the whole image. He, at the end, will be the head of gold in acme, as at the beginning Nebuchadnezzar was so in title and in some distinct measure. This explains Jeremiah 50 : 17–20. The period here in view is when Israel shall be brought again to his land, be satisfied, and his iniquity and sin be no more to be found, for the remnant will have been pardoned. At that same period the king of Babylon and his land are to be punished, as Assyria was of old. " Israel is a hunted sheep, the lions have driven him away : *first*, the king of Assyria devoured him, and *last* Nebuchadnezzar, king of Babylon, hath broken his bones. *Therefore* . . . I will punish the king of Babylon " (see Darby and Amer. R.V.). It is the fact that Assyria was the first empire to devour Israel and drive him out of his land (II Kings 17). It is not fact that Nebuchadnezzar was the last to do so, or did it in connection with the final restoration of Israel, nor was he himself, with his land, punished as here foretold. But the last king of Babylon, the coming Beast, will fulfil this, and the coming destruction of him and his land at one time will fulfil these threatened judgments. Hence he is here named Nebuchadnezzar, as being *par excellence* the head of gold.

Similarly, the inter-tribal conflicts and changes of the Medes and Persian tribes throughout the long period preceding Cyrus are of no moment prophetically and are unnoticed in Scripture. It is when Cyrus seizes Babylon and fixes there his centre, that his kingdom becomes the second empire of prophecy.

So with the Grecian kingdom. The Word of God makes no reference to the long history of the tribes of Greece, nor to the schemes and wars by which Philip of Macedon and his son Alexander at length brought the states under one sovereignty. It is only when Alexander attacks the Persians, and makes himself master of Babylon (the he-goat rushing upon the ram, Dan. 8), that his kingdom becomes the third empire of Daniel.

Thus also is it with the fourth empire. Its ferocity and supremacy are emphasized, but that it would commence, or had commenced, at a city named Rome, is not even mentioned, and what its course would be is unnoticed. It is when the Antichrist shall have made Babylon its centre of universal government that the empire will become what is so vividly and minutely portrayed in prophetic Scripture.

And this essential geographical feature might have been learned from the one fact that, because the four kingdoms were represented by an upright image, therefore the centre of gravity, if it may be so expressed, of each of the three upper portions was exactly over the spot upon which the feet stood. The centre of each empire would be at the same place.   Babylon is Satan's original and final earth centre, as Jerusalem is the Divine centre.   And modern world movements tend unceasingly to the Near East.

It should also be observed that the image is an unbroken continuity from the head to the feet ; there is no break, with later reunion of its parts. Similarly, the fourth Beast continues in view uninterruptedly from its emergence to its destruction, it does not die and come again to life. The phrase, " The reviving of the Roman Empire " is seriously misleading.   There is no *Roman* Empire known to *prophetic* Scripture, though the Romans are mentioned in New Testament *history* ; and the fourth empire has never ceased, though, like the three preceding kingdoms, it has gone and is going through internal changes which are unnoticed as not material to prophecy.   It is the Beast personally, the Antichrist, who having lived, dies, and later comes up out of the Abyss (Rev. 17 : 8–11).   The Abyss is a clearly defined locality, the place of the dead (comp. Rom. 10 : 7 with Eph. 4 : 9.   See also Rev. 20 : 3 ; 9 : 1 ; Luke 8 : 31, and Ps. 71 : 20, where for " the depths of the earth," the LXX has " abyss ").   In what conceivable sense can an *empire* or a *city* or a political *system* go *there*, and come thence again ?

Thus, in Rev. 13 : 2 the Beast (personal) is both lion, bear, and leopard, the symbols in Dan. 7 of the three preceding empires.

The attempt to show that there alway have been in the Roman Empire *about* ten kingdoms, is like attempting to prove that the image had about ten toes, sometimes eight in number, sometimes thirteen, but always about ten, and that its toes grew out all down its legs, in fact formed its legs.   The toes are the extreme final stage, as the head was the first, and the number ten is not merely incidental, as natural to the human form being the figure employed, but is emphasized by being repeated in the ten horns of the beast, where it is non-natural.   As " four horns " proved to be four in number (Dan. 8 : 8, 22), why should not " ten horns " mean ten ?

We therefore reject the term " Roman " empire, and dismiss with it the notion that the area of the fourth empire, or the location of its final ten divisions, can be determined even approximately by what it formerly has been.   The empire has not yet reached its full development, and when it does so it may be as much more extensive than at any time before as each of its predecessors when centred at Babylon became vastly greater than it had been at any previous time.

How, for example, shall Egypt be one of the ten kings that elect the Beast (Rev. 17 : 16, 17), and so be then part of the fourth empire, seeing that " at the time of the end " its king shall attack the Beast and be overwhelmed by him (Dan. 11 : 40–43) ?   Scripture does not seem anywhere to suggest strife between the ten horns.   This is subsequent to his rise and supremacy and to the completion of the indignation against Israel (the Tribulation ; comp. Isa. 10 : 12 and 25), as described in verses

36–39. It is to take place in the era of the darkening of sun, moon and stars (Ezek. 32 : 7, 8), which will be after the Tribulation (Matt. 24 : 29). In relation to the first, second, and third empires, Egypt was never aught but a conquered enemy, and such it appears will be its relation at the end. This destroys the idea that the ten coming kings can be located from what the fourth empire has been in the past. Moreover, never in the past did the fourth empire include all the eastern territory of the second and third beasts, for these reigned to the frontier of India (Esther 1 : 1), whereas the Euphrates was the Roman boundary. Here, then, as to the future, appear two important variations from the frontiers of Hadrian and Trajan.

It has been commonly said that the ten kingdoms will be divided at the end, five in the western and five in the eastern half of the empire, this being inferred from the division of the image into two legs and ten toes. But this is merely human opinion, and no part of the inspired interpretation. The division God emphasized was not of the image into two parts, but of the toes, its final condition, into two elements, iron and clay. Of course, as world empires were being pictured by a human form, two legs with five toes on each leg were an unavoidable feature, but it is significant that the Divine interpretation entirely ignores the legs and passes immediately to the final stage, the toes (Dan. 2 : 40–43).

The corresponding picture, of a beast (c. 7), necessarily does the same, for such a beast was both undivided and indivisible into two parts. Here the legs are not even mentioned, but only the feet, and the Divine interpretation concentrates on the horns, as before on the toes.

If we once begin introducing our own explanations of points which the Spirit of God leaves untouched, where will the process end? If the two legs represent the division of the empire into east and west, and the collapse of these parts means the passing away of the empire, then, logically, we must note and explain the facts that the western half was destroyed A.D. 476, whilst the eastern survived till A.D. 1453. Thus imagination must conjure up the singular spectacle (wholly unperceived by Nebuchadnezzar and Daniel) of half the image standing a thousand years longer than the other half, and standing on one leg! Again, if the two legs of the one vision mean the twofold division of the empire, then the (presumably) four legs of the beast ought to mean a fourfold division.

When divine explanations of visions, or of parables, have been given, our wisdom is to leave untouched details which God's explanations ignore. As has been above remarked, the histories of the empires, however long and chequered, prior to each centring in Babylon, are unimportant prophetically, the great questions being such as these: Where will be the *centre* of the last emperor, who will arise within the

area of the ten (Dan. 7 : 8 ; 8 : 9) ? ; and what will be the *full* extent
of his authority when one of such ability uses such overwhelming strength
to seize dominion ?   What power or union of powers can be supposed
as strong enough to refuse to recognize his overlordship ?   But it appears
that the element of compulsion will not be required at the climax of his
career, for we read that " the whole earth wondered after the beast, and
they worshipped the dragon because he gave his authority unto the
beast, and they worshipped the beast, saying, who is like unto the beast ?
and who is able to war with him ? " (Rev. 13 : 3, 4).

3. It is declared of the Beast that " the Dragon gave him *his* power
and *his* throne, and great authority " (Rev. 13 : 2), and therefore if
Satan's power is universal so will be that of the Beast.   Can we conceive
of Satan being contented with a portion only of the earth, especially
when he shall just have been ousted of his nobler, heavenly sphere?
Did he not show to our Lord " *all* the kindgoms of the world " (the
oikoumenee, the inhabited earth) and say : " To Thee will I give all this
authority, and the glory of them : for it hath been delivered unto me :
and to whomsoever I will I give it " ? (Luke 4 : 6).   Is it not written
concerning Satan that " the *whole world* (κόσμος, kosmos) lieth in the
evil one ? " (I John 5 : 19), and is not this a strictly universal fact ?   It
is the same expression as in c. 2 : 2 : " He is the propitiation for our
sins and not for ours only, but also for *the whole world*."   Three times
Christ termed Satan " the prince of the world," not of " the Roman
world " or " the prophetic earth."

4. Of the fourth Beast it is declared that " it shall devour the whole
earth " (Dan. 7 : 23).   There seems no reason why this should not be
strictly fulfilled in due time.   It is urged that a corresponding term in
the New Testament (οἰκουμένη, the inhabited earth) does not always
imply universality ; but that fact cannot affect the force of an expression
as used in Hebrew and Chaldee six hundred years before Christ, and
before Roman and Greek usage had given a sometimes restricted meaning to a Greek word which properly denoted universality.   The force
of the term in Daniel must be learned from the Old Testament, nor have
we to go beyond the writings of Daniel himself to see the sense in which
he uses it.   In c. 2 : 35 it is said of the stone cut without hands, that is,
Messiah's kingdom, that " it became a great mountain and filled the whole
earth."   This certainly means universality.   The words are thus translated in the Old Testament some twenty-five times, and seem regularly
to imply universality.   Jehovah is the Lord of the whole earth (Ps. 108 :
5 ; Isa. 54 : 5 ; Zech. 4 : 14) ; His glory does or shall fill the whole
earth (Isa. 6 : 3 ; Ps. 72 : 19) ; the waters of the flood covered the face
of the whole earth (Gen. 8 : 9) ; the whole earth was re-peopled from
the sons of Noah (Gen. 9 : 19) ; before Babel the whole earth spoke one
language (Gen. 11 : 1) ; Jerusalem is to be the joy of the whole earth
(Ps. 48 : 2) ; God's watchful eyes " run to and fro throughout the

whole earth " (Zech. 4 : 10) ; His purposes of judgment affect the whole
earth (Isa. 14 : 25, 26 ; 28 : 22) ; Jeremiah groaned that as a prophet
he had been made a man of contention to the whole earth (15 : 10),
which was because he had been charged (25 : 15–33) with messages of
doom (ver. 26) to " all the kingdoms of the world (the usual word for
earth, as in the expression ' the whole earth ') which are upon the face
of the earth " (ground, as in Gen. 2 : 5).

In view of this uniform sense we see no reason for limiting the force
of the word when applied to the fourth Beast, or when used of the
Babylon which is to be, when it, as the capital of Antichrist, is spoken
of as " the hammer of the whole earth " (Jer. 50 : 23), the period being
that when God shall pardon and deliver the Remnant of Israel (verses
19, 20). And so of the third kingdom the first statement made is that
" it shall bear rule over all the earth " (Dan. 2 : 39), which will be fulfilled
in that the last emperor, Antichrist, will arise out of one of the four
regions into which Alexander's empire was divided at his death (Dan. 8 :
8–12). So again when the superhuman king of Babylon of Isaiah 14 is
destroyed (which is to be at the time when Israel receives rest from sorrow
and hard service, ver. 3), it is said : " Jehovah hath broken the staff of
the wicked, the sceptre of the rulers; that smote the peoples in wrath
with a continual stroke, that ruled the nations in anger, with a persecution
that none restrained. The whole earth is at rest, is quiet : they break
forth into singing " (verses 5–7, and comp. Hab. 2 : 3–8). And finally,
in the concluding words of this great prophecy of the doom of the Beast
(Isa. 14 : 26) the term " whole earth " is equivalent to " all the nations " :
" This is the purpose that is purposed upon the whole earth : and this
is the hand that is stretched out upon all the nations " ; for the purpose
of God is to deal at that time with the whole earth, literally and universally, and so Christ said : " But when the Son of Man shall come in
His glory, and all the angels with Him, then shall He sit on the throne of
His glory, and before Him shall be gathered all the nations " (Matt. 25 :
31, 32), which must be taken universally seeing that Christ's authority
is to be universal.

The destruction of the armies of the Beast is described in Rev. 19 :
17, 18, as the " great supper of God." This supper is pictured in
Isa. 18 : 6, and verse 3 shows that that day will affect " all inhabitants of
the world and dwellers on earth." The same era is detailed in Jer. 25,
which first (verses 12–25) specifies numerous kings that shall drink of
the wine of the cup of God's fury, and " reel to and fro, and be mad,"
a Biblical parallel to the pagan proverb, " Whom the gods would destroy
they first make mad." Then follows (ver. 26) the statement that, in
addition to the kings named, there shall drink of that wine of fury, " all
the kings of the north, far and near, one with another, and *all the kingdoms
of the world*, which are *upon the face of the earth* " : and this is followed by
the significant word " and the king of Sheshach [that is, Babylon, see

R.V. marg. and c. 51 : 41] shall drink after them." Thus the judgments of those times, of which the destruction of Antichrist will be the climax, will affect " all the kingdoms of the world which are upon the face of the earth." This phrase is conclusive as to the unlimited area affected, but it is enforced by the further unequivocal statements : " I will call for a sword upon *all the inhabitants of the earth* " (ver. 29), " Jehovah . . . shall give a shout . . . against *all the inhabitants of the earth* " (ver. 30), Jehovah hath a controversy with the nations, " He will plead with *all flesh* " (ver. 31), " Evil shall go forth from nation to nation, and a great tempest shall be raised up from the uttermost parts of the earth.   And the slain of the Lord shall be at that day *from one end of the earth even unto the other end of the earth* " (verses 32–33).

These uiniversal terms dating from five to seven centuries B.C. cannot be restricted by a political usage of a word (*oikoumenee*) in another language by other peoples in a later age.   We shall now examine this word more closely.

5. The Greek word *oikoumenee* means properly the whole habitable earth, and therefore expresses universality (Luke 4 : 5 ; Rom. 10 : 18 ; Heb. 1 : 6 ; 2 : 5).   It is so used in the Septuagint at Ps. 50 : 12 : " *the world* is mine, and the fulness thereof."   Any restricted meaning is secondary, as when it is said of the apostles that they had " turned *the world* upside down " (Acts 17 : 6), or that Cæsar Augustus had ordered a census of *all the world* (Luke 2 : 1).

In Acts 11 : 28 and 19 : 27 the term may have its limited or unlimited force, and seeing that it has two meanings, it is a matter for study as to which it has in any given passage.   Revelation 16 : 14 speaks of " spirits of demons, working signs, which go forth unto the kings of the whole inhabited earth, to gather them together unto the war of the great day of God, the Almighty " (Har-Magedon).   Here *oikoumenee* probably has the limited sense ; first, because a monarch naturally draws his fighting forces from his own proper subjects rather than from outside peoples, upon whose fidelity he cannot wholly depend ; and second, because other Scriptures show that during that same period Egypt, and also Media, and eastern and northern kings, will attack the Beast, and the latter will destroy his country and capital (Isa. 13 ; Jer. 50 ; Dan. 11 : 40–44).   But the facts that some who at first served him later become disaffected, and that his military forces will be drawn from his own original dominions (if this shall prove to be the case), in no way nullify the testimony of Scripture to his earlier universal supremacy, which he will use as opportunity for universal persecution of the godly.

The secondary and restricted sense of any word ought not to be introduced where the primary and usual meaning creates no difficulty, and especially not where *oikoumenee* is joined to words, or is used at the equivalent of terms, which have unlimited force, as in Matt. 24 : 14 : " this gospel of the kingdom shall be preached in the whole *oikoumenee*, for a testimony unto *all the nations.*"   Here the expression "all the nations" is obviously without limit, and does not mean "some of the nations," that is, those in the area of the Roman earth of Christ's day. It is a future day that is in question, the times of the end : "then shall the end come " ; and very certainly the gospel is intended for all mankind, and the people for God's name (Acts 15 : 14) are to be gathered out of "every tribe and tongue and people and nation " (Rev. 5 : 9).

In Rev. 12 : 9 we read that, "the great dragon was cast down, the old serpent, he that is called the Devil and Satan, the deceiver of the whole inhabited earth."   This reference to Satan as the ancient serpent plainly refers back to Eden and all subsequent history, and requires that " the whole inhabited earth " shall be understood in its full sense.

Nor can any sound plea be urged for limiting its force in Rev. 3 : 10 : "Because thou didst keep the word of my patience I also will keep thee from the hour of trial, that hour which is to come upon *the whole inhabited earth,* to try them that dwell upon the earth."   The expression " to be *kept from* " (out of, *ek*) a trial, by no means allows of the sense " to be *enabled to endure* " a trial, but evidently means not to be called upon to meet it.   John 17 : 15 is quoted to the contrary : "I pray not that thou shouldest take them out of the world (*ek tou kosmou*) but that thou shouldest keep them out of the evil one (*ek tou ponerou*)."   Here " the world " is the *sphere in* which men have their bodily existence, and " the evil one " is the *sphere in* which they have their moral existence : " the whole world lieth *in* the evil one " (I John 5 : 19).   To be taken out of the world means here bodily removal from this earth, not being strengthened to endure its bodily afflictions ; to be kept " out of the evil one " means similarly that the inner, the true man, moves no more in the evil one as the sphere of moral life, not merely that the believer is strengthened to endure temptation.   His inner man is translated *out of* one kingdom *into* another (Col. 1 : 13).   The idea of change of location is in all three passages.

Then also we have already seen from a wealth of passages that the time of the end is most assuredly to affect the whole (earth) world without limit, so that to be " kept from that hour of trial " cannot mean to escape from a so-called " prophetic earth " into outside regions, for there will be no regions unaffected by that period.   Nor can " the hour of trial " be the day of the Lord which is to follow the Tribulation, for that day is not one of trial but of judgment.   The terms tempt (or try) and temptation (or trial) do not appear to be applied thereto, for the sufficient reason that the period of testing and proving man is then over, and the time for judgment resulting from that previous testing is then come.   Moreover, that is the day of *the Lord,* whereas it has just before been intimated that Satan, not the Lord, is the agent of temptation (trial) : " the Devil is about to cast some of you into prison, that ye may be tried " (Rev. 2 : 10). Thus the " hour of trial " will be the Tribulation, and it will be as universal as is the earth, for " the whole inhabited earth " (*oikoumenee*) is obviously equal to " those dwelling upon the earth " (*gee*), and since a limit cannot rightly be attached here to the term " the earth " (*gee*), none can attach to *oikoumenee* as here used.

That the edict of persecution will be more strictly enforced at the centre than at the circumference of the Beast's dominions may well prove the case, and therefore it may be that the " sheep " (Matt. 25 : 33–40), who favoured the avowed followers of Christ (" My brethren ") during the Tribulation, will come mainly from those northern and eastern countries whose kings by that time will be disaffected against the Beast. But if this prove to be so, it will further show that even in their areas the edict of the Beast will have authority, and that not even there will the godly " escape all those things that shall come to pass " (Luke 21 : 36).

6. Finally, the application to the rule of the Beast of terms necessarily having universal force requires that the same force be given to all expressions concerning his rule. The following phrases from only one section of the Apocalypse (c. 12 and 13) should be considered as being a connected series, and therefore to be construed together :

(1) 12 : 9—" The old serpent . . . the Devil and Satan, the deceiver of the whole inhabited earth (*teen oikoumeneen holeen*)."

(2) 12 : 12—" Woe for the earth (*gee*) and for the sea : because the Devil is gone down unto you."

(3) 13 : 2—" The Dragon gave him [the Beast] his power and his throne, and great authority."

(4) 13 : 3—" The whole earth (*holee hee gee*) wondered after the Beast."

(5) 13 : 7—" There was given to him [the Beast] authority over every tribe and people and tongue and nation."

(6) 13 : 8—" And all that dwell on the earth (*gee*) shall worship him [the Beast], every one whose name hath not been written in the book of life of the Lamb."

(7) 13 : 12—" He [the second beast] maketh the earth (*gee*) and them that dwell thereon to worship the Beast."

(8) 13 : 14—" He deceiveth them that dwell on the earth (*gee*)."

Now Nos. 1 and 2 show that the *oikoumenee* and " the earth " are coextensive each with the other and with the influence of Satan, which is the " whole world " as we know from I John 5 : 19. " Earth " here is in contrast with " the heavens " and " the sea," thus meaning all the land surface of the globe. No. 3 shows that the Beast will rule this same sphere. Since then the term " earth " is universal, plainly the strengthened term in No. 4, " the whole earth " must be universal. The expression in No. 5, " every tribe and people and tongue and nation " is used in c. 5 : 9 of the redeemed heavenly people ; in 11 : 9, again of the subjects of the Beast : and again in c. 14 : 6, of all who ought to fear God, give Him glory, and worship Him because He is the Creator. In the first and last instances this distributive formula cannot be limited to a supposed Roman or " prophetic " earth, for the heavenly church will not be drawn from such an area only, and that men should worship the Creator is a duty incumbent upon all mankind.

In No. 6, " all that dwell on the earth " are all those whose names are not in the book of life, and in Nos. 7 and 8 there seems no reason for taking " earth " to mean anything less than it means in No. 2, that is, the whole world.

It is therefore not allowable to take the word *oikoumenee*, when used of the rule of the Beast, in its limited sense.   His sphere will be that of Satan, the whole earth : he will have authority over every tribe, people, tongue, and nation :   *oikoumenee* in his time will convey its natural primary, full meaning of " all that dwell on the earth."

Thus world movements are preparing for one world authority ; Satan's sphere is already the whole world ; the Beast will sit on his throne and rule for him ; that Satan and the Beast will aim at less than universal dominion cannot be supposed, nor would any scheme but that of one central world authority promise cessation from world strife, the need and longing of the race.   Then the numerous and various Biblical terms which describe the Beast's kingdom combine to describe world-wide rule.   It would appear that if the non-Scriptural, confusing terms " Roman " empire and " prophetic earth " are avoided, the notion of a limit to the areas of the Beast's authority when at its height will not arise from anything that is said in Scripture.

APPENDIX B

(*to page* 41)

To the Christian it will be matter of genuine sorrow that both the spirit and the law of England, and of the English-speaking world, have set distinctly in the same direction as the totalitarian states.

On May 22nd, 1940, introducing the Emergency Powers (Defence) Act (1940), the Deputy Leader of the Commons said : " Every private interest must give way to the urgent needs of the community . . . it is necessary that the Government should be given complete control over persons and property—not just some persons or some particular class of the community, but over all persons, rich or poor, employer or worker, man or woman, and all property " (*Daily Telegraph*, May 23rd, 1940). And that journal added : " What the measure does is to place the entire resources of the nation, both human and material, at the disposal and control of the Government. Henceforward every citizen will be required by law to perform whatever function the Government may deem necessary for the effective prosecution of the war."

Thus in this once free people, as in some other lands, Socialism reached its goal and the individual was merged in the community. The relationship of the subject to the Crown was virtually put back to where it stood before Magna Charta in 1215, for no Norman king could demand more than *complete* control over *every* person and *all* property in the country. For the present we are all Government slaves, for the very essence of slavery is that the one party claims complete control of the person and property of the other.

This simplifies the duty of the Christian, for at once he has the advantage of the guidance of the New Testament upon the conduct of slaves (Eph. 6 : 5–9 ; Col. 3 : 22–25 ; 1 Peter 2 : 18–25). Ready and faithful obedience is his course, as part of his service to his divine Master, from Whom also his reward will come. Christ allows no rebellion by his followers against the existing authorities, not even though a tyrant like Nero was ruling when the passages cited were written.

Slavery may work harshly (Ex. 1 : 13, 14) or benignly (Ex. 21 : 2–6), and no doubt the Administration here will as yet study to be mild and fair : for example, conscience will still be protected under the Military Service Acts. But however much the Administration here may be better than elsewhere the principle and the extent of the powers taken are as wide as in avowedly totalitarian states.

As yet this legislation is temporary. It remains to be seen how far the former freedom of the individual will be restored. It may be fully, which may God graciously order : but it may be that May 22nd, 1940, tolled the death-knell of individual liberty on earth. *The Times*, while supporting the Act, yet said justly, that "the new Act, printed on a single sheet of paper, comes near to suspending the very essence of the Constitution as it has been built up in a thousand years. Our ancient liberties are placed in pawn for victory : nothing less than the destruction of Hitlerism will redeem them." And when will this be effected ? It did not come with the death of Hitler. He was only one exponent of this political principle which has gripped the modern world. It will not be destroyed until the last world-emperor, the Antichrist, shall have been destroyed by Christ at His coming.

Our province does not take us into the reasons for or the possible political and economic results of this profound change. The strength of the iron element is to remain in the image to the end (Dan. 2 : 41), and of late it has been reasserting itself strongly. Yet on the whole this will make for some kind and measure of order, which is better for society than anarchy. But our concern is with the bearing of the situation on the religious side, with its present effects in other lands and its possible effects here also. Both the Catholic hierarchy and anti-religious politicians will know how to use such powers if and when their opportunity comes. The Prince of this world is steadily and stealthily preparing his whole world kingdom for its final developments. Let the Christian be watchful unto prayer, for it is through many tribulations he must enter the Kingdom of God (Acts 14 : 22).

On October 4th, 1938, speaking in Bristol Cathedral to the Church Congress, the Archbishop of York (now of Canterbury), referring to the Continent, said :

> The totalitarian State involved a conception of personality incompatible with the Christian doctrines of God and of man, for it was bound to regard and to treat the individual as having this meaning and value of his relationship to itself.
>
> The man existed for the State, which was itself regarded as the community organized as a self-conscious unit. Such a theory conflicted with the conception of man as having his ultimate meaning and value in his direct relationship to God. Some forms of this new or revived heresy acknowledged the reality of God, but for all purposes, except the devotional life itself, the State was interposed between God and the soul as effectively as ever was mediæval priest or Pope. As the totalitarian theory militated against the Christian doctrines of God and man, so it was only by renewed apprehension of those doctrines that human liberty could be preserved and made worthy to be preserved.—(*Times*, October 5th, 1938.)

This last sentence is to be pondered deeply. It points to the only possible means by which this or any land can be preserved from lapsing into the degradation and wretchedness into which some lands have fallen, even a genuine and widespread revival of the fear of God. Such as by voice and example contribute to this are in fact doing more for the good of the community than all other persons and measures. The three who went into the fire under the fury of the king did more really to help and bless him than all his statesmen and armies combined.

> In His famous answer to the Pharisees " Render to Cæsar the things that are Cæsar's, and to God the things that are God's," Christ is sometimes thought merely to have made a " clever " answer which embarrassed His questioners : in fact, it was a profound statement of a great truth. Cæsar, or the temporal power, can control our actions, and can assess our taxes : he can punish us, unjustly if he will : he can even put us to death : but there remains, for ever outside his control, the really vital part of our life, our hearts and our thoughts. These are our own, or, rather, for these we are accountable to God alone.—(Dean Alington, *Daily Telegraph*, June 1st, 1940.)

It is written : " They have changed the king's word, and have *yielded their bodies*, that they might not serve nor worship any god, except their own God " (Dan. 3 : 28).

It is written : " *Present your bodies* a living sacrifice, holy, well-pleasing to God, which is your spiritual service. And be not fashioned according to this age " (Rom. 12 : 1, 2).

It is written : " If we died with Him, we shall also live with Him : if we endure, we shall also reign with Him : if we shall deny Him, He also will deny us : if we are faithless, He abideth faithful ; for He cannot deny Himself " (II Tim. 2 : 11–13).

It is written : " Be thou faithful unto death, and I will give thee the crown of life " (Rev. 2 : 10).

This vastly important topic is discussed at length in *World Chaos*.

APPENDIX C

GOG,

Chief Prince of Meshech and Tubal

AN EXAMINATION OF
EZEKIEL 38 AND 39

I. THE PEOPLES CONCERNED

1. *The Chief Races.* By many it has been strongly asserted that the peoples intended by the names in this chapter are Russia and Germany, and that the prophecy is of a confederacy of these northern nations invading Palestine. The view seems based only on similarity of sound between Rosh and Russia, Meshech and Moscow, Tubal and Tobolsk, Gomer and Germany.

In the entire absence of historical support this is too insecure a basis for exposition of Scripture. "Mere similarity of sound is a most uncertain guide" (R. E. Poole, of the British Museum, in *Smith's Dict. of the Bible*, art. "Phut," vol. II, p. 869). Moscow was not founded till A.D. 1147, seventeen centuries later than the prophecy. Both it and Tobolsk are named after the river on which each stands, and the origin of the names of these is not known and offers no basis for any opinion. It is still disputed whether Rosh is a proper name at all, or does not rather mean "chief," and with the accompanying word *nasi* means "chief prince," as the A.V. In the latter case the chief party, Russia, at once drops out of consideration.

Scholars who do not positively reject the proposed identification use upon Rosh and Russia such weak and doubtful terms as "a more probable hypothesis" (*Smith's B.D.*), "dubious" (*Century Bible*), "whence perhaps" the name Russia (Wordsworth). But there is great weight of scholarship against it. Thus the 14th edition of *The Encyclopedia Britannica* says, "The name 'Russia" is derived through *Rossiya* from Slavonic *Rus* or *Ros* (Byzantine 'Ρώς or 'Ρῶσσοι), a name first given to the Scandinavians who founded a principality on the Dnieper in the ninth century, and afterwards extended to the collection of Slav states of which this principality formed the nucleus. The word *Rus* is probably derived from *Ruotsi* (a Finnish name for the Swedes), which seems to be a corruption of the Swedish *rothsmenn*, 'rowers," or 'seafarers '."

So also H. A. L. Fisher, *History of Europe* (1 vol. ed., p. 178), on these Scandinavian settlers on the Dnieper, writes: "To Ruric, the Swedish

201

leader, fame assigns the credit of having founded at Novgorod and at Kief the original centres of a Russian state. So powerful was the Swedish influence, so patient and receptive were the Slavonic populations, who accepted Swedish rule, that the name (Ruotsi) by which the Swede was known to his Finnish neighbours was soon transferred from the master to the subject, and has become the common designation of the Russian people."

Mr. F. F. Bruce's article " The Proper Names in Ezekiel 38," in *The Harvester* for September, 1940, may also be studied with advantage.

There is general agreement that Tubal refers to the classical Tibareni, located in Ezekiel's time between the Black and Caspian Seas ; that Togarmah is Armenia, a little to the south of the former district ; that Meshech points to the Moschi, in the same area as the last ; that Magog meant the Scythians occupying then the Caucasus, though others would say the Lydians. There is also wide agreement that Gomer stands for the Gimirra of the Assyrian records and the Cimmerians of the Greeks, and many think that these became ancestors, not of the Germanic tribes, but of their age-long enemies the Celts and Gauls. There seems no ground for connecting them with the Germans.

Herodotus travelled in the East and wrote his history not more than a century and a half after Ezekiel. One has only to read him to see how scant and uncertain was the information that the most careful enquirer of his time could gain upon the wild regions north of the Black and Caspian Seas which are now called Russia, and to be sure that in his period there could be no ground for connecting the peoples in question with those remoter northern countries. In Ezekiel's day the tribes named were in and around Armenia and Asia Minor, and there seems no evidence that they became ancestors of the Russians or Germans. The " uttermost parts of the north " really known to the dwellers in the Middle East were Armenia and the Caucasus.

In 1940 Germany and Russia were acting together. This did not continue. In 1941 they went to war with each other. Yet it is not beyond possibility that they may again be forced to co-operate. Hence the need of caution in any attempt to forecast events. They may even invade together the Middle East. But the question is, will this, if it takes place, be the invasion of which Ezekiel speaks ? It is unwise to formulate prophetic theories upon a plainly insecure basis, for thus the mind is trained to expect what may never take place, and the real direction that events may take may remain unperceived.

2. *The Auxiliary Forces.* Much is to be learned from the fact that Persia, Cush, and Put are joined with Gog's army (38 : 5). For whereas Togarmah is given as in the " uttermost parts of the north," that is, from Mesopotamia where Ezekiel saw the vision, Persia lies far away to the south-east of Mesopotamia, beyond the Tigris. By the time of the later prophets (Nahum 3 : 9 ; Jer. 46 : 9 ; Ezek. 27 : 10 ; 30 : 5 ; 38 : 5)

Cush and Put are found as helpers of Egypt in war ; but by origin they both were sons of Ham, the son of Noah (Gen. 10 : 6 ; I Chron. 1 : 8) ; and as Nimrod, the first conqueror in Mesopotamia, was a son of Cush, it is seen that their region at that time was adjacent to what later became Persia. Afterward some of them migrated to Libya, west of Egypt on the Great Sea, and to Ethiopia, and in time became subordinate to the great Egyptian rulers. But Ezekiel's prophecy regards the original stock of these peoples in Mesopotamia, adjacent to Persia, and contemplates them as found there at the time that Gog attacks Palestine, and as aiding him.

Thus emerges the material feature that Gog rules Mesopotamia and Persia, that is, the very centre of the Middle East, the centre of the four world-empires of Daniel 2. Now if Gog is really Russia and Germany in combination, this will mean that powers not resident within the area of the image are at last dominant there. Is this consistent with the continuity of the whole image, and with the feature that the ten toes, which are the *final* stage of the whole, develop out of the feet of the fourth empire, not out of regions which have always hitherto been external to that empire ?

The last ruler of the fourth empire, the accepted head of the ten kings, is to rise as a " little horn," an insignificant ruler, and as to locality " *among the ten horns* " (Dan. 7 : 8). These two features are in disagreement with the suggestion that in those end times, after Israel is in peaceable occupation of Palestine, the rule of the Middle East will have been gained by the sovereign of an already mighty and far northern empire.

All this bears against the likelihood of Germany or Russia, singly or combined, reaching that world dominion which each covets. But the soul shudders at the thought of what may yet be involved of destruction and misery for frustrating their fell purpose, and for the retaining of world authority by the fourth empire, and for the fourth beast, its last stage. These suggestions bear also against the likelihood of Italy, being part of the fourth empire, continuing in alliance with Germany or becoming friendly with Russia.*

II. THE PERIOD IN VIEW

No invasion and destruction answering to what is here stated having been yet seen in Palestine the event must lie in the future. As is usual in the prophecies of Scripture, notes of time are given indicating the period for the fulfilment.

1. *The Context.* The preceding chapters (36 and 37) have dealt with the national awakening of Israel, under the figure of the dry bones in the valley becoming a great and living army. Of this, the final statement concerns the putting of God's Spirit into their hearts, and then

* This was written in 1939. The forecast has been fulfilled (1948).

His sanctuary being in their midst for ever. The matter of this future sanctuary, its form and ordinances, then follows directly after the prophecy of Gog, and occupies chapters 40 to the end of the book, which thus are an explanation of the last verse of ch. 37.

But before giving these particulars of the millennial sanctuary the prophet turns back a little to describe the momentous doings that will lead up to that noble climax, and gives in chapters 38 and 39 an account of the great invasion that will become the actual occasion for the personal intervention of the Lord which will bring about the deep moral change required in the people to warrant the external change to follow.

This feature of a prophecy returning to a somewhat earlier point of affairs, and from that point leading on again to the great consummation already foretold, is very frequent in all prophetic parts of the Word of God. It is an unavoidable feature in history, and prophecy is history written in advance.

Thus the preceding and succeeding contexts show that Gog will invade Palestine at the very close of this Gentile age and just before the introduction of the Millennial age. Detail expressions in the chapters confirm this.

2. *Time Phrases.* The term " after many days " in ch. 38 : 8 showed that the event was to be remote from Ezekiel's day.

The phrase " in the latter years," or " at the end of years," is definitely and frequently used of the closing period of God's dealings with Israel leading to their restoration to His favour. It is used first so early as by Jacob, and points to the coming of Shiloh, when " to him shall the obedience of the peoples be " (Gen. 49 : 1, 10). It is the time when the Star shall rise out of Jacob and the sceptre out of Israel (Num. 24 : 17) ; when Israel shall return to Jehovah (Deut. 4 : 30) ; when evil will befall them, and the song Moses taught them apply most fully. Now this song leads on to their restoration and the nations rejoicing with them (Deut. 31 : 19—32 : 43). It is the period when Gentile world rule shall give place to the Stone that shall crush to powder the image seen by Nebuchadnezzar (Dan. 2 : 28) ; and when the mountain of Jehovah's house at Jerusalem shall be the world-centre for all nations (Isa. 2 : 2 ; Mic. 4 : 1–3), after that the anger of God shall have destroyed the wicked, and the intents of His heart have been accomplished in the salvation of Israel under David their king (Jer. 23 : 20 ; 30 : 8–11, 24). " In the latter days " Moab (Transjordania) and Elam (east of Mesopotamia) are to be restored to prosperity (Jer. 48 : 47 ; 49 : 39).

Evidently all this is at the close of this age and the beginning of the Millennial age. This rules out that Ezekiel is speaking of the same invasion as John in Rev. 20 : 7–10, for this latter is to be " after the thousand years are finished." It will have like essential elements to this but is a repetition of it, not the same event.

3. The condition of Palestine and Israel affords another note of time.

The " continual waste " of the land has ended, some power having intervened to " restore it from the sword." Israel has been " brought forth out of the peoples " and they " dwell securely " (38 : 8), indeed, in such sense of security that they are " at rest," satisfied with " unwalled villages," " dwelling without walls, bars, or gates " (11). And this has continued long enough for them to have acquired vast riches, a " great spoil " of silver and gold, cattle and goods, sufficient to provoke and reward a mighty invasion (38 : 13).

This restoration of the land and the nation was foretold explicitly by Moses, and in detail (Deut. 30 : 1–10), and is a chief theme with the prophets. In agreement with Ezekiel as above, Hosea places it " in the latter days " (Hos. 3 : 4, 5), nor does any scripture place *this*, the complete and permanent restoration, anywhere but at the close of the age of Gentile supremacy and the beginning of the Millennial age.

That it is this final restoration which is in view here, not any partial and preceding restoration, is certain from the features that—1. It affects the whole house of Israel (39 : 25) ; ii. That they shall never thereafter be forsaken by their God (39 : 28) ; and iii. That it is the period for the outpouring of His Spirit upon them as a people (39 : 29). It is not, therefore, the Pentecost of Acts 2, for that blessed only a very small minority, and only of those Israelites then in Judea, leaving the greater part of the nation still scattered and unrenewed, and Jerusalem to be again destroyed. It is that enduement of the Spirit before announced by Ezekiel, to be accompanied by the full restoration of the people, first morally, and then in situation and conditions, as in ch. 36 : 22–38, and foretold earlier by Jeremiah (31 : 23–40).

Never since the dispersion of the northern kingdom by Shalmaneser (721 B.C.), and of Judah by Nebuchadnezzar (588 B.C.), have the land and the people been as is here described, and clearly no *such* restoration has been given.

4. It has been thought that these notes of time will apply either shortly before or shortly after the advent of Christ.

(1) William Kelly pictures four chief evil personages acting at the same time immediately " before the millennium." (i) The " beast " of Daniel, the head of the " revived Roman empire," the ten-horned beast, his sphere being west of Palestine. (ii) The " king of the north," Assyria, who will invade Palestine, fulfil such passages as Zechariah 14 : 1, 2, and who will be destroyed by the advent of Christ in glory (3, 4). (iii) " The king " of Daniel 11 : 36 *et seq.*, whom he finds also in Isa. 33 and Zechariah 11, " the idol shepherd," and who is, he thinks, the Antichrist, and will be in league with (i), the " beast." (iv) Gog, of Ezekiel 38, 39. These are all to be destroyed for the deliverance of Israel, and the overthrow of Gog is to be " none other than the last destruction of Israel's foes before the millennium " (*Notes on Ezekiel* 200, and *Notes on Daniel* 191 *et seq.*).

As I have sought to show in my *Histories and Prophecies of Daniel*, I regard Kelly's (i) and (ii) as the same person, yet not the head of a conjectural revived Roman empire, but of all the area included at any time in the four parts of the image of Dan. ii, and also for a short time dominating the whole world. To this sovereign I apply the passages where he sees his number (iii). The distinguishing between western and eastern powers at that time virtually compelled him to regard Gog as head of a remoter and northern kingdom. This required *two* colossal invasions of Palestine, first by the Assyrian and then very shortly after by Gog, for he placed both just " *before* the millennium." This seems untenable, as we shall see later. He has also to suppose this northern power as controlling territories south of Assyria, which seems out of the question in view of the location and power of the Assyrian at that same time.

(2) B. W. Newton placed the invasion of Gog during the earlier years *after* the Lord's descent to deliver Zion from the Assyrian. In his *Thoughts on the Apocalypse*, on Rev. 20 : 7-10, he wrote :

> " Gog and Magog," etc. This must not be supposed to be the same as the gathering against Israel mentioned in Ezekiel 38 ; for that is clearly at the commencement of the millenium—*after* the appearance of the Lord and the conversion of the remnant in the land of Israel as described in Zechariah 12 ; but *previous* to the establishment of the full millennial glory in Zion and in Jerusalem. The period between the day of the visitation of the Lord on Jerusalem, and the establishment of His throne there in peaceful blessedness—in other words, the period between His manifestation as the morning star, and as the sun arising with healing in his wings, is of considerable duration. Many nations are rebuked and judged during this interval ; Moab, for example, and Edom, and the nations mentioned in Ezekiel as in confederacy with Gog : I believe these to be the nations which are now occupying the districts in the centre of Asia north-east of Persia—Bokhara, for instance. I do not regard Russia as coming within the description. I believe the right translation of Ezekiel 38 : 3 to be " chief prince," as given in our version ; nor do I recognize any affinity between Meshech and Tubal, and Muscovy and Tobolsk. Here, however, Gog and Magog are expressions evidently denoting generally *all* nations, and are not used so specifically as in Ezekiel, where the enumeration of the nations confederate with Gog is minute."

This proposal may seem attractive, yet involves serious difficulties.

(i) It seems that the last stage of the image of Daniel 2 will include all territory that had belonged at any time to the four empires, for the gold, silver, and brass are there at the end with the iron to be crushed to pieces by the Stone. If this is correct, then a good part of the area above suggested (Turkestan) will belong to the Beast, for it was part of the second and third empires. How, then, can it at the period in view be ruled by Gog, if he be a distinct outside power?

(ii) In any case, the other territories named, and the coast-lands (39 : 6), as well as Persia, Cush, and Put, were all part of the image, and therefore will be part of the last stage of the fourth beast (Dan. 7), and so will not be held by an outside monarch. Whether the destruction of Gog be just before the millennium or a little after its commencement, it is agreed by these writers (Kelly and Newton) that it will have been preceded by the destruction of the image by the Stone, that is, by the overthrow of the Beast, the head of the fourth empire, the little horn, and the destruction of his armies in Palestine.

The term " isles " is found thirty-eight times, and seems to refer always to the countries bordering the Mediterranean. But let us suppose from Gen. 10 : 5 that it may include the shores of the Black and Caspian Seas, since originally sons of Japhet occupied these. In either case the territories will at the end times all belong to the fourth empire, not to outside powers : yet the coast-lands are to share in the judgment on Gog (39 : 6). Must not, therefore, Gog be the ruler of those coast-lands ? But in this case he will not be the monarch of Germany and Russia, or of remote Turkestan and Central Asia, in contrast to the head of the fourth beast.

(iii) Some of the consequences of the victory of Christ over the Beast in Palestine are given in Isaiah 66 : 18-20. The context gives these particulars :

1. It is a time when Jehovah will pay regard to the humble and contrite (1, 2).

2. But at that time there will again be idolatry in Israel (3, 4 ; comp. Zeph. 1 : 1-5).

3. This will bring a day of tumult in Jerusalem (6 : 17 ; comp. Zech. 14 : 1-3).

4. A temple will have been built there (1, 6).

5. The new and regenerate nation of Israel will come to birth suddenly (7-9).

6. Mourning shall give place to joy and peace, poverty to plenty, distress to comfort, shame to glory (10-14).

7. Jehovah will come, with fire, angels, whirlwind, and will execute far-stretching judgment, especially upon idolaters (15-17 ; comp. Joel 3 : 9-17).

8. There shall be a general gathering of nations and tongues, and they shall see the glory of Jehovah (18 ; comp. Joel 3 as before).

9. From the judgment then executed some from among the nations shall escape and be sent back to tell their peoples of the fame and glory of the Lord who has thus delivered Israel (18-19). These peoples will

include the far-western nations (Tarshish) and also Greece (Javan) and
Asia Minor (Tubal), as well as the distant coast-lands that had not already
seen the glory that had appeared at Zion.

10. The immediate effect will be that the nations will bring the rest
of scattered Israel with honour to Jerusalem as a peace offering to the
King of Israel (20 : before announced, see Isa, 11 : 11, 12 ; 14 : 1, 2 ;
27 : 13 ; 49 : 22 ; comp. Zech 8 : 20–23).

It thus appears that the account of the overthrow of Antichrist will
spread quickly to a great distance, not only through the lands immediately around Palestine, but far away, including those lands and coast-
lands from which the armies of Gog are to be drawn (Tubal), and the
effect will be their submission to Christ.

Now exactly this is to be the direct effect of the judgment upon Gog :
" And I will set My glory among the nations ; and all the nations shall
see My judgment that I have executed, and My hand that I have laid
upon them. So the house of Israel shall know that I am Jehovah their
God, from that day and forward " (39 : 21, 22).

It is really difficult to accept that immediately after this destruction of
Antichrist (according to Kelly), or a few years thereafter (according to
Newton), the severe lesson will have been wholly forgotten and peoples
surrounding Palestine itself, such as Persia, Cush, Put, and the coast-
lands, will join in the attack that Ezekiel describes. The express object
of God in bringing Gog against Israel, even that the nations may learn
effectually His power and glory, will have been served so successfully
that all shall own Him and shall honour His people, Israel. Why, then,
should the lesson need so speedy repetition ? or how could it be shortly
repeated, its end having been gained ?

It is true that various peoples adjacent to Palestine are to be attacked
and punished by restored Israel ; but Isa. 11 : 14 puts these deeds in the
closest time connection with the intervention of the Lord to save
Jerusalem, as one series of connected events, not at some distance of
years later.

(iv) There is this further difficulty. The intervention of Christ to
destroy Antichrist and to save Israel is to be with overwhelming glory.
It is to be a sudden blaze as lightning (Luke 17 : 24) ; it is to be a concentration of the glory of the Father, the Son, and of all the holy angels
(Luke 9 : 26 ; Matt. 25 : 31). It is this out-shining of His presence
that will bring to nought the Lawless One (II Thes. 2 : 8). It is plain
from the prophets that the display of this glory at Jerusalem will be
permanent, and that the knowledge of it as being there will cover the
earth (Isa. 4 : 5, 6 ; 11 : 9, 10 ; Hab. 2 : 14 ; 3 : 3, 4 ; Isa. 40 : 5 ; 60 :
1–3, 19 ; 66 : 18, 19 ; Zech. 2 : 5). It need not take so very long for
Messiah to build the new temple at Jerusalem (Zech. 6 : 12, 13), and
when completed it will be glorified by a state entrance into it of the
Lord of glory (Ezek. 43 : 1–5). But the glory will have been displayed

from the hour of His descent to the Mount of Olives (Zech, 14 : 3–5).

Is it not almost incredible that with the knowledge of the divine glory present at and protecting the city, and with the recent display of its terrific power to blast the enemies of God, as in the case of Antichrist, still a vivid memory, that a fresh invasion should so soon be attempted ?

If it be urged that even after a thousand years of the presence of that glory the nations will nevertheless be so daring and defiant as to attack " the camp of the saints and the beloved city " (Rev. 20 : 7–9), why not, therefore, after only some years of its presence, at the beginning of the thousand years ? the answer is threefold. (i) The men of that later generation will have no such recent display of the blasting power of that glory to deter them. Har Magedon will be but the remote history of a thousand years before, and most of those concerned will have been born since. (ii) As Satan is to be bound from the very commencement of the millennium (Rev. 20 : 1, 2) the nations of this early period will be without his incitement, daring and skill to urge and direct them ; whereas for the later attack he will have been loosed, to precipitate his and their final rebellion and final ruin. It may well be asked whether in his absence, as at the start of the kingdom of Christ, monarchs or peoples will feel equal to such an impious attack and frightful deeds as those of Gog and his armies ? (iii) Scripture does not state that at the time of the later attack the glory of the Lord will be still visible at Jerusalem. The presumption is that the close of the kingdom age will bring many changes. This is the more likely seeing that when these armies attack the city it is not a glory still there that flashes forth to destroy them, but fire that " comes *down out of* heaven " that devours them (Rev. 20 : 9).

III. WHO IS GOG ?

But if Gog be not the ruler of some northern power outside the area of the fourth empire, and if he be in control of the Middle East at the period of Israel's regathering to the land, who can he be other than the last head of the fourth kingdom of the image of Dan. 2, the little horn of the fourth beast of Dan. 7 ? Does Scripture indicate any other such monarch at that exact time ? Let us see whether this supposition answers to the details given.

1. In Ezekiel 38 : 17, God Himself expostulates with Gog in these words : " Thus saith the Lord Jehovah : Art thou he of whom I spake of old time by my servants the prophets of Israel, who prophesied in those days for *many* years that I would bring thee against them ? "

It is of the utmost significance that Gog and his invasion of Palestine were a theme of other ancient prophets besides Ezekiel. Yet no other

Old Testament scripture gives an invader this name.   Is it because of this that this feature has not received the stress due ?

Now of the invasion of the land by " the Assyrian " (Isa. 10 : 5), the " king of the north " (Dan. 11 : 40), the " little horn " (Dan. 7), the " prince that shall come " (Dan. 9), the " northern army " (Joel 2 : 20), and of the " gathering of all nations " (Zech. 12 : 3 ; 14 : 2), many prophets speak and many descriptions are given.   And *no other* invasion of Palestine at the period in question is mentioned.   If, therefore, that of Ezekiel be not the same, then Scripture gives no information which corresponds to the above statement which God makes to Gog.   In other words, if Ezekiel's prophecy does not refer to the invasion mentioned in the other scriptures cited, then it stands alone in the Word, and we are without any mention of what the other prophets declared upon this invasion by Gog.   Apart from the verse quoted from Ezekiel, it would not be known that any other prophecy upon Gog had been given.

But if those other prophecies are unrecorded, what could be the force of protesting to Gog that the most he was doing was to fulfil what God had foretold ?   Indeed, what would be the value of those prophecies having been made ?   The argument from prophecy to the glory of God demands, first, that the forecast shall have been given a sufficient time in advance, and with sufficient particulars, that the fulfilment could neither be a chance coincidence nor an arranged affair ; and second, that the record of the prophecy shall be available for comparison with the events that fulfil it.   It is with design that these things are hidden from the wise and prudent of the world and are revealed unto " babes," for neither the one class nor the other can either contrive or hinder the fulfilment.

2. We must therefore compare these chapters of Ezekiel with those describing the invasion by Antichrist to discover whether perhaps they refer to one event.   But here care is important.   All invasions have certain features in common, such as a leader, armies, arms, an objective —that is, a land to be invaded, and destruction of life and property. It is not such common features, but the distinctive details that must agree to show that two or more accounts deal with the same event. And also there must be no item or items characteristic of any one account which *cannot* apply to the other.

(1) Isa. 10 : 5—12 : 6 is a foremost passage dealing with an invasion of Palestine by the " Assyrian, the rod of Mine anger."   This judgment of the king of Assyria is " when the Lord shall have performed His *whole* work upon Mount Zion and upon Jerusalem."   It is that " destruction which is determined, overflowing with righteousness.   For a *full end*, and that determined, will the Lord, Jehovah of hosts, make in the midst of all the earth."   This phrase is taken up in Daniel 9 : 26, 27, which shows that the latter passage also reaches to the end times of God's dealings with Israel.

The route the Assyrian will take in his march against Jerusalem is given in 10 : 28–32. But at that point the Lord cuts him down (33, 34), and the "Shoot out of the stock of Jesse" (Messiah) bears fruit, even righteousness and peace (11 : 1–9). The earth shall be full of the knowledge of Jehovah; the nations will seek Him (11 : 10); the remainder of Israel will be gathered to Palestine; and the Holy one will be great in the midst of Zion (11 : 11—12 : 6).

This has in common with Ezekiel (1) That the end days of Israel's chastisement are the time; (2) That Palestine is the sphere; (3) That the judgment is wrought by the personal intervention of the Lord, as Ezekiel 38 : 20, "all things shall shake *at My presence*." (4) That fire is a prominent agency in the destruction. Isa. 10 : 17 : "The light of Israel will be for a fire, and his Holy One for a flame; and it will burn and devour his thorns and his briars in one day": Ezek. 38 : 19, 22 : "in the fire of My wrath have I spoken . . . I will rain upon Gog . . . an overflowing shower, and great hailstones, fire and brimstone": "I will send a fire upon Magog" (39 : 6). (5) That in immediate sequence in both passages is the restoration of Israel and the blessing of the nations under Messiah.

If (as Kelly) the Assyrian be an earlier invasion and Gog a later, then it could not be said of the former that by it the Lord had performed His "*whole* work" in Zion and that the "*full* end" had been reached, for the severe punishment of Israel through Gog's invasion would be yet to come.

If (as Newton) the Assyrian be destroyed at the descent of Christ to Olivet (with which we agree), that indeed will be the "full end," the "whole work" of chastisement by God of Israel; but if the *whole* work has thus and then reached its *full* end, how can there remain a subsequent heavy chastisement by the invasion of the land by Gog? A work cannot be completed twice or a full end be made on two occasions. Th refore the Assyrian and Gog, and their invasions, must, it would seem, be identical.

(2) Some further details may be examined.

i. Ezek, 38 : 19, 20 says that at the time of the judgment upon Gog "Surely there shall be a great shaking in the land of Israel; so that the fishes of the sea, and the birds of the heavens, and the beasts of the field, and all creeping things that creep upon the earth, and all the men that are upon the face of the earth, shall shake at My presence, and the mountains shall be thrown down, and the steep places shall fall, and every wall shall fall to the ground."

Just such a shaking, with the same word used, is mentioned in other passages.

Psalm 46 : 23. At the time when Israel shall find God a refuge, a strength, a present help, they say : "Therefore will we not fear, though the earth do change, though the mountains be shaken in the heart of the seas," etc. This is the time when "the nations will rage and the kingdoms be moved" and when "Jehovah makes wars to cease unto the ends of the earth" (ver. 9), and when He is present with Israel (7, 11) "in the midst of the city of God" (4, 5). Thus this shaking has to do (1) with the *last* great war, for then wars are made to cease, and (2) with the personal intervention of the Lord. But, as we saw above from Isaiah, it is the Assyrian king who is destroyed by that personal descent of the Lord to Zion. It is, then, in connection with *his* overthrow that the shaking of all things takes place; hence the king named Gog by Ezekiel must be he.

This same shaking is mentioned in Isa. 24 : 17–23, and is shown to include the heavens also. It is mentioned again in Joel 3 : 16, and in Haggai 2 : 6, 7, 21. In these places also the shaking of heaven is mentioned, and in them also it takes place at the time when the Lord "will overthrow the throne of kingdoms" (notice the singular, throne, a throne which is over kingdoms, the throne of an overlord), and will dwell in Zion. Now the time when "the powers of the heavens shall be shaken" is the time when men shall "see the Son of man coming in a cloud with power and great glory" (Luke 21 : 26, 27). As the Assyrian is to be destroyed when this shaking takes place, and this is at the manifestation of Christ in glory, he cannot (as Kelly) have been destroyed some time earlier and the overthrow of Gog be at the advent of Christ as a separate event. As the shaking and the manifestation apply to both enemies, must they not be the same? for it will not be suggested that there are to be two manifestations of Christ and two universal shakings so close together.

ii. The marked disturbance of the sea, so marked that even the fishes feel it (a *most* phenomenal feature, seeing that they are so accustomed to the movements of the ocean, and to its tempests), is another unusual feature common to Ezekiel and to Psalm 46 quoted. It is emphasized by Christ in the same connexions, that is, with the times of the Gentiles running out, and commotion in heaven and earth, men being "in perplexity for the roaring of the sea and the billows," and it will be directly before His descent: "then shall they see the Son of man coming" (Luke 21 : 24–27).

ii. Ezekiel specifies that the mountains shall be thrown down, and the steep places shall fall, and every wall shall fall. Psalm 46 likewise mentions the mountains shaking and trembling. John (Rev. 6) also mentions this under seal 6, when repeating the Lord's forecast as to disturbances in the heavens, and adds, "every mountain and island were moved out of their places." Men flee to the caves and to the rocks because the "great day of the wrath of the Lamb is come"; of which Isaiah spoke when he said that men would so flee "from before the the terror of Jehovah and the glory of His majesty, when He ariseth to shake mightily the earth" (Isa. 2 : 19, 21).

This is at the time of the seventh bowl of judgment (Rev. 16 : 17-21), which completes the wrath of God upon the Beast and his city Babylon. Then takes place the mightiest earthquake ever known, and which would cause that vast and sudden disturbance of the ocean ; when also " the cities of the nations fall," and as Ezekiel says, " every wall shall fall to the ground " ; and when the " overflowing shower of great hailstones" he mentions falls, as John adds, " every stone about the weight of a talent " (perhaps about a hundredweight). This causes the irreclaimable followers of the Beast to blaspheme God. These are *final* judgments, for by these bowls " is *completed* the wrath of God " (Rev. 15 : 1 ἐτελέσθη), and therefore at the seventh (Rev. 16 : 17) it is said from the throne " It has come to pass " (γέγουεν). But as this is the overthrow of the Beast at Har Magedon (see Rev. 16 : 16), the judgment upon Gog, seeing it is accompanied by the same convulsion in nature, affecting heaven and earth and the sea, and by earthquake, appears to be the same event.

iv. It is further specified that pestilence, blood, fire, and brimstone shall visit Gog and his enemies. Under the same judgment of the bowls these same items are specified—" a noisome and grievous sore " upon the worshippers of the Beast (Rev. 16 : 2), blood being given them to drink (3-7), men are scorched with fire (8), and the Beast and his prophet are " cast into the lake that burneth with fire and brimstone " (Rev. 19 : 20). The full working of the pestilence is given in Zech. 14 : 12 and 15 : " their flesh shall consume away while they stand upon their feet " in their camps.

v. Ezekiel declares that there shall also be destruction by sword : " I will call for a sword against him unto all My mountains." Of the armies of the Beast it is said that they were " killed with the sword of Him that sat upon the horse, even the sword which came forth out of His mouth " (Rev. 19 : 21), that is, by the word of command of Christ. Death in battle by the sword would indeed be a common feature, but the *method* in this case is particularized by Ezekiel as being *mutual* destruction : " every man's sword shall be against his brother " (38 : 21). Now Zechariah follows the description of the pestilence by saying " that a great tumult from Jehovah shall be among them ; and they shall lay hold every one on the hand of his neighbour, and his hand shall rise up against the hand of his neighbour " (Zech. 14 : 13). All is in strict connexion with the final attack on Jerusalem, which is to be followed by the nations submitting to the King of Israel, Jehovah of hosts (16).

vi. At the destruction of Gog all birds and beasts are called together to glut themselves at Jehovah's table (39 : 17-20). The same scene is described at the day when God commands the attention of " All the inhabitants of the world, and ye dwellers on the earth," when an ancient, terrible and conquering nation learns to worship Jehovah (Isa. 18) ; and it is repeated in detail at the destruction of the Beast and his armies (Rev. 19 : 17, 18). Thus it occurs at the time of God's universal dealing with all nations, at the destruction of Antichrist. The largely verbal repetition of Ezekiel in Revelation strongly suggests the event as being the same. And may not the fact of this feast of the birds and beasts coming in the much discussed vision in Isaiah 18 offer the true clue to its application, namely, to Assyria, understanding the Cush of verse 1 to be the area in that direction rather than the area south of Egypt later so named ?

If there are details concerning Gog which *cannot* apply to Antichrist, or concerning the latter which *cannot* apply to Gog, and which, therefore, demand that they be separate persons and their invasions distinct events, we shall be grateful that they be specified, for we have failed to observe any such. But the mass of detail is great, especially concerning Antichrist, and we may have overlooked such contrary particulars. But in the absence of such details, does not the correspondence of so many striking and exceptional features strongly suggest identification ?

The student of any one matter of the end times should labour to form a full mental picture of the whole of that period so as to fit into it easily the matter being studied. He who does this will find the picture so vast, and the particulars so extensive and varied, as may well induce caution, rather than that dogmatism in assertion which has too often marked authors who have expounded the theory of a Russo-Germanic alliance, as, for example, the truly able and learned, but much too positive, William Kelly.

From the above examination it may be seen that :
    (1) The time of the invasions is the same : the end of Gentile rule.
    (2) Israel is dwelling in Palestine.
    (3) The destruction is brought about by the direct intervention of the Lord at His descent from heaven.
    (4) The details of that destruction agree generally and minutely.
    (5) The effect of this judgment in the humbling of the nations is alike.
    (6) The accompaniments are the same : the full restoration of Israel ; the out-pouring of the Spirit ; the Lord dwelling at Zion ; all the earth being taught His glory and being blessed.

IV. WHERE GOG RISES

On the supposition that Gog is the " little horn " of Daniel, Ezekiel supplements Daniel on an interesting and important detail. From Daniel 8 : 8, 9 we learn that the last Gentile emperor will rise in one of the four divisions into which the kingdom of Alexander was divided after his death. From the fact that he is elsewhere called " the Assyrian " and " the king of the north," which term in the prophets means regularly Assyria, it is seen that it will be in the eastern of the four parts. But by Ezekiel it is shown that he will be specially the chief prince of the region now known as Armenia and the Caucasus. It is therefore, it would seem, in that district that he is to be expected to appear as the little horn rising amidst the ten horns of the fourth beast. By the overthrow of three of his neighbours he will, we take it, first extend his sovereignty southward over Assyria and Persia, thus becoming the Assyrian, and making Babylon his capital and the centre of the last world empire, even as it was of the Babylonian, Persian, and Grecian empires of old. And this is the first stage of his career as shown in verse 9 of Daniel 8, even that " he waxed exceeding great towards the south (Mesopotamia), and towards the east (Persia, Cush, and Put), and towards the glorious land " (Palestine).

V. THE WEAPONS USED

It is a deeply significant detail that his forces are armed with the old weapons, not with the modern firearms and machines. It is impossible to " spiritualize " the prophecy at this point, and equally impossible to argue that, of course, the prophet speaking twenty-five hundred years ago did not foresee modern military inventions, but naturally spoke of the armour and arms of his day. It is impossible, because it would have been possible for the Divine wisdom not to have gone into these details of weapons, and so to have left the account indefinite upon this point with the view to future developments in the cruel art of war.

But no; details are multiplied with much definiteness. It is stated that the weapons are such as can be burned, and shields, bucklers, bows, handstaves, and spears are enumerated.

Moreover, no " spiritual " sense can be assigned to the details that this supply of firing will take *seven* years to consume, no more, no less, and that Israel will not need to cut firing from the forests during this period.

Incredible as this literal sense may seem to the modern mind, it appears to fit in naturally and exactly to the state of things in the end days as pictured in the Word of God. Terrific and repeated international wars are foretold as to mark that period, and these will be accompanied by still more terrific angelic and demonic action when " the wrath of God is revealed from heaven " in " the great day of His wrath." The consequent destruction of life and of property will be appalling in extent and area. The second beast of Daniel 7 is told to " devour much flesh " ; the fourth beast has great iron teeth and nails of brass, and it too devours, breaks in pieces, and stamps the residue with his feet.

The rider of the first seal of Rev. 6 goes forth conquering ; the second rider takes peace from the earth, and men slay one another; the third seal shows famine; the fourth horse is of the colour that pictures death by plague, his very rider is the angel of Death, and the angel ruler of Hades, the world of the dead, rides with him to the carnage. By them, during this one campaign, a fourth part of the earth is ravaged by sword, famine and pestilence; and because men decrease the wild beasts flourish. Not to detail all other plagues and destructions, at the sounding of the sixth trumpet alone a third part of men are killed (Rev. 9 : 18).

A fourth of the earth ravaged by one judgment, a third of mankind killed by one other; what will this mean but vast areas devastated and depopulated? and what will this in turn mean if not that the modern methods of production of war machines and material will have become impracticable? As these lines are printed (July, 1942) nearly three years of mechanized and aerial warfare has wrought ruin enough to demonstrate the likelihood of what is here suggested, especially as each nation endeavours most vigorously to destroy the armament factories and food reserves of the opponents. "Civilization" (?) is hastening its own ruin; and in due time men become savages in heart will perforce return to the weapons of the savage, even as they are fast returning to his ways. In both the realm of matter and of morals there is the law that corruption works out its own disintegration and destruction; and in this judgment there is mercy.

Joel 3 : 10, "Beat your ploughshares into swords, and your pruning hooks into spears," refers to exactly the same period, and plainly intimates that the old weapons will be used and that metal will be scarce.

Zech. 14 : 15 shows that animals will be used for war transport at that final conflict. The horse, mule, camel, and ass are named, just as before specific weapons were named. Here the beasts *must* be beasts, and cannot signify motor-cars and lorries, tanks and trains, for the beasts, like the soldiers, are to die by plague.

[Note to present edition (1950).
This discussion was written in 1940. Five years later the ravages of war brought an illustration of what is suggested. In *The Review of World Affairs*, September 29th, 1945, it was said:

The other day an observer of ours stood on the hills near Graz. The Russian army in Austria presented a suprising spectacle. It is not motorized. It moves like an old-time army on small horses and with small-wheeled carts. . . .

It hardly seemed to fit into the contemporary context of vast mechanized armies, atomic bombs, and great air fleets. It was like a scene from an old campaign.

And more recently still, in the autumn of 1947, an authority on atomic bombs was reported to have said that the next war would be fought with atomic bombs and the war after that *with spears* !]

It is therefore to be anticipated that in this, as in all other respects, the word of prophecy will be found more sure than any other utterances, and will magnify the omniscient Author in an exact fulfilment.

Moreover, it is easy to see how great a boon this provision of wood will be to Israel. The tides of battle which will have swept over the devoted land will have seriously denuded it of timber. It is specially and repeatedly pleaded against the Assyrian that he will ravage the Lebanon, the chief forest district of the Holy Land. See Isa. 10 : 34; 14 : 8; 33 : 9; Hab. 2 : 17; Zech. 11 : 1. Bashan, Carmel, and the Jordan area, all timbered regions, are also mentioned as sharing the destruction. Such a timely supply of fuel, already in convenient size and shape, will both be a present, God-provided help in trouble, and will allow time for the forests to begin to recover.

It is to be remembered that by the time in question Palestine, too, will be greatly depopulated. Two-thirds of its then inhabitants will have been cut off, and only a " very small remnant " will survive the judgments of the sinners in Zion. Zech. 13 : 8, 9; Isa, 1 : 9; Zeph, 3 : 11, 12; etc. The fierce fires of the great tribulation will have had the like effect upon those Jews still scattered in the lands surrounding Palestine : it is only a remnant of them that will return unto the Lord (Isa. 10 : 20–23). Nor will one who knows the unbelieving, ungodly state of that unhappy people to-day, and learns from their own Sacred Writings that that state will yet become worse, wonder that only such purging fires await them as a people.

Thus for so diminished a number the supply of fuel can well last for so long a time.

VI. THE EXACT TIME

One other question remains. At what period in the end days, prior to the actual rule of Messiah, can Israel be thought of as settled, prosperous, and feeling secure in their land ? Will not these precise conditions obtain during the first half of the seven years of the firm covenant between them and the Prince that shall come, Antichrist, king of Assyria ? During his rise to world supremacy the whole earth will be swept with uncertainty and distress ; but it is distinctly shown that the establishing of this covenant with their mighty neighbour will give to Israel the sense of security indicated, a false and delusive security indeed, but real at the time. And this will allow of the absorption in money-making for which they are so supremely capable. Thus Isa. 28 : 14, 15 says : " ye have said, We have made a covenant with death, and with Sheol are we at agreement ; when the overflowing scourge shall pass through, it shall not come unto us ; for we have made lies our refuge, and under falsehood have we hid ourselves." The context shows that this will be at the time of that final judgment when " Jehovah will rise up " and will execute His " decree of destruction . . . upon the whole earth " (ver. 21, 22). There is no hint in Ezekiel that at the time of the invasion they will have turned as a people unto God.

Thus they will be lulled into a sense of security. Their phenomenal abilities in trade will soon accumulate wealth : they will deal with Tarshish on the west and Dedan and Sheba on the east (38 : 13). As of old, their land will be the highway from east to west, with the traffic and wealth this will induce. Naturally all this Gog, Antichrist, will know, as Ezekiel says, " In that day when My people Israel dwelleth securely, shalt thou not know it ? " His cupidity, and his hatred of the God of Israel, will incite the invasion and spoliation of the defenceless land. But the issue shall be to teach the remnant to trust in their God, and no more to stay upon him that smote them (Isa. 10 : 20).

Thus the judgments will at last have served their designed end ; the purged remnant will cry unto Jehovah and He will save them. Their and His enemies will be destroyed ; the other peoples shall learn righteousness ; the Spirit will be poured out upon all flesh ; Jerusalem shall be the city of the great King, the centre of universal worship ; and its name from that day shall be " JEHOVAH IS THERE " (Ezek. 48 : 35).

INDEX

Books are shown in italic type.